Mary Kitagawa

ASIAN AMERICA
A series edited by Gordon H. Chang

Mary Kitagawa
A Nikkei Canadian Life

Karen M. Inouye

STANFORD UNIVERSITY PRESS
STANFORD, CALIFORNIA

Stanford University Press
Stanford, California

© 2025 by Karen Midori Inouye. All rights reserved.

This book has been partially underwritten by the Susan Groag Bell Publication Fund in Women's History. For more information on the fund, please see www.sup.org/bellfund.

No part of this book may be reproduced or transmitted in any form or by any means, electronic or mechanical, including photocopying and recording, or in any information storage or retrieval system, without the prior written permission of Stanford University Press.

Printed in the United States of America on acid-free, archival-quality paper.

Library of Congress Cataloging-in-Publication Data
Names: Inouye, Karen M., author.
Title: Mary Kitagawa : a Nikkei Canadian life / Karen M. Inouye.
Other titles: Nikkei Canadian life | Asian America.
Description: Stanford, California : Stanford University Press, [2025] | Series: Asian America | Includes bibliographical references and index.
Identifiers: LCCN 2024009321 (print) | LCCN 2024009322 (ebook) | ISBN 9781503640504 (cloth) | ISBN 9781503641075 (paperback) | ISBN 9781503641082 (ebook)
Subjects: LCSH: Kitagawa, Mary, 1934- | Activists—British Columbia—Biography. | Japanese—British Columbia—Social conditions. | Racism against Asians—British Columbia—History. | Immigrant families—British Columbia—History. | British Columbia—Race relations—History.
Classification: LCC F1034.3.K55 I56 2025 (print) | LCC F1034.3.K55 (ebook) | DDC 971.1004/9560092 [B]—dc23/eng/20240327
LC record available at https://lccn.loc.gov/2024009321
LC ebook record available at https://lccn.loc.gov/2024009322

Cover design: Nita Ybarra
Cover photograph: Mary Kitagawa in a flower field, Magrath, Alberta, 1946. Courtesy of Mary and Tosh Kitagawa.

For my sister Susan

Contents

	Acknowledgments	ix
	Introduction	1
1	Nikkei Canadian Lives before World War II	16
2	An Uprooted Childhood	42
3	Sensing Right and Wrong in Internal Exile	71
4	College and the Beginnings of Political Self-Awareness	109
5	Transformational Relationships	132
	Afterword	162
	Notes	173
	Bibliography	213
	Index	225

Acknowledgments

In contrast to the acknowledgments for my first book, which now seem almost as long as the book itself, I should focus on those individuals who had direct contact with this project.

First, my thanks go to Gordon Chang, editor of the Asian America series, and Margo Irvin, my Stanford University Press editor, for embracing this project with such enthusiasm and for giving me the freedom to write the book I wanted to write. Deepest gratitude is also due to the two anonymous reviewers who read the manuscript with extraordinary care and offered wonderfully precise and productive suggestions. While I didn't do everything they asked, the book is much stronger because of their insights.

When COVID started and everything shut down, Mary kept me company. Our regular video calls helped close the physical distance between us, and her generous spirit and story kept me hopeful during the bleakest of times. Tosh, Mary's husband, would also make the occasional appearance, popping up in the background with historical details and good humor; it's no wonder he eventually became a center of gravity in his own right. He also provided photographs and documents, without which this book would be far poorer.

If not for Chris Lee, I would never have met Mary and Tosh or any of the other Japanese Canadians I interviewed. Chris has remained an influential interlocuter, colleague, and steadfast friend.

Many colleagues (at Indiana University in particular), friends and family from many places—too numerous to name for fear of leaving someone out—have cheered me on and kept me moving. I am grateful for their support. My doctoral student Lisa Doi deserves to be singled out. She tracked down and pored over historical newspapers, scoured memoirs and biographies, and mined the notes and bibliographies of even the most obscure sources on topics related to this project. In the process, she assembled an extraordinarily rich bibliography that wound up reshaping parts of my work.

My deepest gratitude is to Bret, my partner in all things. He was gentle but rigorous in response to a hasty first draft of this book. Since then, he has read and edited every page of every subsequent version, and his prose changes have helped bring Mary's story to life in all its complexity. He also believed in my potential as a scholar long before anyone else did—especially, it seemed, when others had doubts. I could not have written this book without him.

Mary Kitagawa

Introduction

The reader of this book is probably looking for at least one of two things: a biography of the Nikkei Canadian activist Keiko Mary Kitagawa and a history of Nikkei, or people of Japanese ancestry, in Canada. My aim is to provide both, to the extent that this is possible. The history of Nikkei in Canada is in fact many intertwined histories that demonstrate some commonalities as well as numerous differences, including where peoples' ancestors came from in Japan, who recruited them to work abroad, where they settled, when they settled there, the job skills they brought with them, the work they found after arriving, and the social and economic networks available to them. Such differences grow starker once we account for the wartime expulsion of Nikkei from British Columbia in 1942, their exile in the interior of Canada, their government-dictated dispossession, the impoverishment most of them subsequently endured, and their postwar exclusion from British Columbia through 1949. The experience of wartime injustice was one of the few things most Nikkei Canadians have shared since 1942, but they have done so in different ways and to different extents. Indeed, wartime injustice was arguably not the defining feature of Nikkei Canadian history but rather a catastrophic inflection point within a larger sequence of crises, challenges, and at times successes that people of Japanese ancestry, along with their children, grandchildren, and great-grandchildren, have experienced in Canada.

The reader might reasonably ask how one particular Japanese Canadian could bring some of those histories into focus as well as how those histories might help us understand her. The recipient of multiple accolades and honorary degrees, Kitagawa's political work began with her vigorous public support for Japanese Canadian redress, but it has expanded far beyond that effort. Inspired by the example of American institutions, in 2012 she secured diplomas for Nikkei students wrongfully expelled from the University of British Columbia after the bombing of Pearl Harbor. Not content to leave the matter at that, she also secured financial support from UBC that funded the establishment of the Asian Canadian and Asian Migration Studies Program (ACAM). She remained closely involved with both the program as well as the university, leading the effort to hold a 2017 Day of Learning to mark the seventy-fifth anniversary of forced dispersal and its aftermaths. She also lobbied forcefully for a curriculum on Japanese Canadian history and, in 2018, co-taught the resulting course, ACAM 320A (The History and Legacy of Japanese Canadian Internment) with Dr. John Price. Mary also led the 2007 charge to rename a major British Columbia governmental building after Douglas Jung (1924-2002), the first Chinese Canadian member of Parliament, a change that took effect in 2008. (The building had originally been named in honor of Howard Charles Green, a politician who notoriously argued in 1945 that "the Japs must never be allowed to return to British Columbia."[1])

Mary's efforts have also involved a significant interpersonal component. For instance, she has served as an important member of the Human Rights Committee of the Greater Vancouver Japanese Canadian Citizens Association; a community council member of the Landscapes of Injustice Project, a scholarly effort to document the long afterlife of wartime injustice against Nikkei in Canada; and a member of the National Honorary Advisory Council of the National Association of Japanese Canadians. In addition, she and her husband, Tosh, have been longtime participants in the Powell Street Festival, an annual celebration of Nikkei culture in Canada. When the festival faltered in the early 2000s, the two of them helped place it on stable financial and administrative footing. Such efforts have both arisen from and resulted in a breathtaking array of friendships, from the many ACAM students who think of Mary and Tosh as surrogate family members to several descendants of Howard Charles Green. Results such as these are high-profile enough that some people might be surprised to learn that Mary began pursuing them only when she was in her early fifties. In truth, it is probably more remarkable that she began at all, given the relationships that governed much of her life outside the home.

Relational Identity

To understand the matter, it helps to think about identity as being relational.[2] Take a simple question—who are you?—and think through the ways you might respond. Imagine, for instance, that you decide on a common response: you say your name. Your name is not truly your own, though, even if you grew up in a stereotypical "nuclear" North American family whose members remain on good terms. In fact, it is not your own twice over. Your parents may have provided your given name, but your family name is another matter. In most cases, that family name arose and metamorphosed over time. Perhaps one of your male ancestors made shoes or was born to someone named "Anders." Perhaps a grandparent or great-grandparent passed through an immigration center where Anglicization or even complete replacement was the order of the day. Perhaps one of your forebears changed their name out of necessity—for instance, while fleeing persecution. Or perhaps you are named in honor of an Indigenous ancestor, in which case your name likely takes at least two forms: one voiced in that ancestor's language and the other an Anglicized version. Your name is not fully your own. It was chosen by history in consultation with people. Many of those people are long dead, but their decisions continue to shape your daily life in all sorts of ways.

You are yourself, of course, but *who* you are—that is to say, the identity you assign yourself in any given moment—is not entirely of your own making. It continually originates both in the past and in the circumstances you encounter and the relationships in which you participate. In the example cited above, something as fundamental as your name speaks to years or even decades, of conversations, many of which began with the utterance of that name. With each utterance, your sense of who you are underwent subtle consolidation. Again, this presumes a stereotypical family devoid of the many complexities that come with life, and it does so to illustrate that even in the simplest of circumstances, we exist by and through our relationships, which means our identities are necessarily born of those relationships.

Identity is also metamorphic, since the relationships available to us change over time, as do the circumstances governing those relationships. Furthermore, experience can enable us to pursue new relationships. These relationships might require that we sharpen our sense of self, which in turn enables us to pursue more new relationships. That is why you are not who you once were and why you will be different in the future. It is also why, although you will be different, you will not become someone else entirely. The identity with which you enter each new relationship derives partly from earlier relationships and extends some of its previous characteristics into those new circumstances. Nonetheless, you are a moving target, paradoxically consistent in the kinds of changes you might undergo.

And then there is the matter of opportunities, which govern the relationships and the potential identities available to you. A talent for writing will not develop fully if you lack access to a robust and affordable educational system or, more accurately, to the money and relationships that make such a system available. A knack for business or medicine can achieve little if you are regularly thwarted by legal and economic obstacles or, also more accurately, by competitors whose money and relationships enable them to throw legal, social, and economic obstacles in your path. And since the opportunities that do arise will necessarily dictate the number and characteristics of future relationships, those opportunities compound themselves over time. Hence the importance of recognizing structural factors when discussing economic mobility, intellectual development, cultural expression, or political engagement: the distribution of opportunity is unequal, which is why not all things are possible for all people at any given moment.

Now let us apply the idea of relational identity to Mary, in particular in the first two decades or so of her life. Imagine spending your earliest years living in a rural community on Salt Spring Island, which lies across the Strait of Georgia from Vancouver, British Columbia. Imagine that you are one of a handful of children who look like you and that your siblings make up the majority of this handful. A few children who look different in other ways live nearby, but most of the kids in your school and with whom you interact belong to a category that adults, including your parents, call "white."[3] Although she was born in Canada, your mother spent much of her youth in Japan, and your father was born and raised there. As a result, your family and your middle names, your language skills, your speech cadences in English, and many of your social habits differ from those of most children you know. Every relationship in your young life, whether at home or elsewhere on the island, involves at least a measure of translation.

Imagine, at the age of seven, being told that you, your family, and everyone who looks like you are somehow responsible for the recent bombing of a distant American place called Pearl Harbor. The teacher in your oldest sister's class even says this outright, and the claim colors conversations with the people who live around you. Your classmates now hurl insults and assault your siblings; people now vandalize your family's farm under cover of darkness. Imagine your father being abruptly hauled off by the Royal Canadian Mounted Police, leaving you with no idea of whether—let alone when—you will see him again. Imagine being herded into filthy horse stalls, shipped eastward into a strange place called the Kootenays, and then sent with your family to work seemingly endless hours on a sugar beet farm and live in a shack that is somehow worse than those horse stalls. Imagine, in fact, that conditions in Alberta are so bad that your family is shipped back to the Kootenays, where you spend the next few years living in drafty makeshift structures that are more tents than houses.

Imagine being told your family's farm has been sold to a white veteran (a supposedly true Canadian) at a substantial financial loss and that this has been done so that your family can pay for its own expulsion from the province followed by inland exile. Imagine being told after the war ends that you cannot return to British Columbia, including the island where you grew up, because of your ancestry. Imagine being told instead that you should go "back" to Japan, a place you have never even visited. Imagine being told that, if you want to remain in Canada, you must move east of the Rocky Mountains. You are also told that people who look like you, who share your names and language skills and social habits and speech cadences should not gather visibly because that might upset white people.

Imagine that, while the law barring people of Japanese ancestry from moving west eventually lapses, your family lacks the money to return. Impoverished, you all move to a small town in southern Alberta, where you are once again one of a handful of people who look like you. This time, with one or two brief exceptions, your family makes up the entirety of that handful. There are, once again, other people who look different in another way, but they are relegated to something called a "reserve." One or two of them come to your school, but they are not allowed to mix with the white population. Religion also comes into play. Your family has long belonged to the

Anglican church, but that church is active mainly on the reserve. In your town, it is the Church of Jesus Christ of Latter-day Saints, or the Mormons, who rule the roost. There are one or two other non-Mormon kids in your school, and not all of them are in your family. Nonetheless, you remain part of a tiny, highly visible minority that is a subset of another minority.

Imagine that when you graduate from high school, your family has managed to save just enough money to return to the Gulf Islands and buy a new property while also paying for part of your university education. Your oldest sister was not so lucky. Her college years came when the family's finances were at their most precarious, so she had no choice but to work. You, by contrast, have the opportunity to make a move of your own choosing. Like many people of Japanese ancestry your age, you choose Toronto—east of the Rockies, home to a relatively large number of Nikkei Canadians, and supposedly marked by less virulent anti-Japanese sentiment. But money is so tight that you have to work long hours as a nanny, which also involves living far from campus. As a result, you have relatively few opportunities to form relationships with people your age—Nikkei, yes, but also white people and non-white people from other backgrounds.

Every relationship you have had outside your family has been unstable because of all those forced moves. Every relationship you have had outside your family has also been governed by the question of who you are, a question that necessarily creeps back into the home, for that is where the supposed problem lies. Are you Japanese? You were born in Canada, but the Canadian government has told you that you and your family members and other people who share aspects of your background are at best threatening and at worst criminals. They have told you that the land your family owned was not in fact theirs, that you are not to be trusted, that you are a threat to the (white) social and economic fabric, that you cannot gather in noticeable groups, that you are not free to move where you wish in the dominion— that you are, in sum, not Canadian, despite the fact that by law as well as self-identification you are. And even when you succeed by white Canadian standards, some people continue to say it is because you compete unfairly, work too hard, charge too little for your labor, or just generally seek unfair advantage.

Above all, imagine that these conversations, including those involving people who consider themselves your allies, drown out the most important one. That conversation, the one almost nobody outside your family seems to allow, begins with you recognizing that you had not been a criminal at age seven, that you are not a criminal now, and that you had not been a criminal during the intervening years. You know this about yourself, but outside the home there is virtually no one with whom you can have that conversation. And even in the home, your conversations are limited in scope, for all the while your family is still struggling to re-establish itself financially and minimize further persecution.

Many readers might imagine that, as teenagers, they would have become very angry at this string of injustices. They might even imagine themselves becoming activists at an early age. But such a development requires opportunities, most notably in the form of relationships that create a space for what we recognize as activism. Imagine, however, that the conversations listed above are the only ones you had had and *been able to have* throughout your formative years. You might have been angry at the injustices you and your family had suffered, and you might even have had opportunities to voice that anger—at the dinner table. Those opportunities were formative and governed by the expectation of considered, articulate expression modeled by not only your parents but also your siblings, especially your oldest sister. During the family's time in the Kootenays, she was lucky enough to have studied with a high school social studies teacher whose investment in equity and social justice imparted to your sister some of the vocabulary and intellectual framework necessary to put words to the family's situation.

But remember: every relationship you have, whether at home or elsewhere, involves at least a measure of translation. And one of the things you must translate on a daily basis is the slow poison of white nationalism. Identity is relational, and virtually every relationship you have outside the home has been governed by the presumption of your guilt and by the expectation that people who share your background should be eliminated, whether by deportation or by an informal program of ethnic cleansing. Even non-Nikkei who recognize that you were not and are not a criminal compound the problem. They tend not to speak about wartime injustice at all, or if they do, they frame it as a regrettable "military necessity." And when you finally land in Toronto, a place where people are having conversations that run counter to that slow poison, your financial precarity and necessary emotional reserve keep you at a literal and metaphorical distance from those people, those conversations, and those political frameworks. Bearing such relationships in mind, the question we should ask is not why

Mary took so long to become the activist she was, but how she managed to do so at all.

The topic is far from abstract for me. My parents were born around the same time as Mary, and they too were persecuted for being of Japanese ancestry. They were imprisoned by the U.S. government and, as a result, endured different sorts of injustice. Nonetheless, Mary's and my parents' respective injustices shared roots in white nationalism and racial capitalism. Furthermore, Canadian wartime policies were frequently modeled on American precedent, albeit revised to fit the structure of a parliamentary democracy—as, for that matter, were efforts to mitigate and in some cases prevent the resulting injustices.[4] Consequently, even among the important historical differences, I could see similarities. And yet, my parents engaged in little overt activism. They favored redress but were not involved in the political fight. Like Mary, they knew they had never been criminals, despite having been criminalized. Unlike my parents, though, Mary reshaped the experience of injustice into an engine for overt, forceful political engagement. I wanted to know how and why.

That reshaping was necessarily a personal experience, so biography was clearly in order, but biography of a particular sort. Mindful of the separation wrought by our partially shared history, I would never try to provide a comprehensive account of who Mary is and has been. My aim has been only to understand her political formation. That is why this book focuses on relationality: not to delineate the myriad details of a private existence but to track the unfolding of a sensibility and the actions it has animated. Even in her most isolated and isolating moments, Mary has stood in relation to family members, to other Nikkei, to First Nations peoples, to people of Chinese ancestry, to white antagonists, to friends and allies, and of course to various institutions—provincial and federal governments, the Anglican Church, and so forth. Any attempt to understand Mary's political formation should therefore be a study of what E. P. Thompson once called "nodal points of conflict," the intersections where her mind has met and meets the world.[5] Accordingly, this book dwells on what I consider the most important point of intersection, memory—especially the memory of transformative relationships—which has been the driving force behind Mary's activism.[6]

This book takes that point of intersection as a place to begin thinking outward from my own historical frame of reference. Having recognized that a partially shared history separates me from Mary, I now seek to relate that history as well as its attendant gravitational separation to you. Mary herself is something of a crossroads where multiple groups and multiple traditions entangle. Disentangling those groups and traditions has entailed continually thinking in terms of the sharing that divides us. In the text that follows, I have tried to differentiate my voice from Mary's as clearly as possible, but there may be places where the distinction becomes blurred. I can only say that this is because the relationship I have been fortunate to form with Mary has itself been transformative. I have pursued a moving target while myself being in motion.

In the course of studying the development of Mary's political sensibilities, this book also engages with the larger history of Nikkei in Canada. It does so for two reasons. First, although rich, the literature on people of Japanese ancestry in Canada tends to be specialized in emphasis. Interested readers can find excellent work on early immigrant communities, their origins, and their social and economic structure. There is important literature on the forced dispersion, dispossession, deportation, and ethnic cleansing of Nikkei in Canada after the bombing of Pearl Harbor. Valuable work has also been done on the postwar reverberations of such profound injustice, especially concerning the pursuit, acquisition, and continuing impact of redress. In addition, there is a rich body of first-person reminiscences by survivors of wartime injustice, but these necessarily tend to be localized, often accounting for life in a particular place at a particular moment.[7] Bringing together these sources with Mary's own recollections will perhaps enable readers to see some of the histories of Nikkei in Canada, histories that determined the conditions of Mary's life and, consequently, that she has *lived*.

Tracing the histories of Nikkei in Canada as well as Mary's experiences will perhaps also shed light on how Mary's sense of her political self developed over time. Seeing that broader picture is necessary if we want understand Mary's trajectory as an activist. Riyo (Kimura) Okano, Mary's maternal grandmother, was a hard person to get along with, but she loomed large in Mary's childhood and teenage years. For one thing, she raised one of the most important people in Mary's entire life, Mary's mother, Kimiko. But Riyo's impact on Mary was also both more direct and fraught. An early female migrant from Japan, Riyo and her husband, Kumanosuke, lived just up the road from Mary's family before forced dispersal, then at varying distances from them during inland exile, and then *with* Mary's family in a shared house for several years in Cardston, Alberta. During this time,

Kumanosuke died, and Riyo became dependent on her daughter and son-in-law; she eventually spent her remaining years living with Mary's parents back on Salt Spring Island, where Mary spent her summers. If you want to understand Mary Kitagawa, you will need to understand something about her grandmother. And to understand her grandmother, you also will need to understand something about her grandfather, which means you also need to understand something about the earliest Nikkei migrants in British Columbia.

One Nikkei History among Many

The history of Mary Kitagawa is the history of someone who, like so many Nikkei Canadians, continually adapted in order to survive, who constantly had to redirect her attention toward the longer term, and who has striven to think outward from her own experience toward that of others. She gives an answer to the question of how someone might endure profound, repeated, and prolonged injustice and then work tirelessly to preserve the memory of it and to prevent its repetition. The story of Mary Kitagawa also helps us understand how, having been forcibly transformed by Canada, Nikkei have now turned around and begun transforming Canada. Or rather, since Nikkei have been transforming Canada since the late nineteenth century, that story helps us understand how they emerged from inland exile and began helping *accelerate* the transformation of Canada.

To account for that reciprocal transformation, this book redirects our attention away from wartime injustice as a discrete event and the actions of white nationalists as a primary topic, focusing instead on the continuous labor Nikkei Canadians have performed throughout their history. In that respect, this book attempts to recount what being Japanese Canadian has meant to a specific individual over time, in different places, in different circumstances, at different ages. The institutional, civic, personal, and familial insults and injuries visited upon Nikkei after the bombing of Pearl Harbor are central to that attempt. They could hardly be thought of otherwise, so profound was the damage done. But, as readers will see, the fever dream of a white Canada had raged against First Nations peoples, then expanded to antagonize Black, Chinese, and Japanese immigrants, among others. The bombing of Pearl Harbor merely provided a stable, recognizable, easily caricatured target—an excuse masquerading as a cause. Once we bear this in mind, a host of other phenomena come into focus: the accretion and modification of anti-immigrant legislation in British Columbia during the later nineteenth and early twentieth centuries; the seizure of Nikkei-owned properties and their unjust sale to white Canadians during World War II; postwar laws designed to obliterate Nikkei and Nikkei Canadian subcultures; and institutional as well as interpersonal racism that have lingered since the end of the war. Placed against the backdrop of all those phenomena, we can begin to see Japanese Canadianness not as a stable entity that triumphed over a single adversity but as a continual process of identity formation in relation to obstacles and opportunities, suffering and joy, isolation and connection.[8]

To convey the richness of that process, this book tells the story of a particular Nikkei Canadian life, one that has been in many ways exemplary. That life has been exemplary in that it was made possible by the early history of Japanese immigrants to Canada, was shaped by the injustices visited upon Nikkei in British Columbia and Alberta during the Second World War and the 1950s, and has since contributed to painstaking efforts by people of Japanese ancestry to claim their rightful place not only in present-day Canada but also in the nation's history. Recounting those efforts in the context of one Nikkei family will provide us with a ground-level view of one history of Asian immigrants in Canada and of racist efforts to alternately exploit or eliminate those immigrants. Important though legislation and policy have been, these things happen at so large a scale that it is easy to lose sight of their daily consequences.

Mary's life and the broader sweep of history to which it belongs are worthy of study in their own right, but something else is also at stake. For Mary and her siblings, the memories of racialization, dispossession, loss, and suffering—and, importantly, of encouragement to speak their minds thoughtfully—produced an instructive response. They watched their parents move back to Salt Spring Island; struggle to set down new roots in a postwar climate marked by both continuing racism and a keen sense of the humiliation it had visited upon the family; restore the island's Nikkei cemetery, which white locals had repeatedly vandalized; rebuild a family business obliterated by government-sanctioned bigotry and economic opportunism; and then sustain that business in the face of continued postwar racist antagonism.[9] In sum, they watched their family not only acknowledge the limits of their agency but also persist in exercising that agency. Then, as adults,

Mary and her siblings followed that example in various ways. As Mary's sister Rose has written, "Our parents were a powerful team. They were our role models. They taught us never to quietly accept the cruel onslaught of racial hatred, never to act as victims, and always to show a proud face to the world—never a face of defeat. They showed us how to be generous and compassionate towards others."[10]

What is perhaps most striking about Mary and her siblings is the role of memory in their postwar lives, especially the way it contributed to their growing political engagement. Think, for instance, of Mary's success in persuading the University of British Columbia (UBC) to award diplomas to surviving Nikkei whom the university had expelled after the bombing of Pearl Harbor. Mary had been but a small child at the time of this injustice, and she did not know any of those students or their families. But, having witnessed her family's eviction from Salt Spring Island, having watched her mother struggle to keep the children going while their father was being held in an undisclosed location under unknown circumstances, having grown up in the beet fields of Alberta, having watched her older sister Alice endure the torment at which teenagers excel, and having come of age in postwar Cardston, she had a keen sensitivity both to what those UBC students deserved and, more to the point, what they might have felt in the wake of expulsion. Memory was much more than a private cache of experiences. It was a means to generate new relationships, bringing people together across time and space in pursuit of justice.

Memory also was a teaching tool. Since the diploma ceremony was built into the university's regular week-long commencement festivities, Mary rightly believed that the class of 2012 would learn about wartime injustice not only from speeches and official narratives provided by UBC administrators and staff but also from witnessing the actual victims of injustice finally get their due. It is impossible to capture in words the emotional weight of such witnessing, but that was the point. Providing diplomas would not lay wartime injustice to rest. It would bring it back to life, relating the human cost of that injustice to a new generation even as it enabled members of the earlier generation to relate once again to their former classmates, both living and dead.[11] The memory of her own experience allowed Mary to relate to others who had endured similar experiences. That process of relating compelled her to act, and her actions were designed both to address the injustice other Nikkei had suffered and to instill in others a sense of the human toll such injustice exacts not only in the moment but long afterward. Having been forcibly transformed by a generation older than she, Mary sought to transform a generation of Canadians now just coming into its own, to ensure the continued possibility of conversations that had taken decades to initiate.

To capture the full sweep of that metamorphosis, this book unfolds in five chapters. Chapter 1 tells the story of Mary's roots in Canada: the immigration of her maternal grandfather and grandmother, the birth of her mother, the immigration of her father, and her family's earliest years on Salt Spring Island. Chapter 2 recounts the family's growing success on the island, success cut short by the seizure of their property, the separation of the family, and their forced relocation eastward; it also recounts the earliest struggles they had in Alberta and their subsequent time in the Kootenays. Chapter 3 tells of the postwar years in Cardston, where the family began rebuilding its finances and where Mary graduated high school. Chapter 4 tells the story of the family's decision to return to Salt Spring Island, of Mary's university experience, of her marriage to Tosh Kitagawa, and of the family she and Tosh built. Chapter 5 maps Mary's political trajectory from the later 1970s onward, with particular attention to the relationships that transformed her efforts from intuitive, small-scale forms of resistance into large-scale, programmatic projects. The afterword discusses the importance of relationality for understanding how political consciousness both manifests and metamorphoses over time.

The accent in this book lies on lived experience. That experience is, as readers will see, a critical factor in how Mary has, in addition to surviving, come to flourish as a political activist. Because of this emphasis, this book pays less attention to the legislative and juridical processes by which Nikkei injustice and its aftermath have unfolded. Readers will find references to key Orders-in-Council and legal cases, but they should still track down the foundational work of Ken Adachi and Ann Gomer Sunahara, among others.[12]

Some readers will already have noticed that my terminology departs from that of government documents, many newspaper accounts, and even some academic sources, which often refer to wartime injustice in terms of an "evacuation" of Nikkei from western British Columbia or their "internment" after the bombing of Pearl Harbor. I recognize that some contemporary scholars of the topic continue to use the latter term, in part due to its legibility among the broader public. However, as Roger Daniels and Roy Miki have demonstrated, such terms are inaccurate, using euphemism to elide or avoid the truth.[13] And because that truth continues to reverberate in the present, those euphemisms warp the conversations we might have about history and distort the relationships we might seek to pursue. The forced removal of 22,000 innocent people of Japanese ancestry from their homes was not an evacuation, even for those who had the money to move before they were picked up by the Royal Canadian Mounted Police; neither was it an internment. It was a programmatic effort to expel those people from western British Columbia that entailed systematically placing them in interior "ghost towns," labor camps, farming communities, and small towns, as well as cities in Quebec, Manitoba, and Ottawa, where they were subject to restrictions on what they could own and where they could move.

At the same time, though, it also was not incarceration, at least not of the sort Nikkei in the United States endured. Rather, Nikkei who had lived in the western part of British Columbia experienced almost dizzyingly variable mistreatment: a small number were incarcerated, in the strictest sense of that term; some were assigned to labor camps; some were shipped to Alberta, where they toiled in the sugar beet fields for egregiously low wages; others spent the remainder of their lives in former "ghost towns" near the border between Alberta and British Columbia; a lucky few paid their own way to Montreal, Toronto, or other points east. So varied are these experiences that I do not feel I can refer to them as "incarceration," involuntary though the movement of these people was, and confined though Nikkei were due to "exclusion" from the western part of Canada. (I should note, however, that some Nikkei Canadians, including Mary, do at times refer to their experience as incarceration.)

In order to allow for the complexity and variability of Nikkei wartime experience, while also accounting for the involuntary character of it, I have therefore chosen to use "forced dispersal," an umbrella term meant to cover more specific phenomena including outright incarceration, passage through staging areas such as Hastings Park, assignment to work camps, placement on private farms in Alberta or Saskatchewan, and postwar expatriation/ deportation (but *not* "repatriation"). In some places, I also refer to the government's program as one of expulsion from the province. As for post-expulsion conditions, I use the term "inland exile," since forced dispersal combined with continued postwar exclusion from British Columbia alienated Nikkei from the opportunities and relationships they had once been able to pursue in Canada.

A final word about scale. Although exemplary in certain respects, the familial and personal history at stake in this book is also highly particular, in some ways even singular. Consequently, that history is but one of many. Every single Nikkei individual uprooted from the Pacific coast, forced eastward by white nationalism and economic opportunism, stripped of their property and savings in order to pay for their own forced dispersal, subjected to ethnic cleansing, and barred from British Columbia after World War II had officially ended had to marshal all the skills at their disposal and had to draw on all their emotional, intellectual, cultural, and social reserves. Every life impacted by wartime injustice merits consideration. And while many of the histories at stake have been lost to time, readers can still do one important thing. They can multiply the injuries and insults and losses in this book by the roughly 22,000 Nikkei whom the Canadian and British Columbia governments subjected to expulsion, dispossession, and ethnic cleansing. And, having done that, they can then extend their thoughts toward other marginalized groups with whom Nikkei Canadians came into contact: Black migrants who fled the United States to settle on the Gulf Islands in the later nineteenth century, the Doukhobors in eastern British Columbia, First Nations people in southern Alberta and elsewhere, and the Chinese immigrants whom racists and economic opportunists alternately grouped alongside and pitted against Nikkei.

ONE

Nikkei Canadian Lives before World War II

Riyo Kimura would have sensed the difference of British Columbia well before her boat docked in 1903. Having grown up on the island of Innoshima, near her new husband's hometown of Hiroshima, she was intimately familiar with the feel of an estuary. That intersection of fresh and salt water is unmistakable, as bracing ocean breezes punctuate the rich earthy funk of hills covered in lush vegetation and riven by creeks and springs. British Columbia presented a similar circumstance, with vertiginous hills and innumerable protected bays lining the island-dotted waterway stretching from the Salish Sea, past Victoria, through the Haro Strait, and on to Vancouver.[1] And yet, it must have felt strangely alien at the same time. Gone were the familiar *tabunoki* (Japanese bay trees), *tsuburajii* (chinquapin), and Japanese laurel. In their place loomed massive spruce, cedar, and fir trees, while salal, sword fern, kinnikinnik, and Nootka Rose swarmed over every remaining surface. Gone too was the smell of her homeland, replaced with another aroma: ocean, yes, and the mustiness of its intermingling with freshwater environments, but not the same ocean, not the same freshwater, not the same plants and animals. This new, wild land would have been familiar, but only familiar enough to sharpen the sense of what she had left behind, not to mention the magnitude of the challenges that lay ahead—challenges that included the first-time meeting with her husband, whom she had married remotely as a "picture bride."[2]

By the time of her arrival, Riyo's husband, Kumanosuke Okano, had

FIGURE 1. Riyo and Kumanosuke Okano in front of their home, ca. 1925. Photo courtesy of the Salt Spring Island Archives.

lived in British Columbia for six years (figure 1). During that time, he established enough of a foundation to start planning for a family. It had not been easy. The conditions he encountered after emigrating from Japan in 1896 guaranteed that. Virulent anti-Asian sentiment dominated politics in British Columbia, much as it did in the western United States. Then, as now, white supremacists were adept at forming alliances and sharing strategies across regional, national, and geographical boundaries, and their efforts had born significant fruit. As Kornel Chang has demonstrated, two conflicting aims helped produce those alliances. The first was the imperative of forming the American and Canadian nation-states, which would depend on unambiguous and well-regulated boundaries. The second entailed expanding the reach of businesses beyond those boundaries and into new markets, most notably for our purposes by importing cheap labor from across the Pacific Ocean.[3] Racists within the provincial government of British Columbia had long sought to advance the first of these goals by passing measures designed to keep immigrants from Asia from gaining economic or political traction. When the province entered the Confederation in 1871, these measures took on a new urgency for politicians because Canadian law, to which the province became subject that year, failed to satisfy xenophobes in the area. A raft of subsequent provincial acts levied punitive taxes on Asian immigrants and First Nations peoples, barred them from purchasing Crown lands, and severely restricted the kinds of work they could pursue.

The provincial government also passed several acts that repeatedly denied immigrants the franchise; it also attempted to bar people of Japanese ancestry from entering the province—for instance, by implementing a literacy requirement for all prospective immigrants.[4] Most such measures were disallowed at the level of the Dominion government, but provincial officials inevitably redoubled their efforts, either by revising the failed law or by crafting new legislation. Starting with the Qualification and Registration of Voters Act in 1871, the provincial government formally barred from voting all "Chinese and Indians" (i.e., First Nations peoples), including those born and raised in Canada. In subsequent years, it repeatedly reaffirmed this exclusionary policy before, in 1895, passing an amendment to the Provincial Voters' Act that explicitly disenfranchised Nikkei as well.[5] Disenfranchisement was particularly damaging for two main reasons. First, it ensured that people to whom it applied would have no significant representative power. Unable to influence the outcome of elections, they would be of little value to elected officials, whose primary loyalty would therefore necessarily be to white supremacy, regardless of their personal sentiments. Second, it limited the economic mobility of the disenfranchised people, further entrenching the poverty they endured. (Higher-paying professions, which ranged from licensed logging and pharmacy work to legal practice and the civil service, were available only to voting citizens.[6]) The aim of such measures was to force people of Asian ancestry from the province and marginalize First Nations peoples as well as those immigrants who remained.[7]

Although divided about how forcefully to do so, the Nikkei community pushed back against efforts to exploit or eliminate them. As early as the 1890s, for instance, Nikkei miners on Vancouver Island negotiated safer working conditions and held strikes that led to fairer wages, and in the 1920s and 1930s, fishermen and berry farmers pushed back forcefully against legislation designed to drive them out of business.[8] In other cases, the aim was broader, as in 1900, when several naturalized Issei (immigrants, the first generation) attempted to register to vote.[9] They knew their attempts would fail, but their objective lay in challenging the law that barred them from registering.[10] With that in mind, one of the Issei, Tomekichi Homma, filed suit. The choice of Homma was strategic: he came from an elevated class and was an important member of the Nikkei community, having helped found the Sutebusuton Gyosha Jizen Dantai (Steveston Fishermen's Benevolent Society), which he led from 1897 to 1899. For its part, the Dantai helped cover part of Homma's legal costs.[11] Although the case was ultimately unsuccessful, its fate did not spell the end of such challenges. In 1931, Nikkei veterans of World War I secured the franchise in British Columbia after a nearly ten-year battle, and in 1936 the Japanese Canadian Citizens' League, a group founded by Nisei (second-generation Nikkei), lobbied for the federal franchise, anticipating that this would nullify provincial exclusions. The effort, like most of those that had come before it, failed. But its failure was the result of white-nationalist opposition, the power of which merely casts in sharper relief the early ambition and the long-term durability of Nikkei political engagement.

Despite such engagement, many immigrants from Japan had initially approached inequity as the price of pursuing *dekasegi*, or migratory work, that had taken them across the Pacific. Their hope was that moving far from home to earn money would eventually enable them to return with a comfortable nest egg. It was an understandable hope. As Audrey Kobayashi has demonstrated, in some areas the rate of return was nearly 100 percent.[12] Consequently, for many it would have looked as if the model of dekasegi still applied, just over a much greater distance and across cultures. Plus, British Columbia at the time seemed a land flush with inexhaustible resources. Three main lines of work would have been available to those who arrived in the province from Japan around the turn of the twentieth century: mining, lumber, and fishing. Word of the mid-century gold rush still rang in the ears of many a new arrival, while vast old-growth forests seemed almost tailor-made for the lumber trade, and rivers teemed with salmon and bays brimmed with herring and sturgeon.[13]

Once they landed, however, their options narrowed abruptly. Requiring little prior experience, mining and lumber could be decent starting places for the new arrival. That is how Kumanosuke Okano got his feet under him after first landing in the province; from 1896 to 1904, he worked in the lumber industry. However, these fields promised low wages, which was a strong incentive to move up. Like many of his countrymen, Kumanosuke recognized that the prospects for economic success were better in fishing, where he could earn prices near or equal to those of white competitors. Plus, fishing opened up other possibilities. People who had come from Mio in Wakayama Prefecture, perhaps with experience in the production of charcoal, might be able to earn a solid income processing offcuts for the booming canneries—until, that is, coal became the fuel of choice.[14] For people who had come from somewhere like Numazu in Shizuoka Prefecture, there was money to be made as a shipwright.[15] And for those who managed to move out of physical labor, there was the tantalizing prospect of middle-class prosperity. A case in point was Manzo Nagano (1853–1923), the earliest known Nikkei immigrant in Canada. Although he started out as a fisherman, by the early 1890s he had established himself as a respected businessman in Victoria.[16]

For many second and third sons living in Japan at the time, British Columbia must have sounded almost magical, a place where you could practically make your fortune by just stepping off the boat that had brought you. It was an alien land, but one perhaps familiar enough to give an enterprising young man a chance to make his fortune, return to Japan, and buy land of his own. That was the line most large-scale recruiters took, not because it was true but because their bottom line depended on drumming up immigrants who, especially before they were subjected to the tax that had initially applied to Chinese immigrants, brought a healthy profit.[17] Individuals and families, by contrast, recruited workers on the basis of demand rather than arbitrage. Consequently, they tended to operate on a smaller scale and often in a more equitable manner.[18] Even so, early Nikkei immigrants in British Columbia found themselves a world away from home, with little or no ability to speak the main local language, living on the margins of economic and political systems responsive to a hostile white population, and governed by laws that were explicitly designed to prevent Nikkei from making significant inroads. In light of all this, they not only would have to work hard but also be lucky if they expected to replicate the prosperity someone like Nagano had achieved. By 1901, only three of forty-five officially recognized businesses in the village of Steveston, near Vancouver, were owned by Asian immigrants.[19] As a result, for the majority of these early Nikkei arrivals, life in British Columbia entailed a long-term struggle regardless of whether they aspired to return to the land they had called home.

Motives for Emigrating

Why would someone undertake such a struggle? After a brief, difficult first marriage, a subsequent arranged union with Kumanosuke Okano had uprooted Riyo from Japan and brought her to the west coast of Canada.[20] It was an uprooting she could not have avoided. Despite the disruptions wrought by economic upheavals in Japan, kinship continued to determine many of one's options, its power deriving from the belief that one's family encompassed what Audrey Kobayashi has described as "an entire history of relationships, past and future, which define an enduring group under a single roof."[21] Once her family had arranged that marriage, the die was cast. Recognizing this does not really change the question, though. After all, many families allowed their daughters to become picture brides, expecting that the husband would return to Japan and the family would settle nearby. Such an aim was consistent with the tradition of dekasegi, in which people traveled elsewhere for work in order to establish themselves upon coming home. But rewards come with risk, especially in the case of moving from Japan to Canada. So, why would Riyo, like her husband and thousands of other Japanese people, venture so far from home around the turn of the twentieth century?

The abundance of natural resources in British Columbia provided one incentive; the search for exploitable workers provided a second, especially in the wake of the tax on Chinese immigrants. Economic changes in Japan provided a third. After almost 250 years of isolation, Japan was forced into diplomatic relations with the United States during the 1850s. After a period of internal conflict in Japan, the Tokugawa Shogunate, a military dynasty that had controlled Japan since the seventeenth century, was replaced with a new government with a young Meiji emperor as its head. Not content with small efforts at modernization, the Meiji government initiated a series of radical social and economic programs it believed would transform Japan into a modern nation-state that could resist colonization by the West while also establishing itself as a global power in its own right. The project of transformation upended the nation's economy, including in Hiroshima Prefecture, where Riyo and Kumanosuke Okano had grown up. And although they both had been born after that project had begun, they came of age at perhaps its most unsettled moment.

Some Meiji initiatives brought benefits, most notably the establishment of compulsory education. This not only bolstered Japan's global economic prospects, but it also figured prominently in the long-term economic success of Nikkei in North America.[22] In the short term, though, such changes brought little comfort to families, villages, and even entire prefectures that were reeling from massive economic upheaval. Furthermore, in Hiroshima Prefecture, the negative impact of the new Meiji government's initiatives was especially pronounced, largely because of the marginalization of the prefecture's governing elites under the new regime. Pushed to the margins of political life, the prefectural government found itself powerless to limit damage from economic and administrative upheaval.[23]

The tradition of dekasegi in Japan predated the Meiji government, and in earlier times such labor frequently enabled workers to survive, perhaps even thrive. *Watari-dori*, or "birds of passage," would leave home, aiming to return with enough money to perhaps buy land or set up a business. However, rising taxes and inflationary pressures destabilized this model in the later years of the Tokugawa Shogunate. In the early Meiji years, the inelasticity of the domestic labor market combined with Japan's "opening" to the world generated powerful incentives for emigration, which the government had begun to allow. Those incentives included high rates of taxation on land, with a regressive schedule that meant even reductions (as in 1879) did little to lessen the burden. Further complicating things was the fact that, when the central government did cut its tax rates, local governments frequently had to make up the resulting budgetary shortfall by increasing their own.[24]

Inflation compounded the country's economic suffering, and when the Meiji government tried to address this problem, it seems to have made things worse on several occasions. One example is an 1881 collapse in the price of rice, which in real terms caused farmers essentially to pay twice as much tax relative to their output. As a result, many families lost their property, which further hindered economic recovery. As Michiko Midge Ayukawa has suggested, the result was a cycle of economic decline that accelerated in the 1880s: "Prices were falling, as were interest rates; moneylenders were going bankrupt, unemployment was rising, and many farmers were becoming destitute."[25] In addition, cash crop prices, which had become an increasingly important part of the prefectural economy, declined rapidly toward the end of the decade, further impoverishing farmers. And this was the case only for landowners or their first sons. For anyone farther back in the lineage, the prospects were even worse. Second or third sons stood little or no chance of inheriting land and thus of being able to survive in the prefecture.

Industrialization brought further economic pain. Textile production, formerly a supplementary source of income for families, now became centralized and mechanized. Large operations gained from economies of scale, putting an end to spinning and weaving as cottage industries. Those economies of scale made imported cotton economically viable, further depressing incomes in regions that had supplied raw materials for fabric. Similar upheaval happened in other sectors of the economy, such as ironwork, too. By the turn of the century, small producers had largely been eliminated, wreaking havoc at the local level. Not even fishing could escape these changes. The establishment of deep-sea ports at places like Ujina, for instance, obliterated oyster beds in neighboring areas, forcing whole communities to pursue alternative sources of both income and food.[26] Some sectors of the economy, such as growing and processing reeds for the production of tatami mats, remained relative stable.[27] By and large, though, circumstances were difficult, with a tight labor market throughout Japan. With that in mind, after 1885 the Meiji government began permitting emigration, which labor-starved segments of the North American economy happily cultivated. From cane-sugar plantations in Hawai'i and farms in California's Central Valley to timber stands or salmon runs in British Columbia and gold mines in Alaska, *watari-dori* pursued dekasegi outside Japan, with Hiroshima losing the third-largest proportion of its population, nearly 4 percent, between 1899 and 1940.[28] Once these people began sending money home, the rate of emigration only increased, even after word came back that life across the Pacific was much harder than many expected.[29]

By the 1890s changing prospects had led to changing priorities at home, and now the same was happening for Nikkei in British Columbia. The circumstances Japanese immigrants found upon arriving in this new land were egregiously unfair, and they responded by working diligently in the trades that were available to them. As Mitsuo Yesaki noted with respect to salmon fishing, "the Japanese were not necessarily better fishermen. With few other job opportunities, they had no alternative but to work harder and longer for higher catches."[30]

Like their counterparts in the American fishing sector, they also strove to provide mutual aid and engage in collective bargaining, especially as their successes helped transform both the labor market and life in the home.[31] Consider the early twentieth-century village of Steveston, where Kumanosuke and Riyo moved just before the birth of Kimiko, their first daughter.[32] Encouraged by a pair of Nikkei dentists visiting from the United States, Matsutaro Okamoto, a Methodist minister, and Iwakichi Shimamura, a leader among the village's fishermen, persuaded their fellow Nikkei in Steveston to combat high rates of typhus in the community by establishing a medical facility within a mission newly built in 1895.[33] In addition to providing care for patients and serving as a focal point for Nikkei Methodists, the mission also ran the first Japanese primary school in British Columbia. The 1897 founding of the Steveston Dantai, with Homma as its leader, started as an attempt to combat disparities in pay, but the organization soon became an anchor for the wider Nikkei community. When the Methodist mission could no longer meet the healthcare needs of the population, the members of the Dantai funded the establishment and operation of a new, dedicated medical facility in 1898.[34] In so doing, they established the first community-funded healthcare system in Canada, predating Medicare by over fifty years. And, as noted above, the Dantai also advanced the work of more activist members.

With their 1904 move to Steveston, the Okanos joined a community in transition. Shifting from the model of dekasegi toward longer-term residence, Nikkei strove to improve their circumstances whenever and wherever possible. Even so, Steveston retained much of its early rough-and-tumble character. Populated largely by Nikkei bachelors from low-income backgrounds who lived cheek-by-jowl in low-rent bunkhouses, the community seems to have been a little like something out of Wild West mythology. A boat boss named Asamatsu Murakami recalled of the years around 1900, "None of the men had wives then, they were all single. And, as there were no women, they'd get wild. Just a few drinks and they'd start a fight. I saw a lot of fights. Some men killed each other, some were put in gaol. Later, when the brides started coming from Japan, their lives improved."[35]

Exacerbating that roughness was the entrenched poverty among the recent immigrants. Room and board, while inexpensive, still consumed nearly all of a worker's monthly income; clothing and supplies took most of what remained.[36] So, with little opportunity to save for the future, many of the single men tended to put what surplus income they had into the available entertainments of drinking, gambling, and prostitution.[37]

Life for a Nikkei woman in Steveston was no easier.[38] Murakami's account of how things improved there applies to the years after Riyo Okano arrived. (The main influx of picture brides began in 1908, once Canada and Japan had made their so-called Gentlemen's Agreement to limit immigration by men.[39]) Many women objected to having to leave Japan, and some of them refused to remain in British Columbia once local conditions and their economic prospects became clear. In a 1972 interview, Umanosuke and Moto Suzuki recounted these tensions in microcosm. Moto Suzuki suggested that she had been tricked into marrying her husband, adding:

> After we were married my parents said they wouldn't let me go to Canada, and I went back to live with them for a while. They had let me get married only because he said he would stay in Japan. Well, I don't know if he said it or if his relatives did. But it was said that the two brothers would resume the shipbuilding business. I was the oldest of seven children and the first grandchild, so my parents said we want to keep this child close by. His village was next to mine so they said it was almost like living at home, and they let me marry. But then he said he would go back to Canada.[40]

Umanosuke responded, "I had wanted to return to Japan eventually. I would have returned if I'd made any money. But I couldn't make any money, so I couldn't go back." His brother also had no choice, though in a different way. He had sent his two children to be educated in Japan; when his wife decided to join them, the writing was on the wall. He went back and eventually took over the family house and land.[41] (A similar situation arose for Kumanosuke Okano's son from his first marriage. The young man, Ayanosuke, and his wife, Tsuruka, ultimately returned to Japan after an abortive attempt to settle in British Columbia.[42])

The Okanos seem to have had no plans to return to their homeland, and Riyo was undeniably tough and enterprising and bound by the new kinship network into which marriage had brought her.[43] Still, one wonders what she must have thought of this breathtaking, yet mud-caked and fish-stinking land with its vicious white supremacists, rapacious cannery companies, and all those Nikkei bachelors at loose ends. Whatever her opinions, regret was a luxury she could not afford. Plus, the Okanos' circumstances could have been worse. Steveston was a far more appealing place than the average lumber camp. With its relatively large Nikkei population and robust social networks, there would be support for the Okanos as they began to have children. Finances would be a challenge, but the two were making progress. Kumanosuke bought his first fishing boat the year they moved to Steveston.[44] Doing this enabled him to pursue a higher income, though it also came with higher overhead. There was the cost of the boat, but that was only the beginning. He also needed nets, fuel, and a berth, as well as space in which to dry and repair his nets. And finally, he would have to negotiate pricing on his own. The Okanos appear to have sold their catches on Water Street in Vancouver, rather than signing on with a particular cannery in any given season. In another departure from common practice, Kumanosuke did not hire help. Instead, he and Riyo fished for themselves. This enabled the family to avoid having to pay for and manage a crew.[45] Another boon came a little later: after several successful seasons, Kumanosuke was able to buy additional boats, which he rented out to other Nikkei fishermen. This would prove critical for the family's future success. The fleet brought in additional income at the time, and selling it off later provided the Okanos with money to buy their own property in the Gulf Islands, which lay at the western edge of the Strait of Georgia between Vancouver and Victoria.

Establishing a Foundation

Riyo Okano's arrival marked an important turning point in her and Kumanosuke's fortunes. Together, the two of them could support one another, expanding the pool of labor that would contribute to their economic stability. Together, they could avoid the indignities and excesses of a lumber camp by moving into a cannery house, which was common practice for married Nikkei fishermen and their wives.[46] Together, they could begin to build that elusive nest egg that had brought them to Canada. Most important, perhaps, together they could knit themselves into a cluster of communities. Some, like that formed by Nikkei fishermen and cannery workers, were relatively tightly knit. Others were looser but still impactful. For instance, Kimiko, the Okanos' eldest daughter and Mary Kitagawa's mother, recalled playing with First Nations children in the neighborhood around one of the canneries near where the family lived.[47]

Life in Steveston remained challenging, though, even after increasing numbers of picture brides began to arrive in 1908. Housing was still largely a white man's game, even for the fisherman who owned his boat. To live in a cannery house was better than being in a bunkhouse, let alone a lumber camp, but it still was not one's own home. Living in someone else's property required giving up money that could otherwise go toward the family. Plus, life in a cannery house still meant being in the thick of all those single men and their various entertainments, which made it a challenging place to raise an expanding family.

And so, by 1906 the family had moved to a small plot on Duck Bay on the northwest coast of Salt Spring Island.[48] There, daughters Sayoko and Kazue would be born in 1906 and 1908, respectively. The family did not undertake the move casually since their fishing operation in Steveston had become quite profitable. Still, it was time for the Okanos to buy property of their own in a place that would enable them to become fully self-supporting, build equity, begin farming, and continue fishing. A few Nikkei were buying land along the Fraser River, but the plots were large and prices correspondingly high; those plots also required a commitment to full-time farming, with all the risks that entailed.[49] The Gulf Islands, situated between Vancouver and Victoria, had a stronger appeal. Smaller lots could be purchased from private owners for relatively low prices. (Nikkei were still barred from buying Crown lands at the time, so they had to make their purchases on the secondary market.) In addition, given Duck Bay's location, they could work the plot in the off season, and there was also easy access to the gulf and its fisheries as well as to markets in Vancouver and Victoria.[50] One imagines the Okanos felt particular relief about the move after the Vancouver riots of 1907, in which white laborers, egged on by the Vancouver Asiatic Exclusion League and a roster of fiery speakers, attacked people of Chinese and Japanese ancestry.[51] Although Nikkei could find support in various quarters of the white population, British Columbia's racists were organized, visible, and activist.[52]

A Challenging Haven

Since the mid-nineteenth century, the Gulf Islands had been cast in romantic terms as a land ideally suited to the unconventional, the ambitious, the adventurous.[53] From 1860 onward, colonists could acquire land on the islands through a process called preemption. In this case, preemption applies to land that, as far as the law is concerned, has only just come into existence—that is, no one has formally laid claim to it.[54] Accordingly, so long as the land was not demonstrably on an First Nations reserve or did not belong to a recognized settlement, virtually anyone could file a claim to it.[55] Note in particular how this system placed First Nations inhabitants of the Gulf Islands at an inherent disadvantage: any ancestral lands that did not fall within the confines of a reserve were effectively up for grabs by anyone who chose to settle there.[56] So long as the preemptor could show that he had improved that land after submitting his application and so long as he was not absent from his claim beyond a strictly limited period, he could eventually purchase the land at an artificially low price. After that, this person could continue to work the land, or he could sell it to someone else at whatever value he deemed appropriate.[57]

The Gulf Islands ecosystem was rich, but life on Salt Spring Island and its neighbors was still demanding, and many early preemptors eventually relinquished their claims. In an effort to boost occupancy and bolster the growing colonial economy, early leaders of the Hudson's Bay Company courted preemptors from far afield. Most notably, they recruited a significant number of Black migrants from the United States after the Civil War. Promising a life free of American bigotry, the company's pitch assured prospective colonists that British Columbia offered them riches beyond compare as well as a proper chance to capitalize on those riches. Some migrants, such as the Stark family, carved out a place for themselves on Salt Spring Island and even engaged in trade with their Nikkei as well as white and First Nations neighbors.[58] Others found the reality of preemption far harsher than the ideal of the gentleman farmer the Hudson's Bay company had been promoting. Many returned to the United States, while others moved elsewhere in Canada. Few found life in the gulf tenable in the long term, and none found it especially peaceful.[59]

These efforts by the Hudson's Bay Company and, later, the provincial government of British Columbia gave rise to an unexpected frontier mentality. Far from matching the Commonwealth's prevailing ideal of commercial agriculture, life on the Gulf Islands was arduous and frequently precarious. It also was far from color-blind, as Black preemptors knew all too well, though the demands of that life necessitated a degree of cooperation that tempered some of the worst excesses of white racism. As a result, successful preemptors and their followers found a place where they could make a living and do so largely on their own terms. The resulting life might not meet with approval from middle-class white outsiders, but it could be durable, sustainable, and relatively independent.[60] Thus, in their failure to satisfy broader expectations of rural life, the Gulf Islands became a kind of safe harbor in which Nikkei could follow in the footsteps of Black predecessors, establishing footholds on both Mayne and Salt Spring Islands by the turn of the century.[61] All these factors helped people of Japanese ancestry become a third wave of non-natives to colonize Salt Spring Island, starting around 1880.

Riyo and Kumanosuke Okano regularly fished the waters east of Vancouver Island during their time in Steveston. Early in their fishing days, they began visiting Salt Spring Island to gather firewood for sale when salmon were out of season.[62] During their visits, they seem to have become familiar with some of the other Nikkei on the island. There was, for instance, the Tasaka family, which Mary recalls as having been "not only big on charcoal [production] but in producing 18 children."[63] The Tasakas and other Nikkei working the charcoal trade enjoyed such success that in 1902 charcoal was listed as one of the island's biggest exports.[64] The exact relationship between the Okanos and the Tasakas is no longer clear, but it must have been at least somewhat close. Kimiko recalled the Tasakas' operation clearly enough that, when historians sought to reconstruct one of the original kilns, Rose was able to guide them to the spot based on stories her mother had recounted.[65]

Other evidence also suggests that settling on Salt Spring Island allowed the Okanos to knit themselves into another Nikkei community. Around the time they moved, three other Nikkei families also purchased land on Duck Bay. And by 1901, at least sixty-seven Nikkei already lived on the island, many in lumber camps along the southeast coast, and within a few years there was a cluster of families near the hamlet of Vesuvius just to the southeast of Duck Bay.[66] Other families had set up shop elsewhere. Isaburo and Yorie Tasaka, for instance, ran their charcoal-producing operation from their property in Ganges, on the northeast coast.[67] They and other Nikkei families were not going to get rich, but they could participate in a larger sharing economy that governed life on Salt Spring Island at the time.

Mary later recalled that Japanese immigrants and their families on the island "did everything together: picnics, weddings, funerals, helping with building, New Year mochi making, donating to wider community projects like building a school and church."[68] That mention of a school is especially important. Mary is referring to 1939 efforts to build what would become the Consolidated School for the island's children. Nikkei made up more than half the donors to this project; those who could not contribute money helped with construction.[69] Such generosity was not restricted to fellow Nikkei. The school served Black, white, and First Nations children as well. Furthermore, Mary added, "when destitute white people came begging for food or clothing, the Japanese Canadians helped them."[70] This despite the fact that times were tough for Nikkei families, too, as Mary's sister Rose has observed: "During the depression, when people came to their doors seeking food and clothing, our parents and grandparents were very generous—even though they were suffering as well."[71]

While the family had its share of lean years, it did better than many, thanks to Riyo and Kumanosuke's combined economic ambition and financial prudence. Life on Salt Spring Island had always entailed what Ruth Sandwell has called "occupational plurality."[72] In this respect, it fit the Okanos' changing needs as well as their broad range of skills. Duck Bay was well situated for their fishing operation, for instance. Travel to salmon grounds was straightforward, and in the off season, the island allowed them to sustain themselves without having to travel extensively. They could, for instance, pursue herring in the fall and winter, when those fish migrate to inshore waters in the run-up to the spring spawn.[73] In addition, the family could cut timber for farmers trying to clear land. They could harvest and dry nori (seaweed) for themselves. And all the while they could put more of their hard-earned money toward building up equity that would let them expand their fishing operation. Furthermore, like so many immigrants on Salt Spring Island, raising a family further improved their prospects, since children contributed to the labor.[74] As she grew older, for instance, Kimiko began to participate in the family business. When she was five, she began accompanying her father on trips to sell fish on Water Street.[75] He would launch and land the boat, and she would pilot the vessel while he slept.[76] Later, she became the first woman to drive on Salt Spring Island.

Still, life was hard on Duck Bay, especially in the early years, when the Okanos were still fishing. The family's boats and tackle endured wear and tear; at times they also sustained damage. And then there was the fact that fishing is cyclical, with brief periods of intense labor, the value of which hangs on the size and quality of one's catch. The annual sockeye season lasted only two months. Since sockeye were the only salmon that canneries initially processed, this meant that Nikkei had to find other ways to support themselves during the lengthy off season. And even after canneries started buying other types of salmon in the mid-1900s, cycles remained a hallmark of the business. For instance, Fraser pink salmon have a two-year life cycle, so adults travel upriver to spawn only in odd-numbered years, while coho salmon have a three-year life cycle. Furthermore, yields could fluctuate wildly from season to season. The year 1903 saw the average fisherman bring in 861 fish; in 1905 that number soared to 4,043 before dropping to a new low of 426 in 1907. Further complicating matters was the fact that canneries negotiated lower prices in dominant years, so even a big yield brought only moderate financial benefit.

The Okanos put themselves in a favorable position. Having worked their primary boat in tandem, having assembled a small fleet they could rent out, and having established a customer base for firewood, they were able to work their small patch of land on Duck Bay and harvest supplementary foodstuffs. Still, they enjoyed little margin for error, financially or otherwise. Their successes were hard-won; their reserves were modest; the family's well-being was always fragile.

In 1911, the Okanos suffered the first of two gut-wrenching losses. Kazue fell from the family boat and drowned not long after her second birthday. Life on Salt Spring Island may have necessitated collaboration across racial distinctions, but Nikkei were still barred from burying their dead in the local cemetery.[77] That meant the family would have to carry her body across the Strait of Georgia to Vancouver for the funeral, but they would have to move quickly, lest they lose their place in a fiercely competitive and unfair economy. Discriminatory licensing policies designed expressly to stymie Nikkei and advance white fishermen were becoming increasingly common, from restrictions on the use of a motor on one's boat to the price and number of licenses one could own.⁷⁸ And although here, too, members of the Nikkei community fought for fair treatment, they were sailing into a stiff political wind.⁷⁹

Not long after Kazue's death came the second catastrophe. While the family was in Vancouver selling fish, they received word that their property had been the target of arson.⁸⁰ Their houseboat was completely destroyed, along with part of the saltery where they processed their herring catches.⁸¹ The family needed to regroup. They sold the Duck Bay property and moved across the Stuart Channel to Chemainus on Vancouver Island, where they paid to have a new houseboat built.⁸² They also decided, for the safety of their children, to take a break from fishing. Riyo was pregnant, so while construction of the houseboat was under way, she and Kumanosuke decided to return to Innoshima temporarily. There, Kumanosuke's mother, Karu, could care for Kimiko and Sayoko, and Riyo could deliver her baby in safe and familiar surroundings. Once the family arrived, Kumanosuke stayed long enough to help his wife settle in and to get Kimiko and Sayoko enrolled in school. After that was done, he set out for Canada again in order to ensure the continued success of the family's fishing operation. After giving birth to another daughter, Miyoko, Riyo returned to Canada with the infant, leaving the two older girls behind.

Japanese Canadian in Japan

Kimiko Okano would have sensed the difference of Innoshima well before her boat docked. Having spent her entire life in British Columbia, she was intimately familiar with the feel of an estuary. Here, too, she found that unmistakable intersection of fresh and salt water, those bracing ocean breezes punctuating the rich earthy funk of hills covered in lush vegetation and riven by creeks and springs. Once again, vertiginous hills and innumerable protected bays lined an island-dotted waterway between Honshu to the west and Shikoku to the east. And yet, it must have seemed profoundly alien at the same time. Gone were the familiar spruce, cedar, and fir trees; no more salal, sword fern, kinnikinnik, and Nootka Rose. In their place stood *tabunoki, tsuburajii,* and Japanese laurel. Gone too was the smell of her homeland, replaced with another aroma. This new land would have been familiar, but only familiar enough to sharpen the sense of what she had left behind. Unlike her mother, who had left Japan as an adult and had been traveling to be with her husband, Kimiko was just eight years old when she was forced to leave behind everything she had ever known.

Understandably, then, moving to Japan posed significant challenges for her. Over the next seven years she and Sayoko would become fluent in Japanese, but they would lose their command of English. They also would not see their parents again until 1919, when Kumanosuke and Riyo bought the girls return fare. While their parents went back to British Columbia, Kimiko and Sayoko had to stay behind with their seventy-eight-year-old widowed grandmother. Part of this decision had to do with the health and safety of the two girls. After Kazue's death, the fishing boat struck the Okanos as simply too dangerous—this despite the fact that Kimiko had easily proven her skills when she helped her father pilot the family's fishing boat between Salt Spring Island and Vancouver. The practicality and self-assurance she showed in circumstances like that had convinced her parents that it would be best if she watched over Sayoko far from the dangers of open water and the wilds beyond Duck Bay.

For Kimiko, the decision to place her in charge of Sayoko in Japan must have felt almost like being punished for her competence. Still, she gave herself fully to her life in a new country, excelling in school and knitting herself into the local community. She and Sayoko never really bonded with their grandmother, though, so those seven years deprived them of a strong sense of their immediate family. Furthermore, Kimiko's strengths proved a double-edged sword once again when, in 1919, her parents brought her back to Canada. Having committed to life on Innoshima, she found herself unable to converse in English, which she had to relearn on her own, and unfamiliar with the customs of people her age. Furthermore, the family now included a brother, Victor, who had been born in 1916. (Another brother, James, would be born in 1922.) Most distressingly, she had to reacquaint herself with her parents, whom she never fully forgave for their decision to leave her and Sayoko in Japan.[83]

The Struggle to Establish a Durable Footing

With their return to British Columbia, the family faced a growing host of challenges. After 1910, the future of fishing was becoming increasingly uncertain. The trade itself had started to undergo important changes. There was growing talk of closing some fisheries altogether due to overharvesting.[84] Plus, the number of fishing units had been on the rise, while the size of those units had been steadily shrinking.[85] Even as Kumanosuke had begun to assemble a small fleet of ships that augmented his income, market forces were working against the family. The resulting financial pressure worsened already simmering tensions among white, First Nations, and Nikkei fishermen. There had been strikes from as early as 1893 onward, as fishermen struggled to get fair wages for their labor, but groups banded together only intermittently, with race being a critical factor. White fishermen's unions repeatedly voted against allowing First Nations, Chinese, and Nikkei members. (This was one of the reasons for the founding of the Steveston Dantai.) As a result, the various unions often negotiated only on behalf of their members, rather than on behalf of all fishermen.[86] A strike in 1900 brought especially bitter infighting among the unions; it also cost white fishermen the higher wage they would have secured had they cooperated with their Nikkei neighbors.[87] Plus, although the number of Asian immigrants fell and overall economic circumstances improved in British Columbia between 1920 and 1930, white hysteria remained at a fever pitch.[88] That hysteria was especially pronounced in fishing, where Nikkei held 40–50 percent of all gillnet licenses by the late teens.[89] Against this backdrop, Yesaki's observation about the fishing trade takes on a new cast: attempts to suppress Nikkei profits spurred even greater productivity, which further depressed the economic prospects for all fishermen.

British Columbia fishermen of all backgrounds found themselves in a saturated labor market, which cannery owners and racist political leaders used to their advantage. Rather than seek fair prices across the board, however, white fishermen doubled down on their intra-ethnic bonds, inadvertently further weakening their own position. (The British Columbia mining industry had seen a similar behavior, with a brutal labor market and an opportunistic press fanning racist hysteria that ultimately worked against equitable pay.[90]) Attempts to deny Nikkei competitors a collective voice had failed spectacularly; attempts to undercut the Dantai had met with a similar fate. So, racists turned their attention to the playing field itself. In 1912, they secured the first of several restrictions on the number of fishing licenses Nikkei could hold. The restrictions were modest, and people found several ways to circumvent them.[91] Consequently, the proportion of Nikkei fishermen continued to grow, such that by 1919 they held fully half of the available licenses. As word of this figure spread, it provided a rallying point for their white competitors. Emboldened by early restrictions, they called for hearings, lobbied government ministries, and courted racist politicians. As a result, in 1919 the Department of Fisheries made a twofold declaration: Nikkei fishermen would receive no additional licenses for the 1920 season, and starting in 1921 the department would enforce year-by-year reductions to the number of licenses Nikkei held.[92] Thus, even before the strictest anti-Japanese initiatives of the later 1920s and early 1930s, the writing was on the wall. If the Okano family hoped to survive in British Columbia, they would need to do it in another line of work.

Soon after the announcement by the Department of Fisheries, the Okanos sold several of their boats. They used the proceeds to buy two hundred acres of farmland to the southeast of Vesuvius and just inland from Booth Canal, a small intermittently navigable inlet that extends into Booth Bay. They cleared fifty acres, expanded and improved a house that was already there, and set about farming (figure 2).[93] The choice of location was astute. While it was not on the more fertile north end of the island, the land they bought was fairly level, the soil was good, and it had a stable supply of fresh water.[94] Furthermore, the property abutted Sharp Road and had access both to a gravel track called Rainbow Road and to Booth Canal Road. Rain-

FIGURE 2. Kumanosuke, Sayoko, and Kimiko Okano feeding their chickens, 1920. Photo courtesy of the Salt Spring Island Archives.

bow Road connected it with other farms in the area, while Sharp and Booth Canal Roads led to Ganges Road and, via that, to the town of Ganges on the east coast. (A creek that feeds the inlet is still known as Okano Creek.[95])

The Okanos were able to work a fertile plot with good access to markets both on the island and elsewhere. This gave them economic options they had lacked earlier. As the farm became more successful, they gradually scaled back their fishing operation, which they phased out completely in 1924.[96] They also could afford a modicum of travel. Their budget was limited, though, so that travel was limited to family obligations. And so, in 1925, Kimiko and Sayoko returned to Japan for the eighty-eighth birthday of their grandmother (figure 3).[97]

FIGURE 3. Kimiko Okano boarding the ship to return to Canada, March 1926. Photo courtesy of the Salt Spring Island Archives.

An Expanding Family

While the sisters were in Japan, another Innoshima family happened to be holding a wedding ceremony. The bride arrived by boat, bringing with her a large group of family members, friends, and acquaintances. Although the relative isolation of Salt Spring Island seems to have restricted (though not curtailed) the influence of kinship, in Japan family networks continued to loom large.[98] After hearing that Kimiko's family wished for her to marry, a member of the group took the news home to his brother, Katsuyori Murakami, a widower who had lost his wife and son during the pandemic of 1918–1919.[99] The Murakamis were descendants of the tenth-century Emperor Murakami of Japan, but that storied ancestry could not shelter the family's fifth son from the economic and social transformations that had convulsed the nation. By contrast, marriage to the Okanos, who had land and a thriving farm in British Columbia, was a gamble, but it held promise. With that in mind, his family and the Okanos agreed to an *omiai*, or formal introduction of the two. The arrangement turned out to be a stunning success, and Kimiko and Katsuyori married the following January.

Getting Katsuyori into Canada was not easy. After the Gentlemen's Agreement, immigration by men from Japan declined precipitously. One of the important exceptions was a provision for what in Japanese became known as *yobiyose*, after the term for being "called over" to work. The regulations governing yobiyose were strict, requiring not only that the sponsor in Canada be a registered landowner in documented need of assistance but also that the Japanese consulate in the area approve the request.[100] The Okanos were becoming experienced on this front, though, as they had begun regularly employing yobiyose, whom they recruited with the help of the Japanese consulate.[101] They completed the necessary paperwork, and once Katsuyori had consular approval, he entered into a three-year contract of employment, in return for which Okanos would provide housing, board, and a modest income.[102] He landed in Victoria on April 13, 1927, just ahead of further restrictions on Japanese immigration.[103]

Life on Salt Spring Island was no easier for Katsuyori and Kimiko than it had been for the Okanos, and that contract extended from three years into five. But by 1932 it enabled the young couple to buy seventeen acres adjacent to the Okano property on Sharp Road. They were the third Nikkei family to buy into that particular area, followed not long after by Kumanosuke's daughter Sukini (Kimiko's half-sister) and her husband.[104] It was the beginning of a Nikkei enclave that, by 1942, would include no fewer than eight distinct farms and encompass well over three hundred acres.[105] Such success never entailed an easy existence, in part because of friction between the Okanos and the Murakamis. Riyo seems to have had particular trouble with her son-in-law. At least once she falsely accused Katsuyori of threatening her with physical harm; on another occasion, she diverted the stream that fed the Murakamis' property, putting their crops at risk.[106]

Even when relations between the Okanos and the Murakamis were good, life was challenging. As Rose Murakami recalls, "Mother rose at 3:30 a.m., even when she was pregnant, to give breakfast to father. He got up at 3 a.m. to feed the 5,000 egg-laying chickens. After breakfast he would pick strawberries still wet with dew. By 2 p.m. mother had 65 crates packed and ready when the freight truck came to take them to A. P. Slades [a Victoria-based distributor]."[107] Although they hired seasonal workers—mostly Nikkei women from Vancouver Island—to help pick and pack the strawberries, Mary's parents did much of the work themselves. After tending to the young Murakami children all day, Kimiko would pack asparagus late into the night. Each day, a truck would come by to pick up the cut and carefully packed asparagus and eggs, a long-standing arrangement with the grocers in the area.[108]

This hard work was paying off. The farm was productive, and the Murakamis had developed strong connections with regional markets. The family sold raspberries, strawberries, and vegetables to A. P. Slades, who sold them to high-profile retailers.[109] Such was the popularity of their fruit that, when King George VI and Queen Elizabeth visited British Columbia as part of their 1939 tour of Canada, the Empress Hotel in Victoria specifically requested strawberries from the Murakami farm.[110] Katsuyori and Kimiko also sold an increasing number of eggs to a Ganges grocery store run by the Mouats, a prominent white family on Salt Spring Island. After becoming the first woman to drive on the island in 1923, Kimiko made the family's deliveries, barreling down Ganges Road in a Ford truck.[111] It could be difficult to say whether you were safer in the cab with her or standing by the side of the road, but there was no denying that it helped the family tremendously to have her making deliveries.

As they were establishing this economic foundation for themselves,

Katsuyori and Kimiko decided it was time to have children. First came their eldest daughter, Atsuko Alice, born in 1928, followed by Taeko Violet in 1930. (All the Murakamis' children have gone by their Anglo middle names.) The parents were ecstatic when their first son, Ryoichi, was born in January 1933, but joy quickly turned to sorrow. Ryoichi suffered from a congenital heart defect, and although Kimiko did everything she could to keep him alive, he died the following September. By that time, Nikkei on Salt Spring Island had established their own cemetery, where the Murakamis interred the tiny body of their son. Keiko Mary was born in 1934, her sister Takako Rose in 1937, and Katsuhide Richard in 1940. Another son, Yorihide Bruce, was born in 1944, during the family's time in the Kootenays.

Having built a stable foundation on the island, the Okano-Murakami clan helped a number of other Nikkei migrants and their families get established. There were, for instance, the Hiranos, one of two Nikkei families who built houses on the Okanos' land. Two main motives likely governed Kumanosuke and Riyo's decision to allow this. First, there was the centrality of mutual aid for life both on the island and within the Nikkei community. Second, there was the expectation of reciprocity that governed such aid. Life in British Columbia was precarious for most Nikkei, so the Hiranos might someday be in a position to return the favor. We can see the intertwining of these two motives in a critical historical detail. When the time came to build the Hiranos' house, according to Mary, her father provided invaluable labor: "it was my dad who did most of the construction."[112] By then, Katsuyori was married with a thriving farm and a family of his own, but he also was both a former yobiyose and the Okanos' son-in-law. To these two motives we should also add a third: Katsuyori was, Mary stresses, unfailingly generous.

Ruth Sandwell has noted that children were often crucial for the success of migrants to Salt Spring Island, contributing to the household labor pool at less cost than hired help.[113] The Murakami children certainly pulled their weight around the house and on the farm. As Mary recalls, "We were never asked to do any chores. We just did what had to be done without being asked."[114] And yet, life in the Murakami household was not a grind. Work could be made into something more. For instance, as a child, Mary suffered from asthma, which meant the family had to keep the house as clean and dust-free as possible. The Murakami children, inspired by their

FIGURE 4. Katsuyori, Kimiko, Alice, Violet, Mary, and Rose Murakami in front of their Sharp Road home, summer of 1938. Photo courtesy of the Salt Spring Island Archives.

parents' upbeat attitude, made a game of their chores. With dust rags tied to their feet, they would polish the floors by pretending to skate from room to room.

Resourcefulness was the order of the day, in play as well as in work. Mary recalls, "We were far away from other families, so we played mostly by ourselves or helped with the chores. We were never bored because it was safe to wander around: [we] went down to the canal, created our own fun, visited our grandparents, played with our dog [named Mune], went into our forest to look for flowers."[115] The family had other animals, too. In addition to the five thousand chickens, they also had a horse. Although Katsuyori originally purchased it to draw the plow in planting season, Mary remembers the animal as something of another playmate for the children.[116]

Life on the island extended beyond the family. When they were old enough, each of the Murakami children began attending school. There, they sat in class alongside children from the island's various communities—some First Nations, some white, some Black, including, in the case of Kimiko and her siblings, members of the Stark, Wood, and Whims families.[117] Island-wide events, such as the annual Fall Fair, would bring citizens together. Mary recalls walking to the fair, where her family entered their flowers, vegetables, and berries in competitions.[118] Beyond the local sharing economy, Nikkei on the island also had their own community activities. There were births, weddings, and funerals. New Year's would see families gather to make mochi (a delicacy made from pounded glutinous rice) and trade stories. As the 1930s drew to a close and with their family and the Nikkei community finally having carved out a place in British Columbia, the Murakamis set their sights on a landmark moment: spring of 1942, when they would finally finish paying for their land (figure 4).

TWO

An Uprooted Childhood

An officer with the Royal Canadian Mounted Police (RCMP) abducted Mary's father on March 17, 1942. He did it in accordance with a government directive, but that technicality in no way lessens the violence of either the directive or its implementation.[1] As the RCMP truck approached the family farm, Katsuyori gathered his children and reassured them that all would be well, encouraging them to keep their spirits up and to help the family weather the nightmare that had begun with the bombing of Pearl Harbor the previous December.[2] He then exited the house, heading toward the vehicle. He was moving slowly, having recently undergone an appendectomy.[3] With heedless malice, the Mountie shoved his charge, causing him to fall and strike his face on the bed of the truck. Mindful that the family was watching, Katsuyori hurriedly got up and told them he was okay. The children loaded what little he was allowed to take into the truck, and Alice asked the Mountie if her father could perhaps ride in the passenger seat to ease his postoperative discomfort. Not only did the officer refuse her request, but he also shifted gears roughly as he drove away, causing the truck to jerk forward and nearly toppling Katsuyori yet again.

The Murakamis had been bracing themselves for more than a month, but the reality of the abduction and the brutish way the Mountie conducted himself terrified them. Mary later recollected, "In my seven-year-old mind . . . as my father was being taken onto the truck, I saw the gun in the holster of the RCMP officer, and I thought for sure that he was being—because of the way that he was being manhandled—I thought for sure that my father was being taken away to be shot."[4] Readers familiar with the postwar narrative of Canadian tolerance and social liberalism might be tempted to think of the RCMP officer as simply a bad apple, the lone perpetrator of a discrete misdeed.[5] For a young girl accustomed to men who exhibited gentler, more measured behavior, though, the Mountie came across as a raw existential threat. Furthermore, we must also remember that this officer was performing an operation dictated by government policy. From hurried proposal and intemperate debate through hasty implementation, that policy validated, enflamed, and institutionalized anti-Japanese hysteria. Consequently, such hysteria, which might otherwise seem like it was just improper behavior, was an extension of government policy. Actions such as the Mountie's were therefore never really departures from an otherwise supposedly humane, if ill-advised, policy. As Kirsten Emiko McAllister has observed, they were simply the purest, most explicit expressions of a larger state-sponsored project of violence.[6] After all, even the physically gentlest expulsion from British Columbia was still an exercise in abduction and extortion. Most Nikkei in internal exile may have moved out of British Columbia on their own two feet, and all of them paid much more than their own way, but that movement and that payment were never theirs to choose. They always occurred under threat of more overt violence and even greater personal cost.

We should also recognize that Mary's response was not the outsized worry of a young child confronted with wanton violence. It was reasonable, especially given the circumstances. Abductions of Japanese-born men were taking place throughout the province, and they came after an extended period of profound uncertainty and growing local aggression. Nikkei life in British Columbia had always been tenuous, and everyone immediately recognized that the bombing of Pearl Harbor would further enflame anti-Japanese sentiment. Racist politicians and civic leaders had long sought excuses to further entrench and, if possible, expand their policies, even in the face of resistance from Ottawa and, at times, locals. Looking toward the prospects for conflict with Japan, the provincial government actively pursued various anti-Nikkei measures linked to the presumption of pro-Japanese loyalty from 1938 onward.[7] Spurred in part by such measures, in October 1940, the Canadian government formed the Special Committee on Orientals in British Columbia. In theory, that body was supposed to keep the government apprised of developments in the province, and it eventually produced an explicit statement that Nikkei and their families posed no danger to the nation. Nonetheless, to placate far-right politicians and newspapers, it also recommended that Issei and Nisei be required to formally register, a policy subsequently implemented by the government of Prime Minister William Lyon Mackenzie King.

Under the pretext of providing an accurate headcount of the population, registration went forward with relatively little complaint being raised, perhaps in part because Italian and German immigrants were subject to similar measures.[8] Rather than relieve tension in the province, though, registration seems to have had the opposite effect, much as anti-Asian legislation had done in the United States.[9] The very existence of the special committee lent credence to the claim that "orientals" were a problem in need of solving. Further aggravating the situation was the fact that at the end of 1941, Canada, as part of the British Empire, was at war in the Pacific. Japan attacked Hong Kong on December 8, the day after bombing Pearl Harbor, and before the month's end, its military had overwhelmed Canadian, British, and Indian soldiers as well as the Hong Kong Volunteer Defense Forces. For most Canadians, the question was not whether the national government would or even should move against people of Japanese ancestry, but how.[10]

After ferocious debate behind closed doors, Ottawa bowed to British Columbia racists on January 14, 1942, announcing five key measures, including the formation of a committee to dispose of nearly 1,200 fishing boats the government had seized from Nikkei fishermen on December 8, as well as the eviction of all Japanese nationals from so-called protected areas in British Columbia.[11] Still, it remained unclear exactly what the new measures would entail. The boundaries of those protected areas had yet to be established. What would they ultimately encompass? Also, some "enemy aliens" would be allowed to remain in those areas, provided they held police permits. Who could get such permits, and how? There was to be a civilian corps for which Nikkei Canadians could volunteer. What sorts of work would it perform, and how might one join? More importantly, what incentive might there be for volunteering beyond the demonstration of loyalty to Canada? And as for the committee in charge of the Nikkei fishing fleet, what would govern whether that body leased, chartered, or sold the boats outright? Furthermore, if the RCMP was to oversee restrictions against Nikkei, such as the control of gasoline and explosives and the confiscation of radios and cameras, what protection could the community expect from a growing tide of local aggression? Last, but certainly not least, looming over all of this was the implicit question of whether further measures would be coming.

Compounding the problem, white authorities shuttered every Nikkei newspaper save one, *The New Canadian*. In an attempt to address its suddenly much larger readership, this paper ran an editorial below an article about the January 14 announcement. Entitled "Keep Cool and Keep Calm," it urged readers to bear in mind that "Ottawa's announcement is only the general plan of what is to be done. The important and effective details are yet to be decided."[12] But the editorial staff of the paper could not entirely silence the worries of a people under threat. On January 16, the paper observed that "the entire Japanese Canadian community in British Columbia is anxiously awaiting further word from Ottawa as to the details of the new regulations announced Wednesday morning. There is no person of Japanese origin not affected, some only slightly, but others for whom the whole future is a huge and almost terrifying question mark."[13] That question mark would grow larger and more terrifying as, with each issue, *The New Canadian* chronicled the stutter-step advance of anti-Nikkei policies. Ambiguity was the order of the day; as the national government continued to dither, a vacuum developed into which all manner of speculation rushed.[14] In mid-January, the paper posited that restrictions would be scaffolded depending on one's nationality and asserted cautious optimism about that scaffolding.[15] Later that month, it directly rebutted the claim that all Nikkei would be evicted from the province.[16] It surveyed the dimming prospects for Nikkei in the United States on January 30, acknowledged on February 9 that all Japanese nationals between the ages of 18 and 45 would be removed from British Columbia and sent to interior labor camps, and assured readers on February 16 that expulsion would apply only to "those [men aged 18–45] born in Japan and not naturalized."[17] Corrosive uncertainty persisted until, finally, on February 26 it became official: Canada would force everyone of Japanese ancestry to leave all but the easternmost part of British Columbia, regardless of nationality.[18] By the end of April, no one in the Murakami or Okano families would be able to call Salt Spring Island home.

With that announcement, the large and terrifying question mark that had loomed over many now loomed over all, and few if any answers to what had become existential questions were forthcoming. Nikkei had set down deep economic and social roots in the province over the six decades since they first began immigrating. Who would care for their businesses, their homes? With the forced removal of all Nikkei from the coast, relatives and community members could not step in, as some had proposed when it seemed only Japanese nationals would be subject to removal. Presumably, the Custodian of Enemy Property, established in 1916, would take control of these assets. But what would that office do, and how? Combined with politicians' and newspapers' shameless courting of anti-Japanese sentiment, the sheer number, variety, and value of properties virtually guaranteed chaos.

If the community's experience with the Japanese Fishing Vessel Disposition Committee had given any indication, the outlook was bleak. In the two months after their seizure, nearly two hundred boats had sunk due to negligence, and more than three months ultimately passed before plans for recovery and repair were in place. Furthermore, in the interim the committee began moving more and more toward outright liquidation of the Nikkei fleet rather than leasing and preservation.

There also were questions about the prospects of the community itself. Civic and religious organizations had already come under intense scrutiny in what would eventually become a concerted effort to purge Nikkei of their language, religious practices, and community groups. As was the case in the United States, this external pressure exacerbated intergenerational tensions, as many younger members of the community, less tied to their family's cultural origins, found themselves at what seemed like a cultural advantage.[19] Worse, no one could say how forced removal from British Columbia would impact individuals and families, which meant that the fabric of Nikkei life was threatened at literally every level. And one place where this threat made itself felt especially keenly was in the prospect of family separation.

The majority of Issei had not been naturalized. But many of them had married and had children, and those children, having been born in Canada, were British subjects. Consequently, they were governed by the same laws and, in theory, enjoyed the same protections as their white fellow subjects. What would happen to their families? Would they be sent to the labor camps where their fathers and husbands had gone? If not, where would they go? And what, if any, provisions would there be for communication, let alone visitation? For Nikkei, family life itself was under direct institutional threat. But even the most basic aspects of that threat remained vague because the government repeatedly failed to provide clarity.

The Murakamis had braced themselves for Katsuyori's abduction after two critical episodes. The first was when the RCMP formally interviewed him in order to gauge what sort of threat he, as an Issei, might pose. The second event that led them to pack his things was when the Salt Spring Island representative of the Custodian of Enemy Property, Gavin Mouat, warned them to be ready.[20] He could not tell them when the RCMP would come, just that he expected they would. And that terrifying ambiguity had come to define every aspect of the family's daily life.

Into the information void crept all manner of speculation, especially given the dark rumblings from Europe that had begun seeping into the public consciousness. On February 26, 1942, for instance, *The New Canadian* ran an alarming proclamation in large font on its second page: "Streng Verboten / Ihre Aufmerksamkeit." The two German phrases, "Strictly Forbidden" and "[For] Your Attention," were followed by this declaration:

It Is Prohibited and Ordered That:
1. No civilians will be permitted on the streets between 8pm and daybreak.
2. All owners of motor cars, trucks, and buses must register same at Occupation Headquarters where they will be taken over by the Army of Occupation.

Readers of the *Vancouver News-Herald* might perhaps have recognized the reference. Alarmed by fascist gains in Europe, the *News-Herald*, the Kiwanis Club, and several local businesses joined the Vancouver Junior Board of Trade in holding a Streng Verboten Day that was meant to give British Columbians a taste of what life under totalitarianism would entail. For the predominantly white participants, the event was a clever way to model a dark future under Nazi rule, sell war bonds, and, in some cases, advertise their wares.

For readers of *The New Canadian*, however, the resonances literally hit home. The paper's banner headline for February 26, running above articles in both English and Japanese, reported "Ottawa Orders Dusk to Dawn Curfew." Furthermore, Ottawa had just issued formal statements that all Nikkei would be required to surrender all motor vehicles—not just boats—along with cameras, radios, and firearms. As the editors of *The New Canadian* observed in an article explaining their use of *Streng Verboten*, it was a "strange coincidence" that saw the Junior Board of Trade's stunt take place alongside new orders from the Dominion government that implemented precisely the sort of repressive measures that were supposedly only the work of fascists. Lest readers miss the point, they added the words "Strictly Forbidden" above the government's announcement that it would seize Nikkei-owned vehicles. Young Mary was hardly alone in contemplating the possibility of previously unthinkable violence at the command of the Canadian Government.

In Want of Compassion

Difficult as they were for Mary, the challenges of that time were even worse for Alice, who had only recently turned thirteen. Too young to have the autonomy of her parents but old enough to grasp the darkness and injustice of the time, she bore an especially heavy burden, and she bore it daily. On December 8, 1941, a teacher singled her out in class and accused her of starting World War II. Another teacher refused to come to work, claiming she feared a Japanese submarine would torpedo her ferry from Vancouver Island. There was even unhinged talk of a submarine making its way up Booth Inlet to the Okano farm.[21] Encouraged by these and other adults, Alice's classmates turned on her. Mary later recalled that

> they started abusing her physically. One day she was going . . . out of the school to go home, and she saw this pile of rocks, and she thought, "Oh, that's strange." But then she walked by it and started walking home. Well, she used to take the shortcut through the forest. And then, a bunch of boys appeared and started stoning her. She said she was hit all over her body, her head, everything. And she started bleeding, you know.[22]

Fortunately, Alice had speed on her side. A fast runner, she was able to escape. More torment awaited her, though. The next day, one of the boys pushed Alice's face into a water fountain, smashing her mouth against the spigot. Only institutional racism put an end to the assaults when, after a few days, the children and their Nikkei classmates were forbidden to attend school.[23]

Despite such hardships, the Murakamis persisted. They had to. Crops needed tending and animals needed care if the family was to survive. The house was not going to maintain itself, and someone had to check on the Okanos, who had recently retired. And then there was the community more generally. Not all white people on the island shared the hysteria that had come to define government policy, but allies were necessarily a loose coalition of people who, because of the island's sharing economy, were as dependent on their bigoted neighbors as they were on the Nikkei whose businesses they supported. There were nearly eighty people of Japanese ancestry on the island at that time, and the Murakamis were keenly aware of how fragile the group and its position had become. Consequently, everyone in the family buckled down and continued doing their share while also trying not to let the growing tide of verbal and physical violence infiltrate their home. And so, Alice kept her suffering to herself. After the first assault by her classmates, for example, she made a beeline to the family's chicken house to get cleaned up, hoping to prevent Katsuyori and Kimiko from learning about the incident. They in turn sheltered the children, insofar as they could, from the gossip and insults that proliferated with each passing day.[24]

Still, even before the RCMP came for Katsuyori, the Murakami parents could only do so much. As racist islanders increasingly turned on their Nikkei neighbors, the tide of insults and injuries rose. State-sponsored bigotry gave an air of acceptability to action at street level, fueling a shared, if unofficial, effort to speed the expulsion of Nikkei islanders from their homes, their businesses, and ultimately the community itself. Some of those efforts were informal—a whispered slur in the grocery store, someone shouting outside the house at night—but others took on the aura of institutional approval. For instance, soon after the Murakami children were barred from the school that their parents and grandparents had helped fund and build, the family received a visit from the island's Anglican minister. He told them to stop attending services. Everyone in the family had been baptized and raised Anglican; they attended church regularly, and the Nikkei community had helped fund the purchase and installation of the organ in a building they themselves had helped construct.[25] Nonetheless, the minister told them they were no longer welcome in that house of God.[26]

These developments were profoundly disheartening, especially for a practicing Anglican family in the run-up to Christmas. But none could compare to the violence of Katsuyori's subsequent abduction. The family had anticipated something like this since the expulsion of all Japanese males aged 18–45 had been announced on February 7. But little information had been forthcoming about the conditions Japanese men could expect or how long they would be gone. *The New Canadian* ran occasional general updates from one labor camp or another, providing important reassurance that the men were alive and making the best of a horrible situation. On March 14, for instance, it ran a piece that said, "'Tell the folks back home that we are getting along fine, and we hope that everyone is keeping his chin up'! is the message that Yosie Yasui sends along from Rainbow, B.C. in the heart of the Canadian Rockies." The essay then went on to provide an account of life in a Nikkei labor camp, striving to keep up morale among those back home: "The boys are taking everything in their stride. They are trying to make the best of their stay here, and on the whole are quite content. The officials, too, have been very co-operative, they do everything possible for us." And, knowing how little information was available on the ground in British Columbia, Yasui concluded with a postscript: "We have seen a number of trains carrying groups of our compatriots eastward."[27] Barely three days later, the RCMP provided a radically different image of the government's program when its officer assaulted Katsuyori, who then effectively fell off the face of the earth. In the weeks to come, the family would have nothing to supplant the image of him putting on a brave face in response to state-sponsored violence.

Consolidation of the remaining Murakamis became critical as anti-Nikkei agitation gave rise to formal persecution. On March 4, 1942, Order-in-Council P.C. 1665 went into effect, requiring that Nikkei surrender any and all land to the Custodian of Enemy Property. (Fishing vessels and liquid assets had fallen under other restrictions.) This was, the order stipulated, purely "a protective measure," though many already knew not to put excessive faith in that assertion. Coming amid continued uncertainty, the order worried Kimiko. Each new measure up to then had brought nothing but increased trouble, and demanding control of private property must have felt like a prelude to theft. Fortunately, she had known the Custodian's representative on Salt Spring Island, Gavin Mouat, for decades. So, when the government order came down, she took what little comfort she could in the belief that the roots she and Katsuyori had labored to establish in the island community might help safeguard their hard-won gains.[28]

Besides, there were bigger fish to fry. As Rose has noted, Kimiko had become "an instant single parent with five children" after Katsuyori's abduction.[29] In this new role, she had simultaneously to wind down the operation of the family farm, to prepare the house for the family's expulsion from British Columbia, and to care for the children, who ranged in age from one to thirteen. There were neither options nor time to weigh them in the spring of 1942. Just about the only thing that had become clear was that the family needed to fortify themselves in the present and to plan for the worst. With that in mind, they settled into a routine, adapting it as circumstances demanded. Alice stepped in to perform many of her father's tasks on the farm.[30] She also lent a hand on the Okano property. The Okanos had retired, but their property still demanded upkeep, even with the help of their sons, who had taken over the farm, and the sponsored laborers Kumanosuke and Riyo had become accustomed to hiring.[31] Alice's help became especially important after Kumanosuke lapsed into what Mary has since suggested was a depressive episode: long an avid reader, he now simply sat quietly every evening, hollowed out by the folly of Japan's militarism coupled with the prospect of losing all he and Riyo had built.[32]

As the departure deadline of April 21 approached, Gavin Mouat visited the family again, this time telling Kimiko that she would have to sell the five thousand chickens she had raised. Word had spread that Nikkei were under the gun, and a buyer took the ferry over from Victoria, anticipating a rock-bottom price. Fortunately, Kimiko was a shrewd negotiator. Pointing out that the hens were about to lay their eggs, she was able to increase the price slightly; she also managed to keep a few chickens to sustain the family until departure time arrived.[33] Kimiko was also a prudent planner. Having watched government officials as well as many of her white neighbors lurch into rabid racism and shocking opportunism, she took the money from that sale and stitched it into a belt, along with a modest sum she withdrew from the family's bank account as a precaution. Although she later regretted not closing the account entirely, her precautions turned out to be a saving grace in the months ahead.[34] The Canadian government froze Nikkei assets, which it then channeled into special accounts from which it doled out modest allowances with which families would then pay for necessities. And because the government was essentially relying on those assets to pay the costs of forced dispersal, getting an increase in the allowance was virtually impossible.[35]

As she did with the family's money, Kimiko also tried to do with the house. Nobody knew how expulsion from the province was going to play out at the governmental level, but it was increasingly clear that a majority of the island's white community had closed ranks against their Nikkei neighbors. Furthermore, few people had faith that the Custodian of Enemy Property would execute its protective task properly. As a result, there was little reason for the Okanos and Murakamis to believe the reassurance by one islander that "not one chopstick" would be moved during their absence.[36] With that in mind, Kimiko hid as many of the family's valuable items as possible in order to safeguard them against theft. Alice, following suit, even hid her father's beloved violin in the attic.[37] And finally, though she could hardly carry what she had packed, Kimiko also squirreled away a block of butter, keeping it close throughout the family's expulsion from Salt Spring Island. Such efforts to protect the family have loomed large for Mary, providing formative moments to which she could return time and again as her own political consciousness developed.

April 21, 1942

Mary's memory of the family's expulsion from Salt Spring Island remains vivid:

> Normally, our farm would have been full of sounds: the chickens, our dog, our horse, and all the people working there. You know, it was full of life. And, on that day, when we were leaving, as we left our house . . . it was this eerie silence of [an] ominous future. And then, as we were getting into this car of a friend that came to pick us up to take us to the boat, the *Princess Mary*, my oldest sister noticed that our dog that we had given away was under one of the steps, and she had given birth to these puppies. And [Alice] and I ran over there, trying to . . . well I mean, she had nothing to eat, right? Because she had escaped from the people that we had given the dog to. But this friend, Mervin Gardiner, who was taking us to the boat said, "Don't worry. . . . I'll take the dogs home and I'll look after them." So that gave us a bit of peace.[38]

A large crowd had gathered at the Ganges wharf, but no one spoke. The white islanders were not there to say goodbye, just to watch.[39] And once they had watched the *Princess Mary* depart with their former neighbors, some of them got down to business: it was time to loot the Nikkei homes they knew were now unguarded.[40] One of them got a violin for his cunning.

Torazo Iwasaki, who owned a large farming operation at the north end of Salt Spring Island, had anticipated this sort of behavior. He left the boat when it stopped at Mayne Island, insisting that he return to his home, and it took some time for his family members to coax him back on board.[41] By contrast, Gavin Mouat, the Custodian's representative on Salt Spring Island, seems not to have been so concerned, even though most of the properties entrusted to him were extensively vandalized. Such was the extent of the damage to Iwasaki's property, which abutted Mouat's own, that he was even reprimanded by the Custodian's office in Vancouver. Tasked with finding renters to occupy the properties in their owners' absence, he found occupants for just under half, and one of these complained about how Mouat's livestock encroached on the land she was farming. As time went by, the Vancouver office expressed frustration with Mouat's general unresponsiveness.[42] Worse was yet to come.

Like so many, the Murakamis were repeatedly uprooted over the years that followed. The Canadian government moved the family eight times between 1942 and 1945; even though the Second World War was over, Ottawa displaced the family a ninth time in 1946. The economic devastation of internal exile and dispossession dictated a tenth move in 1949. Only in 1954 was the family able to return to the west coast, where they could finally try to set down roots again. The intervening twelve years seemed a period of continuous movement. The Murakamis would land somewhere and set about making the place habitable, only to find themselves having to move yet again. The interval might be days, it might be weeks, it could even be a few years. No one ever knew ahead of time.

To help the reader keep track, here is a brief summary of those movements. After their expulsion from Salt Spring Island, Kimiko and her children passed through an improvised staging area at Hastings Park, a temporarily repurposed exposition site in Vancouver, before being shipped to Greenwood, a decrepit former mining town (of the sort known among survivors as a "ghost town") roughly six miles (eleven kilometers) north of the border with the United States in central British Columbia, where they arrived in early May of 1942. The following July, they were shipped to Magrath, in western Alberta, where they had to work in the sugar beet fields. First, the family worked briefly alongside the Okanos on a farm owned by a family named Keeler; soon after, they moved to a farm run by a man with the name of Jensen.

In November of that year, the family had to move again, this time to the Kootenay Rockies at the eastern edge of British Columbia. There, they passed through Bay Farm, Popoff, and Slocan City, sites run by the British Columbia Security Commission (BCSC), the administrative body tasked with overseeing the forced dispersal of Nikkei. Along with Lemon Creek, these three sites made up what the BCSC called Slocan and Extension, a cluster of four camps along the Slocan River at the southern tip of Slocan Lake. Other former residents of Salt Spring Island also landed in the area, including Ruth Hirano, whose family had lived on the Okano property and whose house Katsuyori had helped build. From January 1943 through August 1945, the family was then placed in Rosebery, less of a town than a sparsely populated railroad siding on the northeast shore of Slocan Lake. After World War II ended, Ottawa presented Nikkei with a stark choice: move east or be deported to Japan. The family decided to move east, at which point the government temporarily placed them in New Denver, a former mining town roughly five miles (eight kilometers) south of Rosebery. They stayed there through May 1946 before moving to Magrath and the sugar beet fields once again. Finally, in 1949 they relocated to Cardston, in southern Alberta, where they would remain through 1954. As for what happened to Katsuyori, that will become clear later.

Hastings Park

The name alone would have brought all manner of entertainments to mind before the outbreak of the war. Since opening in 1888, the 150-acre site had come to exemplify liberal capitalism and its benefits.[43] Starting in the early twentieth century, it was home to an annual summer fair run by the Vancouver Exhibition Association, as the organization was called at the time.[44] By 1929, an amusement park called Happyland was open for business. Just to the northeast of Happyland were the Livestock and Horseshow Buildings, which housed animals brought for display in the summer fair. To the southwest stood the Machinery Hall (1913), later known as the Manufacturers' Building, which housed production- and transportation-themed exhibitions. Those with an interest in "domestic arts" could visit the Women's Building, an Art Deco structure built in 1936 that had started off as the Industrial Building. Another popular venue was the Automotive and Ice Rink Building, built in 1933 as part of a worker's relief project. It housed exhibits and booths for the summer fair; starting in 1936 it also provided a venue for professional hockey. Summer 1941 saw the opening of the Garden

Auditorium, a luxurious Streamline Moderne facility that was built as a performance venue and dance hall.[45] And then there was the Exhibition Park Race Track, a five-furlong flat course. This facility entered its heyday after 1946, but even in the early years it drew large crowds that sat in the grandstands backing onto Happyland. Among the regulars were many Issei and older Nisei, but younger Japanese Canadians would also have been familiar with the course, having participated in high school championship footraces that were held there.[46]

For Nikkei in 1942, however, Hastings Park had transformed into a monstrous, distorted version of itself. The Canadian government had been planning to rent a portion of the site for military use, but after the bombing of Pearl Harbor, it decided to make the entire park a staging area for the mass expulsion of Nikkei from the province.[47] Instead of trumpeting the promise of supposedly Canadian liberality, the bold Art Deco façade of the Women's Building and the sleek elegance of the Garden Auditorium were now part of a de facto short-term prison through which more than eight thousand innocent civilians passed. Some stayed a few days, others for weeks. But for all, the space in which they found themselves was profoundly jarring. The central field of the race track now held cars and trucks that had been seized from their Nikkei owners. The Livestock Building became a housing area for women and children under 13. Boys aged 13–18 found themselves lodged in the Women's Building, while the Automotive and Ice Rink Building housed men over 18. Separated from wives and families, these men had little to do. Newspaper reporter and activist Muriel Kitagawa (1912–1974) declared that "the men looked so terribly at loose ends, wandering around the grounds, sticking their noses through the fence watching the golfers [to the northeast of Hastings Park], lying on the grass. Going through the place I felt so depressed that I wanted to cry."[48] On the day before the Murakamis arrived, Kitagawa also noted that the Livestock Building had only ten showers for some 1,500 women.[49] Imagine what it would have been like for the children, too. Every time they set foot outdoors, they would have seen the park's four roller coasters, a flume ride called Shoot the Chutes, and the midway of Happyland, all brought to a standstill by the hostilities for which their own country had chosen to punish them and their families.[50] Even the main gate to the park bore the unmistakable mark of this transformation, its role as grand welcome now inverted by the presence of a newly built guard house.

Hastings Park had been repurposed quickly and with little regard for the welfare of its occupants. Instead, it was laid out for maximum administrative efficiency. For example, the decision to split the camp's population into three groups was a regulatory measure imposed by white bureaucrats. It also was another case of administrative policy implicitly validating the racist claims that policy supposedly addressed. Segmenting Nikkei society this way would, officials suggested, help ward off "decadence" of the sort that British Columbia racists and their allies had long claimed was endemic to immigrant communities.[51] The concentration of each group in a single, contained location and the relegation of specific activities to particular sites also facilitated surveillance.

The stability of families and communities was an afterthought—if even that. The Livestock Building, for instance, featured a feeding area, but that was limited to infants and very young children. Everyone else ate in a common mess hall that was segregated, with men and boys over 13 in the north end and women, girls, and younger children in the south end. Nikkei could pursue a limited number of leisure activities in the Manufacturers' Building, but doing laundry meant going to yet another building just east of the on-site administrative office. And since observation and regulation came first, families suddenly found themselves unable to function without permission from their white overseers.

Harold Miwa, who passed through Hastings Park as a teenager, later described the situation this way:

> You can't just go walking into the building to see mom; you had to have a pass to go to see your own mother. So to get a pass, we had to go to this office building and then request a pass. And okay, you got one hour and he'll [*mimes looking at his watch*]. You got ten to twelve; okay, ten to one—you've got one hour. Okay, go on in and you get your pass. And as you go to the building there's some kind of a guard sitting there, a man, and you show him the pass. Fine, you go inside, then you look and you go see your mother. Then you're talking to them or whatever and the hour goes so fast sometimes, you know. So when you're wandering around, the matron within the building . . . they say "let me see your pass," so you show them the pass. It must be two o'clock and [they say], "you've overstayed, get out." Then you have to leave: get out, get out.[52]

On a later visit to the administrative office, Miwa clawed back a little control for himself and his fellow Nikkei. When the secretary in charge of the passes stepped away from her desk, he grabbed a stack of forms, which he sold, completed, to friends and acquaintances for a nickel each.[53] They got a lot more than one hour for their money.

Hastings Park was, of course, never meant to house people, let alone for the long term. According to administrative documents from the time, it was meant to serve only as a "manning pool," or staging area for the movement of large groups. But since Nikkei had already been criminalized on the basis of race, their welfare while on site was of relatively little concern to the government. There was that "leisure" zone in the Manufacturers' Building, in addition to a small shop where Nikkei who had managed to save some cash could buy a few necessities. But Ottawa signally failed to provide for the day-to-day needs of its occupants. Take, for instance, the initial absence of any school facilities on site. Childhood education had long held high value in Japanese culture, but Nikkei parents also recognized the economic importance of schooling for advancement within Canada. Consequently, they vigorously demanded the establishment of an educational system for their children. Due to the chaos of expulsion and the intransigence of white administrators, that establishment did not begin until April 1942, and in-person teaching did not commence until the following month.[54]

Once schooling got under way, instructors ran into all sorts of problems. Some had to do with facilities. Aside from the kindergarten, which was in the Manufacturers' Building, most classrooms seem to have been set up in the Garden Auditorium, which was a congenial space for dancing and musical performance, but less so for instruction (figure 5). Several classes were set up next to one another in the performance hall, with students sitting on the risers, trying to focus on their teacher while tuning out the teacher leading the class next to them. A few others were tucked in under the dormers upstairs, the pupils struggling to follow their lessons in the hot, stuffy space. And, through it all, the indefinite nature of people's stay at Hastings Park eroded their investment. The park itself did much the same, according to Roy Yasui, who was a teenager at the time: "There was a futile attempt to teach us but it was impossible since there were too many places to hide at Hastings Park. We spent most of the time exploring the park."[55]

FIGURE 5. A circle of Nikkei children in a former British Columbia Electric Company display in the Manufacturers' Building, Hastings Park, 1942. Photograph by Leonard Juda Frank. Photo courtesy of the Vancouver City Archives.

Important though education was, the Canadian government's racist project generated a multitude of even more pressing challenges, foremost among them the establishment of living quarters. All the buildings at Hastings Park were ill-suited to the task of housing human beings, and some were outright uninhabitable, especially from March into April 1942. The Murakamis arrived having dressed for travel, their shoes polished to a high shine, only to find themselves relegated to the Livestock Building. Although this facility had been in use only since the summer of 1941, straw crunched underfoot, the smell of animal waste permeated every surface, and dust filled the air.[56] This was especially worrisome for Kimiko, since Mary's asthma had long dictated that the family keep their house immaculate.[57] And stretching from wall to wall, filling the space with barely room to move between them, were ranks of bunkbeds. As Mary later recalled, the earliest arrivals at Hastings Park lived through a critical moment in the site's preparation. "They weren't really ready for us because they were still filling those ticking bags with straw. And they gave us two army blankets, and there were no pillows."[58]

Total strangers of all ages now lived right up against one another, with no privacy whatsoever. And as the Murakami children tried to adjust to this dehumanizing new environment, the reality of their situation impressed itself upon them in a constant stream of alienating stimuli: the insistent stench of livestock, column upon column of bunkbeds, the sound of voices echoing off every surface, and on the evening of the family's arrival, the sound of a people in agony: "As we entered, we could hear some of the elderly women crying and sobbing."[59] And then there were the toilets—or, rather, the *absence* of toilets. For Mary, this aspect of Hastings Park became irrevocably fused with the destruction of family life:

> We didn't have toilet facilities. . . . Some women and children had to live in the stalls where maggots were still coming out. And just at the entrance of the stalls, there was a trough where all the animals' feces and urine were flushed away, and that was our toilet. There was no privacy, and so a lot of us didn't want to go, you know, go to the toilets. Because everybody was there, sharing, you know, the same thing. And it was, you know, it was so dehumanizing.[60]

Eventually, administrators modified the facilities, setting up cubicles, adding toilets, and improving the washing facilities. But they did so reluctantly, and for the most part after repeated formal complaints by Nikkei.[61] In the interim, Kimiko did what little she could, taking the children outside the building every day to air out their clothes and clear out their lungs.[62]

Nutrition was another failure. On the day the Murakamis arrived, there was not enough food to feed the people the RCMP had hastily bundled into confinement. As a result, women and young children in the Livestock Building were going hungry. On this point, though, the family was fortunate: Kimiko could use that block of butter she had tucked into her belongings. It was especially important for Richard, who was just over one year old and getting hungrier by the minute. Now and then she would let him eat a bit of the butter, soothing him enough to help the family get through its first night in this surreal place.[63]

When there was food at Hastings Park, it was dreadful, and not just for a family accustomed to growing, harvesting, and preparing its own meals. The BCSC boasted of having served over 1.5 million meals for just nine cents per meal, but the human cost defies comprehension.[64] Stewed prunes, gruel, and sundry other lukewarm substances were trucked in from an off-site industrial kitchen. Dysentery became commonplace, and diarrhea the norm for many.[65] Mary would later recall how diligently Kimiko protected her children from such hazards, insofar as she could:

> My mother was told that if she registered with the RCMP and promised to come back at a certain hour of the day, that she would be allowed out of the compound. And so, she did this as much as she could. She would take us down to Powell Street because some of the restaurants, Japanese restaurants were still open, so she would feed us there. Because she had enough . . . sense to get as much money out of the bank account [as she could, putting it in her belt]. . . . [But] a lot of people couldn't, so they had to . . . just continue eating that slop.[66]

Others were fortunate enough to know people in the vicinity who had not yet been forced from their homes and could come by with food. As Frances Kuniko Nakagawa later recalled, "Friends and relatives from Steveston and Vancouver came to see us with obento, but they could not enter the exhibition grounds and we could only meet with the fence between us."[67]

As always, Kimiko's foremost goal was the preservation of her children, but if we look at the larger picture, a pattern becomes visible. From prepping the house, setting aside cash, and packing that block of butter to airing out the family every day and securing permits to venture outside Hastings Park for proper food, we can see a pragmatic and principled response to state-sponsored violence and disempowerment. Though not so mischievous as Harold Miwa, Kimiko too was working to reclaim as much agency as she could. There was little she could do about the seemingly endless string of Orders-in-Council. But, like most of the other eight thousand Nikkei shunted through Hastings Park en route to inland exile, she recognized the importance of looking forward, trying to anticipate what fresh injury might come next, and bracing for it.

Waiting for Word in Eastern British Columbia

For children like Mary and her siblings, the early hours and days of expulsion made themselves known at every level of existence: the riot of smells inside the Livestock Building; the feel of a lumpy straw-filled mattress and scratchy government-issued blankets; the taste of portion-controlled meals made of the cheapest materials; the merciless exposure of your neighbors, a horror matched by the knowledge that you were equally exposed in even your most private moments; and the sound of hundreds of confused, humiliated, enraged voices morning, noon, and night. Even time itself bore the mark of injustice, becoming either cruelly concentrated or maddeningly open-ended. To seek a visitor's pass to another building was to set the clock ticking on interaction with family or friends. But to be in Hastings Park at all was to be in limbo, waiting for days or weeks or months—it seemed no one knew, especially in those early days—to be shipped God-knew-where, God-knew-when. And when Nikkei were finally shipped out, that did not bring an end to their waiting.

The Murakamis found themselves in Greenwood on May 2, 1942, twelve days after being forced from their home. When the plan to ship Nikkei to Canada's interior first became public, many inland communities declared themselves unwilling to accept any of the internal exiles. By contrast, the mayor of Greenwood, W. T. McArthur, recognized the economic benefits a large influx of residents would bring. Its copper-mining days long past, the town had something like two hundred residents at the end of 1941.[68] The main commercial area on Copper Street had become a shadow of its former self; buildings stood empty, and many had fallen into disrepair. No new industry lay on the horizon. The town was simply too far from any large urban area, and the roads leading to it were narrow and snaked through vertiginous mountain passes, as did the railway. A captive population promised a much-needed influx of labor and money that otherwise would never come. With that in mind, McArthur held a town meeting at which the majority voted in support of bringing Nikkei in. As a result, Greenwood eventually housed roughly 1,777 people for varying durations.[69]

The townspeople may have voted to bring in Nikkei, but that seemed to have been the extent of their preparation. Mary recalls, "When we first got off the train, there was no one to meet us there. And so, we dragged our one suitcase [each] into town, which was not too far from the train station. And the [BCSC] Commissioner finally saw us coming, so he took us to the undertaker's house, where the undertaker's wife boiled up some eggs for us and gave us toast."[70] The new arrivals moved into the town's many abandoned buildings, which were identified by numbers rather than names (Building 1, Building 2, etc.).[71] Space was at a premium. According to Tamiko Haraga, who arrived in Greenwood as a teenager, "each family had one room. Small families had a room approximately 10 feet by 14 feet. Our room was larger, about 12 feet by 20 feet, because there were eight of us in the family."[72] Dust and cobwebs covered every surface, and Nikkei had to buy their own supplies. Mary recalls that "the women . . . didn't have any pots and pans and cleaning things, so they had to go down to the store to buy them. And all the young people and mothers, they cleaned up the place. And we were assigned to a little cubbyhole where there were no beds or anything; there was just an empty room, a really tiny empty room. And we slept on the floor, lined up like sardines."[73] The occupants of each building had to share a small stove positioned in a common area, which compounded the difficulty of feeding one's family.[74]

These worries receded relatively quickly, though, since Greenwood turned out to be just another way station for Kimiko and the children. A letter arrived toward the end of May, just a few weeks after they arrived. It had been censored, but gist was clear: Katsuyori was alive. He and about two hundred other Nikkei men had been shipped to a labor camp along the Yellowhead River.[75] Working about 100 miles (160 kilometers) west of Edmonton, they were tasked with clearing a route for the Yellowhead–Blue River Highway, which eventually would become part of the Trans-Canada Highway. The family was relieved to receive word from Katsuyori, but for Kimiko and Alice, the update would have brought other worries. *The New Canadian* had been running a series of reports from these labor camps, and although the tone of the reports was sunny, there was no mistaking that the life in question entailed grueling work and primitive living conditions (figure 6). Ever mindful of morale, Katsuyori put forward the plan for reunification: per Ottawa's demands, the family could be reunited if they moved to Magrath, Alberta, to work on a sugar beet farm. He had agreed, he wrote, and would meet Kimiko and the children there in the summer.

Word quickly spread about how backbreaking and poorly paid the work in Alberta was. According to Tom Tagami, who was sent to Slocan as a young man, the Anglican Reverend "G. [Goichi Gordon] Nakayama would film the people working on the sugar beet farms, and then visit Slocan to show the films he had taken. We saw the awful conditions they had to put up with, and no one wanted to go east. But people had no choice—they could either go to the prairies or to northern Ontario, where the work was cutting four-foot pulp wood in snowy, minus 23 to 25 degrees (Fahrenheit)

FIGURE 6. Katsuyori Murakami with Ron Inouye and Phillip and Luke Murakami, sons of Sukini (Okano) and Morihei Murakami (no relation to Katsuyori), at the Yellowhead Pass Prison Road Camp, April 19, 1942. Photo courtesy of the Salt Spring Island Archives.

weather."[76] For the Murakamis, though, that relay of information was not yet available. They were among some of the earliest families shipped to Alberta from the Kootenays, and word had only just begun to make its way back. Indeed, Nakayama did not travel through the area until 1943, well after the Murakamis had moved there.[77] All they knew was that this might be their only opportunity to be together.

To help tide the family over, Katsuyori enclosed a $20 bill in his letter. Kimiko and the children did not know it at the time, but he had been earning only 25¢ per hour, and the Department of Labour charged him both for his meals and for basic health care.[78] As a point of comparison, in the early 1900s Nikkei migrants had earned $2.40–$2.85 a day for their risky, arduous work in the coal mines near Hardieville, Coalhurst, Staffordville, and Lethbridge.[79] Now they were earning less than that for labor that was nearly as challenging, especially as the crews passed over the Continental Divide. At lower elevations the snow might be only a couple of feet deep when trampled underfoot, but at Blue River it loomed over the men, and temperatures could sometimes stay well below freezing for weeks on end.[80] In his letter to Kimiko and the children, Katsuyori mentioned none of the hardships life in the labor camp entailed—the weather, the arduous labor, the meager pay, the continuing postoperative difficulties he was having, the lack of proper health care, or the fact that his difficulties had necessitated a transfer from construction work to duty in the kitchen. Instead, he concentrated on the prospect of being reunited with Kimiko and the children. All they had to do, he noted, was agree to move eastward to meet him.

Relocation to Southern Alberta

While copper had given rise to Greenwood, water gave rise to Magrath. Toward the end of the nineteenth century, the Canadian government offered economic incentives to settlers who could work the fertile Alberta plains. But working the plains would take more than just planting and tending crops. It also would take irrigation, for while water was plentiful in the so-called Palliser Triangle, over 80 percent of surface water lies to the north of agricultural settlements and flows northward toward the Arctic Ocean.[81] What little surface water is available tends to freeze in the long, cold southern Alberta winters. These conditions had not been an obstacle for the Indigenous Kainai people, who had developed sophisticated survival strategies over generations. With the arrival of white migrants, though, the Kainai were marginalized in order to invent an "open" prairie ready for farming.[82] This then turned water into a problem that irrigation was meant to solve for the constellation of settlements dependent on agriculture—most notably the hamlet of Magrath and the neighboring towns of Cardston and Raymond.

The move to Magrath would allow the Murakamis to be reunited. It also would place them near the Okanos. Kumanosuke and Riyo had been sent to Magrath from Hastings Park earlier that spring. Unable to afford a move farther east and thus caught up in the government's sugar-beet labor plan, the two had no choice. They would have to pursue farm work once again, but now on behalf of someone else, the Keeler family, who owned the property.[83] By then in their seventies, Kumanosuke and Riyo found the prospect of farming daunting enough, but beet farming is especially laborious. Consider the initial phase of the process. To ensure a good yield, farmers would plant vast numbers of seeds set in rows about 30 inches apart. Once the seedlings took root, field workers would then go down the rows, using a hoe to "thin" the crop down to small clusters of plants every 8–10 inches. Other workers would follow behind them, paring down those clusters to a single plant. The process was so time-consuming and so labor-intensive that families would put their children to work. For families where an adult's skill with the hoe allowed them to thin down to individual plants, that merely freed the children to work in some other capacity.

As Yukinori Peter Takasaki recalls, beet farming was "truly physical abuse" in the years prior to mechanization, and weather only compounded that abuse.[84] Early in the growing season, for instance, one might also encounter heavy rainfall, which turned the fields into thick, boot-thieving bogs topped with a slippery glaze that could sweep your feet from under you. Conditions were so bad that *The New Canadian* reported on this additional difficulty Nikkei faced during their first season in southern Alberta: "Sugar beet workers on the prairies met extremely wet conditions, making the work much more difficult for the inexperienced workers as the beet plants must be thinned at the two-leaf stage."[85]

The threat posed by weather was significant, too. *The New Canadian* went on to add that such bad weather also "cut deeply into the possible earnings of Nisei beet workers."[86] The rain could, for instance, starve the crop by leeching nutrients from the soil, or it could cause rot. No less important, by making the soil itself harder to navigate and harder to work, it drastically slowed the pace at which people could work. This was almost as big a threat as the potential loss of crops, for time was of the essence. Nikkei earned an average of about $30 per acre for the entire season. But the pay was on a contract basis, which meant they had to complete tasks on a deadline dictated by the life cycle of the plant. Fail to tend the crops on your contracted acreage, and you would not get paid. As a result, labor in the beet fields ran from dawn to dusk. And when they were not working in the fields, the workers sought paid work elsewhere, because that $30 an acre was not enough to buy the food, clothing, and other necessities a family would need.[87] By comparison, at least some of the Nikkei who had worked on farms run by members of a Christian sect called the Doukhobors had earned a higher wage ($35) over a shorter period (two months).[88] Agricultural life in southern Alberta had never been easy, but it was particularly harsh for Nikkei displaced from British Columbia, stripped of their property, deprived of control over their finances, and subject to labor terms set by the government and beet growers.

At least the Murakamis would be together. They also would be near their extended family. On July 23, 1942, Kimiko and the children arrived at the farm where the Okanos and one of their sons were working. Katsuyori had arrived earlier that month, but there was no time for celebration. The Murakamis departed the next day for a farm closer to Magrath, one owned by a man named Lalovee Jensen (1907–1985), whose family was well established in southern Alberta.[89] After studying animal husbandry at Brigham Young University in Provo, Utah, in the early 1930s, Jensen returned to Canada to make his way. He bought a share in his father's farm and began building on the gains that operation had made.[90] His farm raised livestock as well as various crops, most importantly beets. Such was his success that, in 1954, he became president of the Alberta Sugar Beet Growers Association, a position he held for the next twenty years. But in 1942, trying to expand a promising but still fragile operation, he faced the same labor shortage as virtually every other farmer in the region. Indeed, Alberta had been desperate for a durable workforce from as early as 1903; hence the observation by David Iwaasa that, in the early twentieth century, "as long as they [Nikkei] were essential as a source of cheap labor, they were at least tolerated in Southern Alberta, albeit sometimes grudgingly."[91]

White people in both British Columbia and southern Alberta had displayed divergent attitudes toward people of Japanese ancestry. But in Alberta, circumstances lent that divergence a different character. Prairie life in the early twentieth century had brought relatively few non-white immigrants, and most of those were of Chinese ancestry.[92] The earliest records are few and far between, but it appears a handful of Nikkei were in the region before 1905, when Alberta became a province.[93] Numbers increased slowly, with 247 Nikkei recorded in a 1911 census, and 473 by 1921.[94] By the summer of 1941, that number reached 578.[95] By contrast, people of Chinese ancestry had lived in the province far longer, and exclusionary legislation designed to mimic American measures had already relegated the majority of them to the economic and social margins of society.[96] As a result, Nikkei provided a visible but also relatively unthreatening minority against which to build whiteness. Thus, early-twentieth-century opposition to Nikkei in the area tended to be muted and localized.

In fact, until Japanese imperial aggression came to be seen as a threat to the British Empire, Nikkei in southern Alberta had managed to build a generally favorable public image for themselves. They did so in large part thanks to the efforts of a community that formed in the predominantly Mormon town of Raymond, just to the southeast of Lethbridge. The foundation of that community was laid in 1909, when Nikkei were brought in to work land on behalf of the Knight Sugar Company.[97] Knight ultimately failed, but several of the Issei who had come to work there remained, buying land and setting up operations of their own. By 1914, the community had grown to such an extent that members formed the Raymond Nihonjin Kyokai (Raymond Japanese Society), which served both to advance the needs of community members and to liaise with white economic and political groups.[98] By 1929, the Nikkei community in Raymond had grown to such an extent that it led to the founding of the Raymond Buddhist Church, which operated out of a building purchased from the Raymond Second Ward of the L.D.S. Church.[99]

Still, the relative success of Nikkei in the province was a double-edged sword. The *Alberta Farmer* and the *Calgary Herald* made the opening of the Raymond Buddhist Church part of a favorable article about people of Japanese ancestry in the province.[100] And as Iwaasa has suggested, many of the Mormon pioneers who helped establish Magrath, Cardston, and Raymond had arrived in the province with the Midwestern persecution still very much part of the faith's living memory.[101] But economics brought out fault lines that tested the limits of faith. Beet farming is extremely labor intensive. It also is seasonal, meaning that people working the fields one year frequently would find more dependable and often better-paying work elsewhere. As a result, labor shortages were a chronic problem.

Coupled with the fact that profit margins were slim, large growing operations had a strong incentive to seek the cheapest workers possible. This gave rise to arguments such as that offered by Charles A. Magrath (1880–1949), first mayor of Lethbridge and eponym of the community where the Murakamis found themselves. In July 1908, the *Lethbridge Herald* recounted a debate over how the sugar beet industry could meet its labor needs. Immigrants, it was agreed, were the only people likely to labor so hard for so little compensation. The real question was mainly one of racialization, and the paper summarized Magrath's contribution thus: "The fact is that they are employing Japs because they could not get anyone else. No fair minded man could deny them the right to get the labor wherever they could."[102]

While Alberta may not have exhibited the same virulent racism as British Columbia, voices against Nikkei in the province were strong. Laborers, for instance, recognized cheap labor as a threat. During a strike by Central and Eastern European farmworkers in 1935–1936, rumors swirled about the hiring of Nikkei scab laborers in other industries, the implication being that beet farming would soon follow suit.[103] They found themselves making arguments that were surprisingly consonant with those of growers who either ran smaller operations or simply bought into anti-Nikkei sentiment. In some locales, such growers came close to carrying the day in debates about the mass importation of Nikkei forced labor.[104]

Another strike in 1941, coupled with the onset of war, settled the matter. The labor market in southern Alberta had become unsustainable, and Nikkei who had formerly led stable lives in British Columbia were now in desperate straits.[105] As Ottawa began announcing various anti-Nikkei measures, the Alberta Sugar Beet Growers Association sent a delegation to meet with members of the BCSC. The association framed its work as a patriotic act. Pointing to the claim that expelling Nikkei from the coast was a military necessity, they argued that putting people of Japanese ancestry to work in the beet fields was for the good of the nation. The association recognized that stirring up further anti-Asian sentiment would only strengthen the farmworkers' hand and complicate the task of bringing in this captive labor force. It therefore stipulated that any Nikkei brought into

Alberta by the BCSC should be expelled from the province at the close of hostilities. A telegram to the Minister of Labour argued in March of 1942: "Regardless of considerable opposition we believe saner citizens for patriotic reasons would support policy of bringing Japanese families here under strict supervision of Security Commission in accordance with Commissioner's commitments to us if you as Minister of Labour would assure us that both Japanese Canadian Citizens and Japanese aliens would be removed at close of emergency."[106]

Mary and her family would likely not have known much of this at the time, but they nonetheless experienced the fallout of these historical currents on a daily basis, and their experience has continued to reverberate decades later. For instance, two of Mary's most vivid memories of that summer in Magrath are architectural. She remembers the shack where her family had to live, calling the roughly 10- by 15-foot space a "little box." While the housing that many Nikkei encountered in the province may have been unsuited for occupancy in wintertime, the Murakamis found themselves living in a structure that Mary describes as "not fit for human" use at all. It seemed to have been built merely to enclose a space and little or nothing beyond that, containing "nothing—no beds, no cooking facilities." So primitive was the structure that one of the first things Katsuyori did was ask Jensen to drive him into town, where he purchased—at his own expense—lumber and other supplies with which to make the space habitable for his family.[107] Mary even remembers the color of the place, though for a specific reason. The building stood near a pigpen, making it a convenient gathering area as the heat of summer intensified. Drawn by the waste from the hogs, thousands upon thousands of flies congregated on the outer walls, cladding the shack in a shifting black mass.[108] Mary also remembers the owner's house, large and white and ornate.[109]

Even though Katsuyori did what he could to improve the Murakamis' living quarters, the family found itself worse off than they had been in New Denver. In the Kootenays, they could forage for greens. Here, virtually everything they ate had to come from a can, since there was no way to store anything fresh. Water for bathing and cleaning came from an open pond the family had to share with animals.[110] Tending to sugar beets is exhausting, labor-intensive work, and Katsuyori had yet to fully recover from his appendectomy and the subsequent strains of forced labor on the Yellowhead–Blue River Highway. As a result, he became weaker and weaker as the growing season went on. Furthermore, the family would receive just $35 an acre for their labor, and that money would not come until after the harvest. Mary recalls that Jensen added insult to injury: "he was telling the people of Magrath to 'treat the Japs like criminals.' "[111]

In order that her parents and siblings might survive the summer without completely draining what remained of their savings, Alice took a job with the Magrath Trading Company, which was run by James Alfred Ririe (1884–1973). That job turned out to be pivotal, for it brought the family into a relationship that both opened up economic opportunities and demonstrated the renewed possibility of humane treatment by a white person. Ririe's parents had numbered among the first arrivals in Magrath when they emigrated from Utah in 1899. Ririe returned briefly to Utah to study business at Brigham Young University before returning to Alberta and joining the family business.[112] "He was a very kind man," Mary recalls.[113] Sensitive to the many challenges facing the Murakamis, he hired both Alice and Katsuyori to work part-time at his store during the interval between planting and harvest. In addition, "he would find other jobs for the whole family. Like, for instance, in between the thinning of the sugar beets and the weeding there would be a space of time where we didn't have to do the sugar beet work, so he would find other work . . . for instance, picking beans. He didn't have to do this, but he would wake up early in the morning—like about 6 o'clock" to take the family to those other farms. He would then pick them up later for the trip home.[114]

Between Katsuyori's continuing deterioration, the insults and injuries of life on the Jensen farm, and the kindness J. A. Ririe showed the family, it became clear that something not only had to change but perhaps also could. To bring the family back together, Kimiko and her husband had acceded to the government's demand that they take up work on a beet farm. Having made that decision, they bore the hardships such work entailed. They even took on extra work to survive. But the Murakamis were hardly resigned to their circumstances. On the contrary, as Alice would soon demonstrate, thoughtful resistance not only was possible but also could be effective.

THREE

Sensing Right and Wrong in Internal Exile

As the summer of 1942 ground on, it quickly became clear that the Murakamis could not survive in Magrath. Weakened by his appendectomy and his time in the Yellowhead–Blue River Highway labor camp, Katsuyori was in no condition to withstand the rigors of beet farming, especially when coupled with the privations of life on the Jensen farm. Alice was only fourteen, but she recognized the urgency of the situation.[1] As a young girl on Salt Spring Island, she had grown up in a household shaped both by hard work and by its resulting agricultural and economic success. Now, as an adolescent she was experiencing firsthand the fragility of that success in the face of racist aggression. And yet, having encountered the kindness and generosity of the Ririe family, she also recognized the possibility that help might be at hand. With that in mind, she wrote an urgent appeal to the BCSC representative in Lethbridge, detailing the conditions her family lived in and asking the representative to intervene. Such was Alice's eloquence and logic, Mary recalls, that it provoked a site visit. Swinging his jacket to ward off the flies, the BCSC representative "didn't even go into the shack there." He took a quick look around the property and decided to move the family to the Kootenays.[2]

Dire living conditions may have necessitated their removal from the farm, but crop yields and a white farmer's financial prospects governed the timing of that removal. Alice's letter was eloquent, and the Murakamis' circumstances were undeniably inhumane, but it is likely that Lalovee Jensen also weighed in on the matter. For one thing, his reputation was at stake.

He may have denigrated the people from whose labor he profited, but he had to continue working with white landowners and businessmen in and around Magrath. For another thing, like other farmers who had applied to import Nikkei workers, he had a financial stake in their output. To judge from the timeline of events, the BCSC took that stake into account. The RCMP did not put the Murakamis on a train to Nelson, British Columbia, until November 1943, after the harvest.[3]

Still, the family left Magrath just a few months after they had arrived. In the course of November, they migrated northward along the Slocan River, passing through two sites, Popoff and Bay Farm, named for the properties on which they had been built. They then spent about a month in Slocan City. Finally, in January 1943 the BCSC placed the Murakamis in Rosebery (figure 7). They would remain there through August 1945, but the damage for Mary had already been done; faced with the likelihood of further moves, she resolved not to form any close bonds with other children.[4] Mary's only stable relationships were with her father, mother, and siblings, and it would be over a decade before she found a significant point of social contact with someone outside her immediate family.

Wartime Life in the Kootenays

The move from Magrath brought better conditions for the Murakamis, but the family still faced big challenges. Rose wrote this description of their home in Rosebery:

> The tiny shacks, built row upon row especially for us, were not ready for occupancy—but in the freezing weather we were forced to live in them. Our shack, number 208, was 14 by 28 feet divided into three tiny rooms. It had a camp stove, a small two-burner kitchen stove, and a wooden sink. It had no electricity, and the communal water tap was outside. The shack had only green shiplap boards for the outside walls, no inner walls and a roof but no ceiling. Father again built some furniture.[5]

Throughout January and February, families struggled to stay warm in their skeletal homes. As the shiplap dried, it began to shrink, a process speeded by the belated arrival of stoves that further desiccated the already parched winter air. Heat escaped, cold crept in. And although each shack was small, the stoves were unable to keep pace with the bitter cold. Rose recalled that

FIGURE 7. Katsuyori, Kimiko, Alice, Violet, Mary, Rose, and Richard Murakami in Rosebery, 1943. Photo courtesy of the Salt Spring Island Archives.

in the small rooms, beds had to be pushed against the walls, and on winter mornings the bedding was stuck frozen to the wall. The cracks in the walls and floor were stuffed with whatever was available to keep out the cold. Father scrounged scrap lumber and tarpaper to make the inner walls. He split cedar shakes from downed trees to cover the outside walls.[6]

It could have been worse. While the Murakami family was large enough to get its own shack, smaller families had to share these cramped, drafty quarters.[7]

Even with Katsuyori's improvements, the shack was inadequate for the circumstances. Winter in this region is always cold, and the year the Murakamis moved in was no exception. *The New Canadian* reported that January temperatures at nearby Kaslo reached a record low of –17 degrees Fahrenheit, and life virtually shut down for a time after a big mid-month snowfall:

> Mail was held up, roads were blocked, water-pipes frozen, and most important of all, stocks of firewood melted away as stoves and heaters were stoked up to maximum efficiency. For days Kaslo workmen were dispatched to a point 17 miles [27.2 km] south of the city, to clear the highway to Nelson. Similarly blocked roads and winter conditions were reported a week ago from Slocan, New Denver and Sandon.
>
> Evacuees from the mild coastal strip were particularly wondrous and a trifle fearful of the biting temperatures. The majority lacked necessary garments for such weather, and in all the identical houses in Rosebery, New Denver, Slocan and Tashme, it was a case of huddling around the stove in vain effort to keep warm.[8]

The paper tried to make light of the situation with a joke about how locals kept calling the weather "most unusual," but there is no mistaking the misery of the situation. And it was even worse for the Nikkei whose roofs collapsed as snow accumulated.

Food was another problem. Before the war, Nikkei had been self-reliant, producing their own fruit and vegetables, catching their own fish, and raising their own livestock. This had kept the cost of living relatively low while also enabling the community to establish an efficient, interconnected economy, which forced dispersal destroyed.[9] Furthermore, white shopkeepers along Slocan Lake, like those in Greenwood, recognized that these internal exiles were a captive market, and they priced their goods accordingly. At the same time, arrangements with the BCSC's stranglehold on Nikkei funds meant that even those who had built up reasonable savings could barely afford the cost of living. Aside from eggs, canned meat became the main protein for most Nikkei in the area. Fresh cuts of beef and chicken were simply too expensive. Getting adequate fruit and vegetables was also difficult. As a result, Mary remembers, the family foraged during the warmer months, gathering dandelions and other edible plants that grew along the road and in the margins of local farms.[10]

Of course, foraging could only provide so much, and in the depths of winter it was not an option at all. Furthermore, Nikkei had arrived in the Kootenays long after planting season had passed. Fortunately, another marginalized community in southern British Columbia, the Doukhobors, saved the day. Such were the fairness and generosity of this group that Mary, like so many who endured inland exile, still recalls them with great warmth: "These people were so kind! And they would bring vegetables to the Japanese Canadians in Greenwood and sell it to us for a really reasonable price; they didn't take advantage of us. And that's how we were able to eat vegetables and fruit: because the Doukhobor people brought it to us."[11]

Committed pacifist Christians, the Doukhobors had fled persecution in Russia at the turn of the twentieth century, initially settling in Saskatchewan. After conflict with the provincial government over education, military service, and communal living, the group moved to eastern British Columbia. There, their troubles continued, even as leaders attempted to make their belief systems more legible to outsiders. (The actions of a radical subset known as the Sons of Freedom further inflamed tensions, particularly in the 1950s and early 1960s.[12]) This, as Julie Rak has suggested, was the critical issue: "Not only were Doukhobors opposed to a separation of church and state, but they also opposed the ideas of church and state in and of themselves. This meant that Doukhobors effectively became subjects who could not be written into the Canadian national script except as curiosities or as a threat to nationhood."[13]

Rak's emphasis lies primarily on how Doukhobor historical description has evolved under the pressures of marginalization. However, her suggestion also points to a critical commonality: both the Doukhobors and their newly arrived neighbors had become targets of oppression because they were unwilling or unable to conform to the ideal of middle-class, capitalist whiteness. That is why, in the summer of 1943, the supervisor at Lemon Creek, J. S. Burns, ordered the construction of an expensive fence expressly to keep the Doukhobors from entering the site, doing so at the same time as he denied a significantly cheaper request to upgrade the safety of a school building so that it might be used as a community recreation hall. By way of justification, he claimed the fence would counter the group's supposed penchant for thievery and vandalism.[14] Nikkei quickly came to know better, though; some even took matters into their own hands. According to Ayukawa,

> Doukobour [sic] farmers used to drive their wagons to Lemon Creek to sell us cabbages, potatoes and such. They were our saviours but the authorities tried to keep them out by building a log fence on the road-side. But overnight the fence was destroyed. There were suspects, but no proof. High school students were blamed and the school was closed until someone admitted guilt. I don't know who the culprits were, or whether they were caught, but after a week the high school reopened.[15]

Links between the two communities soon expanded further. Several Nikkei even worked on Doukhobor farms. Tamiko Haraga (1925–2014), whose family was expelled from Steveston to Greenwood, later wrote: "I went to work for a Doukhobor family [that lived nearby] with my younger sister and a few of my friends. Doukhobors owned most of the farms in the Grand Forks area. They were nice, honest and hardworking people." Understanding the importance of reciprocity, she added, "We also had to work hard."[16] For her part, Ayukawa also noted that "later some Doukhobors became very friendly with us. We used to walk along the railway tracks to pick and buy their cherries. Some young men enjoyed their saunas and even learned 'The Volga Boat Song' and sang it at concerts. Baseball games between the Lemon Creekers and Doukhobors were often held."[17]

Injustice has a long afterlife. The infrastructure built for Nikkei would eventually be repurposed for the suppression of Doukhobor culture. If the community in general "opposed the ideas of church and state in and of themselves," many of the Sons of Freedom took that opposition to its logical conclusion, refusing to send their children to Canadian schools. For their convictions, between 1953 and 1959 the government seized their children and the children of their coreligionists who were in prison. Implemented by the Department of the Attorney General, the Department of Education, and the Department of Welfare, the seizure program saw these children shipped to New Denver, where they were confined to a sanitarium that originally had been built in 1942 to house Nikkei.[18] Designated specifically for Nikkei afflicted with tuberculosis, the building soon became known as the San and, over time, became a cultural hub as well as a medical facility, providing a site where community members could garden and perform the annual Bon Odori (festival for the dead).[19] For Doukhobor children, the building had no such resonances. It did, however, bear one imprint of its history: administrators and staff continued to regularly call the facility the San or the Sanitarium in official correspondence as well as in daily practice.

A Child's Life in Slocan and Extension

By contrast with Magrath, life in Slocan and Extension was much better for Mary and her siblings. This was so because, as many who spent their childhoods in the sites along Slocan Lake have remarked, parents strove to protect their children from the full weight of injustice. Students through grade eight attended schools that Hide Hyodo (later Shimizu), building on her experience as primary school supervisor at Hastings Park, had helped set up at each of the sites.[20] High schoolers on Slocan Lake trekked to Lakeview Collegiate, which the United Church had established in New Denver. Getting this patchwork system up and running was an arduous task complicated by two main factors. The first was an argument between the British Columbia Department of Education, which refused to fund schools for Nikkei children, and the BCSC, which reluctantly took on that expense. The second factor was wild variation in the available infrastructure. In Kaslo, where vacant buildings were plentiful, setting up a school for younger children was relatively straightforward. In Lemon Creek, by contrast, where a dedicated structure had to be built, the delay lasted over a year.[21]

Heavy involvement from Nikkei families as well as from non-Nikkei volunteers proved essential. Parents provided what few resources they had, in addition to lobbying their local BCSC representatives.[22] Nisei, most of whom had only just finished high school, signed on to lead classes for which they often had to learn both the course material and the lesson plans. As early volunteers moved eastward, new recruits had to be found. Fortunately, in addition to members of the community, a number of non-Nikkei began arriving in the region, all of them driven by political conviction. Some were conscientious objectors whose instructional work was a condition of their release from prison; others, such as Mildred Fahrni, who taught social studies at Lakeview Collegiate, were dedicated activists working to offset the injustice they saw unfolding.[23]

Fahrni was especially important for Mary's sister Alice, whose memory of the Jensen farm loomed large: "We were treated like animals, like slaves," Alice later remarked.[24] For Alice, the new social studies teacher differed profoundly from so many of the white people she had encountered since the bombing of Pearl Harbor: "I'll never forget Mrs. Fahrni. She had her hair short and she was very slender. She used to talk about the CCF [the Co-operative Commonwealth Federation] all the time, and she called it the 'Carrot Chewers' Federation.' She used to explain about Gandhi and the other peacemakers. Deep inside she really believed in all the things she taught."[25] For Fahrni, work at Lakeview Collegiate was not just an exercise in mitigating the suffering of her Nikkei charges. It was the chance to implement social change by teaching the mechanisms of that change to her students. As Alice later recalled, "she didn't refrain from putting the facts before us. . . . I was fifteen at that time, and it really got me thinking. A lot of the younger children didn't understand what position we were in vis-à-vis the government."[26] As another Lakeview Collegiate student, George Masuda, observed, "She was a staunch CCF'er and that came across clearly in the classroom."[27]

Life outside school had its own rewards. It is perhaps difficult to imagine children and young adults at play during forced dispersal, but that is what extracurricular life in the Kootenays sometimes allowed (figure 8). It did so, however, due in part to the efforts of adult Nikkei. Mary points out that "it's amazing, how people in this kind of condition . . . persevere and try to create a community . . . so that the children will feel as if it's normal. So, as children, I'm sure you've heard stories . . . of children, even today saying, 'Oh, we had a lot of fun in the camps!' Of course we had a lot of fun because our parents, you know, suffered to create this atmosphere for us."[28] Not that the atmosphere was free of disagreement. Ayukawa recalls how members of the Parent-Teacher Organization at Lemon Creek objected to plans for grade eight students to celebrate their graduation with dancing. When the ceremony finally rolled around, dancing was in the cards, but debate resumed about how long each song should last.[29]

FIGURE 8. Mary and Bruce Murakami in Rosebery, March 2, 1945. Photo courtesy of the Salt Spring Island Archives.

Adult intervention had its limits. In summer, children quickly learned the best swimming holes on Lemon Creek and the Slocan River; during the winter, they also learned that slow spots on the river were navigable on ice skates, though chiefly in the morning.[30] Since candles were in limited supply, bonfires became social hubs. Roy Yasui recalls that "the grownups would take turns telling scary stories but some of them were humorous, historical or about famous Japanese persons."[31] And then there were the innumerable games children played, from marbles and blindman's bluff to baseball and, Mary recalls, Auntie-I-Over: "We used to pick teams. And one would be on this side of the shack, and the other would be on this side.

And we'd throw the ball over the roof, and if the other side caught the ball, then they would run and try to hit us with the ball. And if we get hit, then we have to go to the other team."[32] Beyond such casual play, a child's life was, for Mary, emotionally isolated outside her family because, having been moved so many times, she had lost faith in the durability of her friendships: "Well, in Rosebery, we stayed from 1943, January, to 1946, when we moved to New Denver. That was the only period of stability, you know, as far as not being moved around. All the rest of the places, the times with the people were very short. So, when we started getting moved around, I just decided I wasn't going to have any friends. I wasn't going to get attached to anybody."[33]

Two slow-moving catastrophes disrupted the stability Kimiko and Katsuyori had established for their family during the early days in Rosebery. The first came just after they had arrived. Order-in-Council P.C. 1665, issued the previous March, had tasked the Custodian of Enemy Property with holding Nikkei land, trucks, boats, and cars as "a protective measure." Now, however, there was Order-in-Council P.C. 469, which empowered the Custodian to sell off any and all property owned by Nikkei. Months in the making, it went into effect on January 19, 1943, less than a year after expulsion. Proceeds from each sale were either disbursed by check, in the case of Nikkei living outside the system of forced confinement, or, for those still under the control of the BCSC, deposited into the account being administered by the commission. The order served multiple purposes. It validated expulsion by implying Nikkei were "enemies" whose property could thus be sold, further offsetting the costs of expulsion. It eliminated the task of managing Nikkei-owned properties, ensuring continuity in sectors disrupted by expulsion (e.g., berry farming, where Nikkei farms were critical). And it helped to ensure people of Japanese ancestry would not return to the coast by depriving them of places to which they could return, with a key part of this last plan involving redevelopment of the Powell Street area, which had become a Nikkei Canadian cultural and economic hub, into an industrial zone.[34] And while many whose property was sold without their consent may have received an approximation of market value, even in the best of cases the sale was forced, the government refused to allow most Nikkei to dispose of the resulting funds as they wished (or, just as often, needed), and anyone who hoped to own property after the war would have been at the mercy of whatever market awaited them.[35]

The New Canadian, which had urged readers to "keep cool and keep calm" as racist fervor reached a fever pitch the previous spring, pulled no punches this time. Leading with a series of incisive questions about the economic and political ramifications of the order, it declared "the answers are needed quickly, for while the most staunchly loyal and tolerant of us may do their best to swallow with good grace this last dose of bitter medicine from their own government, a policy as indefensible as this from any point of view except the dictates of a race war, is certain to provoke a strong reaction." Having called Order-in-Council P.C. 469 what it actually was—part of a race war—the paper continued:

> On the face of it not the slightest shadow of a democratic principle is attached to this action. And in many cases it may well be the last straw which can be added to a war burden which has mounted higher and higher and heavier and heavier upon the backs of Japanese Canadians since Pearl Harbour. For although everyone of common sense was willing cheerfully enough to assume a heavy load because of the extraordinary conditions precipitated by that black day, it is yet to be shown to the satisfaction of any informed and thinking person that that burden has not long exceeded the bounds of justice, of reason, or even of necessity.[36]

Such arguments initially fell on deaf ears outside the Nikkei community, where news that the war had turned against the Axis Powers dominated the papers. And even when non-Nikkei began to push back that following spring, their actions met with significant resistance from both Ottawa and British Columbia racists. Nikkei groups such as the Japanese Canadian Committee for Democracy and non-Nikkei allies such as the Cooperative Committee for Japanese Canadians undertook legal challenges, but these encountered bureaucratic slowdowns that ensured sales would be fait accompli before any judgment might be rendered.[37]

Speed is relative, though. While Ottawa and its representatives moved to sell off property as quickly as they could, the Murakamis could only watch and wait until November 3 of that year, when their land, that of the Okanos, and everything that stood on that land were unceremoniously sold off.[38] For example, Katsuyori had bought two plots from a Salt Spring Islander named T. Frank Speed. The first of these measured ten acres and had cost $1,100 in 1931, while the second purchase had added seven acres for $704 in 1938.[39] Katsuyori had cleared the land at a cost that, including physical labor, exceeded the resulting increase in potential sale price.[40] Moreover, the property had gained significant value, especially considering that the site had both electricity and piped-in water serving the four-bedroom house Katsuyori had built with the help of a carpenter. Nonetheless, an August 18, 1942, appraisal provided to the Custodian by Gavin Mouat's office suggested the Murakamis' farm was worth a scant $1,310.87, with the house supposedly providing $1,000 of that value. This appraisal also assigned assorted henhouses and the like an additional value of $239.13. That total was subsequently reduced to an even $1,300 by one I. T. Barnet on the nineteenth of the same month. When the dust had settled from the sale, a pair of veterans had taken possession of the two lots for a meagre $1,284.

As for the money from this sale, that was doled out to the Murakamis and Okanos from accounts managed by the government, a mechanism designed to ensure that they and other Nikkei families would pay for their own forced dispersal. Impoverished, stripped of land they had cultivated and on which they depended, they now had no prospects for returning to British Columbia, and that was if the ban on their return were ever lifted. They would have to look and work elsewhere.[41] By contrast, Gavin Mouat, the Custodian's representative on Salt Spring Island, made a killing, and not just from the sale of the Murakami and Okano properties. Salt Spring Lands, a company of which he was part owner, paid a pittance for the large plot of land owned by Torazo Iwasaki. As the agent for the sale, Mouat earned a 5 percent commission. He started logging the area almost immediately, and in later years he sold off the land for development in profitable bits and pieces.[42]

For Katsuyori and Kimiko Murakami, life in the Kootenays was a series of seemingly insurmountable challenges—the move from Magrath, getting their bearings in yet another new community, making their shack habitable, searching for food, continuing to manage an artificially low income, getting their kids into and through school—all set against the backdrop of the forced property sale. It is therefore understandable that they did not recognize the second catastrophe until it had fully unfolded. As they settled into Rosebery, the family began noticing changes in Violet. Initially, it appeared she was suffering from some kind of intermittent problem, seemingly a minor injury or perhaps an inflammation. Always athletic, she began to have trouble moving. Mary recalls, "At that time, we noticed that, you know, when she was running . . . the way she was running, suddenly her hip would lock, and she can't move."[43] Over the coming months it became clear that something more serious was going on. As a young child, Violet had displayed a special talent for languages, and she remained an excellent conversationalist. But in school, she began having more and more trouble with her homework. Her difficulties grew so pronounced that by 1945 the family stopped sending her to school.[44]

They had no satisfactory options. Medical care in New Denver and the surrounding communities was stretched to the limit. The Sanitarium was the sole specialized institution, and it was dedicated to treating TB patients. That left all other matters to a handful of nurses and general practitioners. Expulsion from British Columbia had expanded the area's resources. Matasaburo Uchida, a general practitioner who had built a substantial practice treating Nikkei in Vancouver, played an especially important role both at the Sanitarium and throughout the region. A number of other physicians, including a dentist and an optometrist, also contributed their services, as did a host of dedicated Nikkei nurses.[45] Nonetheless, the rationing of supplies, the rudimentary facilities these people had at their disposal, and the health care needs of over 2,500 Nikkei of all ages meant that the emphasis lay on triage and low-level interventions, such as a surprisingly large number of appendectomies and tonsillectomies, rather than diagnosing and treating a young girl whose symptoms were intermittent, complex, and slow to emerge. There was also the matter of cost. Until 1949, health care in the area was priced according to a "hospital ticket" system. The holder of a ticket could receive basic care for $3.00 per day, which was a princely sum for the Murakamis, especially when they thought their daughter's problems might simply pass.[46] As the scope of Violet's difficulties became clear over the next couple of years, the family decided it was better to keep her home, where she could help around the house, and where they could protect her from trouble that might arise.

Fractures in a Community under Duress

As in any community, especially one under such corrosive institutional pressure, social order was fragile. The fabric of Nikkei life occasionally frayed in low-level, even amusing ways. Roy Yasui recalled that kids living near a Slocan Lake tributary called Carpenter Creek would regularly fish using improvised tackle.[47] They had to be careful, though, since this was apparently forbidden: "When the Mounties caught us fishing they would row out to deep water and throw our fishing lines overboard." For adults, the stakes were higher, though perhaps not in the way white authorities initially anticipated. "When the adults were caught they would be sent to the jail in Nelson which was sixty miles [99.2 km] away. Consequently, only the bachelors went fishing. They wanted to be caught because jail food was much tastier."[48]

In other cases, the erosion of social order was more consequential. Ayukawa recalls that "there were always tales being told of knots being knocked out of the walls separating the men from women and also men in charge of the bathhouses who were peeping-toms."[49] Even darker tales circulated as well, most notably one about a sexual predator active in the Extension. The rumor did not reach everyone, but it was consistent in identifying a prominent Issei as a pedophile. The person in question had helped many Nikkei navigate forced dispersal, including life on the sugar beet farms of Alberta. Worse, he was a man of the cloth who had also conducted extensive missionary work throughout the Pacific Northwest from the late 1920s through the bombing of Pearl Harbor. During the war, he traveled widely outside British Columbia, visiting every site associated with inland exile and usually staying with Nikkei families. No one reported the man to the authorities though. Criminalized by the Canadian government, which used the RCMP to arrest and monitor them, Nikkei could not trust law enforcement. They understandably feared that reporting a high-profile member of the community would only cause more trouble. Subject to wartime censorship, they also had no stable, reliable means to spread word of internal threats. They could only warn those close to them and trust that the rumor mill would get the information to those who needed it. That trust was ill-founded, as it usually is, but it was all the community had in the wake of criminalization, expulsion, and fragmentation.[50] And so, for those in the know at the time, the man became anathema. For instance, the Issei parents of one young boy in southern Alberta warned against any contact with the man's family. After being paired with the man's daughter, the boy asked to switch seats at school, and he never interacted with her or her brother again.[51]

1945–1949: *The War Drags On*

World War II ended in 1945 for most Canadians, but not for Nikkei. The cessation of hostilities merely heralded a new phase in their criminalization. In the spring of 1945, alarmed by Constitutional protections that had recently been confirmed for Nisei in America, the government of Prime Minister King implemented a "loyalty survey," which was designed to force the emigration of Nikkei or, for those who did not leave, to disperse them across Canada. It did so by requiring that respondents choose between being sent to Japan at some future date (a process the government called "repatriation" but was in truth expatriation) and agreeing to move further eastward. Financial incentives accompanied expatriation, while Nikkei who opted to remain in Canada would have to relocate at the government's direction and could not count on long-term employment or housing.[52] And while broad public disgust eventually put an end to the government's plan, return to the West Coast remained out of the question.[53] Ottawa still appealed to its racist ministers—most famously Ian Mackenzie of British Columbia, who promised to purge all Nikkei "from the Rockies to the sea"—by annually extending wartime restrictions even after the defeat of Japan.[54] The strategy persisted through 1949, even in the face of increasing public discontent, when the federal government finally allowed the restrictions to lapse.[55] But even if the law would have allowed the Murakamis to return, like virtually all Nikkei expelled from British Columbia, they lacked both property to return to and the money to do so.

Destitute and faced with the threat of deportation, in the wake of the survey the Murakamis opted to return to Magrath, where they landed on a farm owned by a man named Bondaruk. Later, they worked on a farm owned by one of the Spencers, a prominent Magrath family. The move allowed them to reconnect with Riyo and Kumanosuke as well as Kimiko's brothers, James and Victor, who had remained on the Keeler farm. The Murakami children were older now, able to help with work in the fields. For Mary, this also meant she began to register aspects of life that might have eluded her at an earlier age. She noticed, for instance, a change in the fabric of her community. A large number of Nikkei from the Gulf Islands had found themselves shipped to Magrath, and so some of the pre-war patterns of life reasserted themselves. To be sure, there was no disguising the impact of forced dispersal, the demands of sugar beet work, and the vast distances between the farms where people found themselves. According to Mary, "there wasn't anything like the community that we left behind . . . because everybody was working." Even so, some of pre-war social practices reasserted themselves: "When I went to my Auntie's place . . . between the hoeing and weeding time, I noticed that a lot of the older men were playing that *hanafuda* [a traditional Japanese card game]."[56] Nonetheless, for Mary, such moments were more than cultural touchstones. They also provided powerful physical reminders of her outsider status: "I still remember the men smoking, which I hated because I was asthmatic, and it wasn't good to be sucking up all that smoke."[57]

The family's finances remained precarious during this period. For instance, the slow-motion train wreck of dispossession did not end with the forced sale of Nikkei properties in 1943. It was followed by the Royal Commission to Investigate Claims of Japanese Canadians for Property Losses, more familiarly known as the Bird Commission, after its chair Justice Henry Bird (1892–1971), who had been appointed to the British Columbia Supreme Court in 1942. Active from 1947 to 1951, the Bird Commission was nominally a way for Nikkei to recover at least part of what the government and British Columbia racists had stolen from them. In practice, Ottawa employed the commission both as a fig leaf to mask its ethical and legal failures and as a means for drawing a line under the domestic oppression it had engaged in during World War II.[58] Some financial good did come of the commission's proceedings: the former owners of properties sold to the director of the Veterans' Land Act (VLA) for subsequent resale to white veterans received additional compensation equal to roughly 80 percent of the wartime sale price. In most other cases, however, the commission took the word of appraisers and Custodian representatives at face value, compensating former owners around 10 percent of the sale price.[59] It was only in egregious cases, such as that of the VLA, that the commission would offer significantly more.

In August 1948, while the Murakamis were at work in the beet fields, a hearing took place regarding a claim they had filed for compensation. To pursue that claim, the family had been required to provide a dollar amount for the commission to review. This was no small matter, since it entailed accounting for expenses dating back more than twenty years on a property the Murakamis had never expected to sell. Still, Kimiko and Katsuyori carefully laid out the expenses they had incurred in the course of acquiring their property and building their business. Difficult as it was to provide that accounting, the hearing itself promised to be even more so. Identified in legal documents as the owner of the properties, Katsuyori would have to testify in person. An interpreter was made available so that he would be able to answer questions, but speaking to white officials about a matter of such importance still brought tremendous pressure. Katsuyori was self-conscious about his command of English, so Kimiko was usually the public face of the family.[60] Scheduling was also a problem. The commission operated during normal business hours, but the family worked some twenty-five miles (forty kilometers) away in Magrath. Citing the demands of his job and the need to travel by bus, Katsuyori wrote to request an afternoon hearing, which the Lethbridge representatives of the commission grudgingly provided.[61]

In their claim, the Murakamis estimated that their land was worth $3,000 at the time of its forced sale, and they assigned a value of $4,560 to the buildings (including the house). Since the Custodian sold both property and buildings for $1,284, the Murakamis claimed a loss of $6,276. In addition, they estimated the additional loss of $400 worth of furniture, tools, and equipment stored in the house at the time of expulsion, for which the Custodian had provided only $169.15. In their claim, the Murakamis noted that they had proposed "a very small value for our household goods, tools, poultry equipment and farm equipment."[62] Throughout the hearing, the representative for the Bird Commission repeatedly called the family's figures into question. He wondered at length why Katsuyori had not kept records of every purchase and had not documented the hours and relative cost of his labor. Katsuyori replied that there had been no need for such financial defensiveness because he had never intended to sell the property. In the end, the commission recommended compensation totaling $1,087.41—just over 80 percent of what the family had originally received.[63] While nowhere near the sum the Murakamis had calculated, the commission's award indicates that its representatives found the sale to have involved an artificially low price.

That indication would have been a cold comfort at best, though. Life on the farm was hard, and the shack in which the family lived was once again inadequate. At least they found their employer more reasonable and their circumstances somewhat more manageable. As a result, they were able to begin rebuilding the nest egg that forced dispersal and inland exile had destroyed. What they would do with that nest egg was a bone of contention, though. Kimiko wanted to move the family east, where they could start anew, but Katsuyori was determined to return to Salt Spring Island and rebuild the life he and his family had worked so hard to make for themselves.

Meanwhile, the Okanos were headed elsewhere. Kimiko's brother James moved with his parents to nearby Cardston, where they settled in a large, two-story grey house just south of downtown.[64] There, in the spring of 1948, he and a Nikkei partner from Magrath co-founded the Du-Eet Cafe, which also sold baked goods and candy to take away (figure 9). Located at 325 Main Street, the cafe stood in the heart of a thriving commercial district that included retail businesses, a feed shop, a hardware store, a car dealership, and a large grocery store (one of several in the town).[65] The cafe was the family's first venture after forced dispersal, one that had the potential to remake their fortunes. After all, Cardston had roughly twice the population of Magrath; it was home to the sole Mormon temple outside the United States at the time; and it sat on a major thoroughfare leading to Waterton Lakes National Park, a popular vacation site near the American border.

Established as a reserve in 1895, made a national park in 1911, and then expanded in 1914, Waterton Lakes National Park had become a popular

FIGURE 9. Exterior of the Du-Eet Cafe in Cardston, Alberta, 1950. Photo courtesy of the Salt Spring Island Archives.

tourist destination in the early twentieth century. A breathless article in the *Calgary Daily Herald* counted some 15,000 visitors to the park in 1920, up from some 1,200 in 1915.[66] Several factors drove that increase. One was the rise of outdoor vacations, which had become an increasingly important part of the Canadian imaginary. To spend a day or two "roughing it" in the staggering beauty of the Canadian Rockies was seen as a bracing, wholesome respite from work.[67] This ideal became a reality for an ever-larger segment of the provincial population in the later 1940s, a development driven at least partly by the spread of personal transportation, improvements to roadways, and government intervention.[68] Provincial Highway 5 had undergone significant improvement in the later teens, bolstering links with cities and towns in southern Alberta, while subsequent road construction eventually connected the park with British Columbia and with the United States. And as for roughing it, one could camp under the canopy of the heavens or, if seeking a lesser roughness, spend a night at the Prince of Wales Hotel, which the Great Northern Railway Company opened in the park in 1927.[69] The hotel went a long way toward making the park a destination for American as well as Canadian tourists. Located at the crossroads of Provincial Highways 2 and 5, Cardston would not necessarily draw its southern neighbors, but it was ideally situated to serve visitors from Alberta and points east.

Cardston understandably fired the imagination of Okano and his partner, who seem to have anticipated their business might become a hub for Nikkei in southern Alberta. There was Raymond, which had a relatively large and long-standing community of Japanese origin, but there also were the various smaller Nikkei communities, which had formed in places like Coaldale and Magrath, scattered throughout the province. With that idea in mind, the two men placed an advertisement an April 1948 issue of *The New Canadian* suggesting that readers, "visit us when you're out to Waterton Lake."[70] That appeal turned out to be optimistic. Nikkei living in Raymond had established a solid economic foundation for themselves, but beet farming was no kinder to them than it was their white neighbors.[71] What little economic surplus they had accumulated was better saved in anticipation of hard times. As for Japanese and Japanese Canadians living in smaller southern Alberta towns, the vast majority were effectively stranded there by forced dispersal and dispossession. Unable to move eastward, they could scarcely afford to vacation regularly at Waterton Lake.[72]

Having failed to drum up a Nikkei customer base, the Du-Eet needed to pitch itself beyond an Asian Canadian, let alone purely Nikkei, audience. Indeed, while Cardston itself had had small Chinese Canadian populations at various points in its history, in the late 1940s and early 1950s the Okanos and Murakamis seem to have been the only Asian Canadians both living and working in town.[73] By contrast, local white people and, to a lesser extent, residents of the Kainai Reserve were plentiful. If the Du-Eet Cafe was to survive, it would have to serve the broader population of Cardston and its surrounding district.

Survival proved difficult, though. Running a cafe was risky, even though restaurants of this sort were often fixtures of small-town commercial areas. Profit margins were slim, and a restaurant's long-term prospects often hinged on establishing an early aura of success.[74] Furthermore, in a number of small towns, racial stereotypes also played a role. Cafes run by Chinese immigrants were often tagged as "decadent," and many white-owned competitors attempted to trade on their use of "all white help."[75] The Du-Eet Cafe seems not to have run into this last problem, but nonetheless it faltered during its first year. Within months, the partner withdrew, leaving James and the aging Kumanosuke to manage the business on their own. Money was running out, and it looked as if their fledgling venture might soon fail.

Hoping to turn things around, James approached his sister for help. Mary recalls, "My uncle kept coming to Magrath, where we lived, and . . . begging for money . . . [and] his sister said no."[76] Knowing the welfare of her family was at stake, Kimiko worried that lending James money might undo what little progress the Murakamis had made in recovering from wartime dispossession. Regardless of where they went, they would need savings when they left Magrath, and that departure was finally on the horizon. Besides, it was not clear that financing the Du-Eet Cafe would necessarily fix its problems. (Cafes may have been fixtures in many small Alberta towns, but they failed far more often than they succeeded.[77]) Katsuyori, however, felt duty-bound to help his in-laws and former sponsors, and eventually he carried the day: "My father, who's always so soft-hearted, said, you know, 'Lend it to them, lend it to them.'"[78] This went on for the better part of a year, and eventually the Murakamis realized that they would have to take over the business if they wanted to recoup what they had lent. And so it was that in January 1949, the family moved to Cardston, settling into what the children began calling simply the "grey house" on south Main Street with Kumanosuke, Riyo, and James.[79]

The Beginnings of Economic Recovery

The move turned out to be pivotal. Cardston had begun to emerge as a leading small town in southern Alberta. One early factor in this was the Edmunds Act, a prohibition against polygamy that became U.S. law in 1882. Hoping to accommodate practitioners of plural marriage and to establish a foothold outside Utah, the Mormon Church directed a senior member named Charles Ora Card to lead an expedition north from Utah in September 1886. The following spring, after an abortive attempt nearer the U.S. border, Card and a second group settled on the banks of Lee Creek (sometimes called Lee's Creek), which provided a reliable supply of water, ran through fertile land, and crossed a surveyed roadway. This location would enable the community to establish economic foundations as well as engage in travel and trade with relative ease.[80] Such was the success of the town that in 1923 it became the site of the first Mormon temple outside the United States. Consequently, while Cardston never approached the economic or political prominence of Lethbridge, it nonetheless became a center of religious gravity.

Around this same time, officials also set about consolidating Cardston's economic advantages, most notably by ensuring that a major north-south thoroughfare passed through the center of town. As railroads ceded their economic power to the automobile, this increased and consolidated the flow of traffic from surrounding areas through the business district.[81] In so doing, Cardston became a nexus for tourism, for religious pilgrimage, and for trade. By 1948, the town was estimated to have a substantial population (2,500 people, in comparison to Magrath's 1,400).[82] Given all this, one can understand James Okano's early optimism. The Du-Eet Cafe, which sat one block from the town hall and just over two blocks from the temple, was ideally situated to draw on a steady stream of customers from the surrounding area as well as from within Cardston itself.

With the arrival of the Murakamis, that ideal soon became a reality. It did so in part because the family could now save on labor costs. As had been the case on Salt Spring Island, here too, the whole family helped run the business. "We were brought up to, you know, no one asked us to do anything. If there was a task to be done, we did it," Mary recalls. "Our family was a team; we functioned as a team."[83] James helped in the back of the house, Violet served meals and bussed tables, and Kumanosuke ran the cash register until his unexpected death the following November.[84] School schedules and other outside demands meant the family still had to hire waitresses, but Rose and Alice waited tables and Mary worked in the kitchen and washed dishes.[85] (Eventually James designed and built a high-volume dishwasher that did the majority of that work.[86]) Bruce was still quite young, so he usually stayed home with Riyo. Richard pitched in where he could at the restaurant. He also worked as a pinsetter in the nearby bowling alley.[87]

At the heart of the business stood the Murakami parents (figure 10). Once again, circumstances forced Katsuyori into the kitchen, as they had during his time working on the Yellowhead–Blue River Highway. This time, he discovered a hidden talent for baking: "My father had never been a baker. I mean he never even used to come into our kitchen, and all of a sudden, he's thrown into this—luckily, he's very flexible, you know." Such was his talent that before long the cafe started selling out of baked goods.[88] Kimiko, for her part, was able to draw on kitchen skills she had honed on Salt Spring Island, but she had to scale them up dramatically to meet the demands of a restaurant: "My mum took over as the cook; she took two shifts. I don't know how she did it because she was just a tiny woman. She was only about four-foot-nine. And she worked from early morning, the breakfast shift, right through to the dinner hour. . . . And she'd never worked in a restaurant before. The only cooking she ever did was, you know, cooking for us."[89]

Other restaurants stood close by, and they offered many of the same mid-century-diner staples.[90] Despite the competition, though, the Du-Eet Cafe began to thrive. As Mary recalls, "I guess they liked the food, the atmosphere, whatever. Like, every meal was just jam-packed, and people were waiting to get in. So, each, like, breakfast, lunch, and dinner were really, really busy."[91] Some of the cafe's visitors were just passing through, but those were largely seasonal. More important by far were the locals, many of whom soon became regulars. "There were a lot of people who came daily, you know. Even in between [meals], they would come for a cup of coffee or something—milkshake, whatever."[92] The cafe's regulars also extended

FIGURE 10. Katsuyori, Kimiko, and Bruce Murakami in front of the Du-Eet Cafe, 1950. Photo courtesy of the Salt Spring Island Archives.

beyond the white, mostly Mormon population in and around Cardston to include marginalized groups. Mary recalls that the Du-Eet Cafe "catered to the townspeople and tourists coming in during the summer, and the First Nations people and the Hutterite people, you know, when they came into town from the outskirts."[93] Customers even included important political and cultural figures, such as Chief Shot Both Sides (Atso'toah, 1874–1956), who was then the head chief of the Kainai Nation.[94]

Nikkei Life on Main Street

Despite the evident popularity of the Du-Eet Cafe, as Mary was quick to note, Katsuyori and Kimiko "didn't interact with the Cardston society or anything like that."[95] Much the same seems to have been the case for the Okanos. Both families made nominal inroads into the social fabric of Cardston, but these seem to have been driven largely by economic and political necessity. Consider, for instance, the decision to enroll the Du-Eet Cafe in the Cardston Senior Chamber of Commerce in 1949. Membership in this organization placed the Du-Eet Cafe in a circle of businesses closely aligned with town government, which was itself also a member.[96] But there likely was more at stake than aligning the business with a local power base. There was visibility itself: at least some white North American businessmen viewed participation in a Chamber of Commerce as a proxy for the willingness to "assimilate."[97]

Social groups carried similar weight. For instance, James Okano joined the Cardston Rod and Gun Club around the same time. No record survives regarding his motivation, though he may partly have been following the lead of his brother, Victor, who joined that organization in 1945.[98] But why would either of them have joined in the first place? The answer was likely as much political and racial as civic and social. Small-town life in mid-century Alberta was indelibly marked by an ideal of sociability. Service organizations and clubs flourished, encouraging a sense of social cohesion while also advancing the interests of local business.[99] Rod and gun clubs were no exception. Having arisen amid concerns about the rapid depletion of wild game, these organizations cast themselves at least partly as stewards of wildlife, establishing rules for sportsmanlike behavior that would both promote the bracing purity of wilderness excursions and act as a bulwark against unsustainable practices.[100]

The need for stewardship was undeniable in southern Alberta by the later 1940s. The once plentiful trout in Lee Creek had declined noticeably in the preceding decades, and business leaders across the province voiced concern about not only dwindling food sources but also declining rates of tourism, which threatened other sectors of the economy.[101] In response, fishing and hunting clubs arose with the often-explicit mission of preservation under the guise of fair play. The Cardston Rod and Gun Club, for example, established a rearing pond designed to replenish depleted numbers in Lee Creek. Such efforts were a point of pride for club members, who also made much of their association with Ducks Unlimited as well as their campaigns against the local magpie and crow populations.[102] The ethos at work was one that Fred Bradshaw voiced in 1918, when he served as Chief Game Guardian of Saskatchewan: "A true sportsman is usually a good citizen. He looks upon the game laws as his code of ethics and tries to live up to them."[103]

But the definition of a true sportsman, like that of sustainability, was flexible, driven largely by the question of competition. The Cardston Rod and Gun Club, for instance, referred to magpies and crows as "predators" that had to be "kept within reasonable bounds" if the duck population was to thrive.[104] But while sportsmanship was the province of the human, not all humans were thought to possess it in equal measure. In early twentieth-century Canada, it had strong racial and economic components. Of particular importance to these clubs were hunting freedoms that First Nations peoples possessed by treaty. Clubs asserted that these freedoms threatened the rapidly diminishing wildlife populations that exemplified the "Last Best West."[105] They repeatedly called for an end to those freedoms under the guise of asserting "fair play" for all.[106] As were Nikkei in Canada and in the United States, Indigenous peoples were cast as enjoying an unfair advantage. Like their Nikkei counterparts, First Nations groups were often described as either desperately in need of white "civilization" or else, ruined by contact with their white neighbors and overseers, borderline irremediable. The Indian Agent in Morely, Alberta, wrote in 1903, "as long as they can hunt you cannot civilize them."[107] Positioning themselves explicitly as stewards of wildlife and of fair play itself, rod and gun clubs also positioned themselves implicitly as stewards of the Indigenous peoples who both depended on and supposedly threatened that wildlife. In the process, they allowed supposed leisure pursuits to become proxies for racial, economic, and political belonging.

For James and Victor Okano, that belonging would always have been approximate and contingent. After all, there was no disguising the fact that they were part of a racialized group that had been explicitly criminalized, forced from British Columbia, placed in Alberta over the objections of prominent citizens and newspapers, dispossessed, impoverished, and then barred from returning to the west coast. This, though, was the character of Nikkei life on Main Street in postwar southern Alberta: existence in a racial and cultural borderlands. The Murakamis and Okanos might pursue some of the jobs and achieve some of the financial goals associated with mainstream postwar existence, but theirs would always be a kind of half-belonging.

Still, the families improved their circumstances in every way they could. First, they moved from the Grey House into another home, one the Widmer family had recently vacated.[108] Mary knew Sylvia Widmer from high school, but the family gained broader recognition as owners of Central Service Company, a Chevrolet and Oldsmobile dealer located near the Du-Eet Cafe.[109] The Murakamis were still extremely frugal, of course, always mindful both of Katsuyori's desire to go west once more and of the precarity of any gains they might make. With that in mind, most of their meals took place in the restaurant, the better to save on labor as well as cost.[110] In addition, Kimiko made clothing for her children; "she even sewed a suit for my younger brother [Richard]."[111] Mary took after her mother, sewing many of her own clothes. Sometimes she would buy fabric at the local shop; more often, though, she would order from the catalogs circulated by T. Eaton's.[112]

Combined with their newfound economic success, living lean enabled the family to build up surplus against future demands. It also allowed them to make a decisive change in their financial fortunes through two smart, interconnected investments. First, they bought the building at 325 Main Street, which gave them control over the physical form of the Du-Eet Cafe. This purchase then led to the second investment. Around 1952, while they were living in the Widmers' former home, Katsuyori and James began to expand the back end of the restaurant. Rather than build added capacity, though, they built living quarters. Mary recalls that "we each had a bedroom because it was a long, long building that we added to the restaurant. . . . It was quite a few rooms, you know, like an additional bathroom. Geez, there were . . . I can't remember how many bedrooms there were." Alice had moved to Chicago the previous year, but the living quarters still had to house Katsuyori and Kimiko Murakami, their five remaining children, and James and Riyo Okano. As was the case with Kimiko's sewing, the expansion of the building took place outside regular business hours to avoid disrupting the Du-Eet's slim profit margin.[113] Needless to say, the workload must have been exhausting: "They were like magicians; they were able to do a lot of things that you wonder how in the heck they did it."[114]

Work and Play

The move from Cardston meant that Richard, Rose, Violet, and Mary all had to start at new schools in the middle of the year. For Richard, the transition was especially difficult. According to Mary, "he had a hard time adjusting at that time when we first went, and he used to cause a lot of trouble in his class, and he was thrown out of his class, you know, on and off." Displaying early signs of a hard-won independence that would prove invaluable later, he took this as an opportunity to pursue his own interests: "Instead of sitting outside of the classroom, he used to take off and go fishing in the creek."[115] Something bigger was at stake, too, for Richard had developed night terrors. At some point, while the family was still living in the Grey House, he began to wake suddenly, screaming at the top of his lungs.[116] There were multiple factors in this, the most important of which would only come to light decades later.

Despite the difficulties he faced, Richard formed friendships. One in particular stands out for Mary now:

> There was a family living behind our restaurant, you know, on the next lot. And this kid was only . . . ten or eleven years old. But his parents owned a farm, and he was allowed to drive the truck. . . . And, you know, when you put a little kid in a truck . . . he would have a pile of cushions. And this was a four-on-the-floor—right?—you had to change gears. And then at that time there were no seatbelts or anything. Richard would be in the passenger's side, and Jimmy would be the driver. And they would go all the way to the farm, which was quite far, and do whatever chore that Jimmy had to do. And they would come safely home again.[117]

Even so, there was no denying that repeated uprootings and the fragmentation of the British Columbia Nikkei community after 1942, among other factors, took a heavy toll on Richard.

For Alice, life in southern Alberta provided daily evidence of the position Nikkei were in vis-à-vis the Canadian government and its white supremacist policies. Wealthier families who could afford to move east, for instance, were sending their children to college. Impoverished by expulsion and dispossession, the Murakamis were in no position to do this, despite the academic promise Alice had shown from an early age. Her years in Magrath and Cardston were thus primarily spent helping the family rebuild its financial foundation. Still, smart and resourceful, she nonetheless set about making plans for when her parents would be on stable economic footing. Of particular note were her efforts at correspondence. "I don't know how she got a hold of this pen pal," Mary recalls. "In fact, she had two pen pals in the U.S. Army." Laughing at the memory, she adds, "And I used to see her writing, you know, letters to him and to this other guy."[118] Matters progressed to the point that each of the men visited the Murakamis while they were working on one of the sugar beet farms. Although living in awful conditions, the family put their best foot forward: "One day while we were in Magrath, her husband-to-be came to see us, and it was terrible because we lived in this shack. There was hardly any room for us alone, so he comes, and he's given one room."[119] Destitute they may have been, but they still sought to host each of their Nikkei guests from the United States appropriately.

Doing so was a point of pride for Kimiko and Katsuyori, but it also was an acknowledgment of just how difficult cross-border romance was for Nikkei at that time. Forrest La Violette (1904–1989), an early scholar of Nikkei in North America, observed that broken engagements and the like were a hot topic among Canadians of Japanese ancestry. In at least some cases, the failure of those couples stemmed directly from bureaucratic obstacles. The U.S. government, for instance barred Nikkei Canadian citizens from staying in the United States long enough to find a spouse. For their own part, La Violette wrote, "the Canadian immigration authorities would not permit an unmarried 'Oriental woman,' even though an American citizen, to enter Canada for permanent residence." Adding insult to injury, "in June 1946, almost a year after V-J day, the American Consulates in Canada were required to send to the State Department in Washington the applications for permits for Canadian citizens of Japanese ancestry to enter the United States. This usually required about six weeks while any other Canadian could cross the border, for less than 29 days, with only a birth certificate."[120]

Despite such obstacles, Alice and her fiancé, Ted Tanaka, prevailed. Their marriage took place in Chicago in January of 1951. None of Alice's relatives could attend. Acquiring visas would have been a significant challenge, but there was a bigger problem. The Murakamis had begun to reestablish themselves financially, but they were in no position to rest on their achievements. As Mary put it, "nobody went because we couldn't leave the restaurant."[121] Instead, Alice and Ted returned briefly to Cardston, where a bridal shower was held on the following Valentine's Day. Some thirty guests attended the shower at the Pioneer Home, a local landmark, and it featured vocal as well as instrumental performances. Mary has no recollection of the event, but according to the *Cardston News*, "a dainty lunch was served after which the bride opened gifts, assisted by her friends, and thanked all most graciously."[122] In the end, it was a bittersweet moment, with Alice building a life of her own but moving to Chicago and eventually to California to do so. Fortunately, Mary was able to visit Alice several times in those early years. And later on the Tanakas would bring their family to see the Murakamis on Salt Spring Island in summertime.[123]

Nikkei Girls at Cardston High

For Mary and Rose, who were in high school, the challenge lay less in disruption to their social and academic lives than in navigating racial and religious boundaries. They were reminded of this on their very first day of school in January of 1949: "When my sister Rose and I went to register at the high school, we were really afraid because two boys came out from the classroom . . . to have a drink at the fountain, and they looked up and saw the two of us. And then they said, "Japs!"—you know, really loud. And, you know, right then and there we were scared; we didn't know what they were going to do to us."[124] Incidents of this sort appear to have been relatively infrequent, and the two boys even became friends: "Rose would chum around with these boys. We'd see her on the handlebar of the bicycle, where the boys would, you know, would pedal her around town. . . . [They were] the ones that called us 'Japs' at the beginning."[125] Still, it was the beginning of a twilight existence in which Mary and Rose would find themselves embedded within and yet still on the margins of mainstream small-town life.

The family's emphasis on education went a long way toward helping the girls coexist with their white Mormon neighbors. Mary describes Rose as having gone from strength to strength with relative ease, even as she casts herself as an undistinguished student.[126] She recalls a mathematics teacher with whom she had particular difficulty: "He had three or four brilliant boy students, and he was only interested in them. And so, students like me, who wasn't very good at math, would go to ask him—you know, we'd get up to go and ask him a question—and then he would say to me, . . . [*sighs*] 'You again.' And so, I would just turn around and walk back to my seat. And so, I never learned anything from him."[127] And yet, as her sister Alice had in Slocan, Mary did find supportive teachers in Cardston. For instance, one teacher, Arminto Kearl (1909–1998), created a girls' group that Mary recalls fondly. And Mary's scholastic performance was strong enough for her later to gain admission to Trinity College, the Anglican division of the University of Toronto.

Mary recalls that she and her sister "got along well because we did well academically."[128] The importance of scholastic life in mid-century Cardston was profound, and that importance left a lasting impression:

> The thing I remember most is . . . we would come home to the restaurant, have a snack, and then race for the library. Everybody fought to go to the library because, if you don't go there in time, you don't have a seat there. And the library was always full of students, so in order to get a seat there, you had to get there quickly. And so, Rose and I would just gobble something down and then take off and go to the library. And we would stay there until we had to go back to the restaurant and help with the dinner crowd. And after we helped with that, we used to do our homework.[129]

This ethos would have warmed the hearts of administrators in the provincial Department of Education, which took out an ad on the front page of the *Cardston News* in December 1950 telling readers that "your right to know is the door to a better economic, social and cultural life, and education is the key to that door."[130] More than propaganda, though, the idea that you had to scramble for a seat in the library after school also tells us much about the social and cultural life of a mainstream high schooler in postwar Cardston.[131] To participate in that life was to be demonstrably, visibly studious. Hence Mary's remark about getting along, Doing so was not a measure of efforts to become part of the community. Rather, it stemmed from the family's long-standing investment in education and from their determination to recover from forced dispersal and dispossession. Mary and Rose simply found a point of contact with their neighbors, the majority of whom were driven by the Mormon community's belief that academic strength was necessary for the well-being of the individual and of the community.[132]

Although the demands of school and work at the Du-Eet Cafe were considerable, the girls still managed to participate in a few extracurricular activities.[133] Mary became a member of the Cardston Junior-Senior High School newspaper staff.[134] And Arminto Kearl organized summer recreational trips for the group she had formed: "She used to take us to Waterton Lake and camp overnight, and we would have fun . . . at the lake. And I remember, you know, cooking breakfast in the morning and things like that."[135] Enjoyable though such trips were, they belonged to a broader culture of white, Anglo-Saxon, Protestant uplift. As Donald Wetherell has suggested regarding earlier summer camping expeditions by groups such as the Young Women's Christian Association or the Canadian Girls in Training, trips of this sort "did not merely provide a week's summer entertainment; they reinforced and sustained moral values and combined education with pleasure."[136] Having been raised in an Anglican household, Mary seems to have found this part of the project unremarkable. Still, it is worth dwelling briefly on the moments of self-sufficient joy that trips like this provided. For someone like Mary, who in the Kootenays had resigned herself to an essentially solitary existence even among other people, the social side of these trips must have felt like a strange luxury.

And then there was basketball. Rose and Mary joined the Cardston High School team, the Cougarettes. Practice was right after school, so both girls would spend an extra hour on campus before heading to the cafe and then the library. Neither girl was especially tall, but each found a place on the team.[137] This was due at least partly to the vice principal of Cardston Junior-Senior High School, Shirley Gibb, whom Mary recalls as having been a welcoming, supportive coach.[138] The highlight of their time on the team came in March 1953, when the Cougarettes traveled to neighboring Vermilion High School, where Rose helped them win the provincial championships in two back-to-back games.[139]

A Dawning Political Sensibility

Mary had not enjoyed a particularly strong sense of belonging prior to her arrival in Cardston. More than half of her life had been spent in ethnic enclaves produced in part by racist hysteria. From the moment they entered Hastings Park in 1942 until they finally left the Kootenay region in 1949, the Murakamis had lived with fellow Nikkei not by choice but by government fiat. They, like other families, found themselves in Greenwood or Rosebery purely because Ottawa needed a place to keep them. Mary interacted with children her age, of course, studying for school or playing games. But those connections were largely superficial since she had long since learned that the BCSC might decide to move a family from one site to another with little notice and seemingly no rhyme or reason. As a result, in the Kootenays she might have been surrounded by people who looked like her and whose families had similar social dynamics, ate similar foods, navigated similar emotional challenges, and endured the same injustices. But she remained alone among them, always ready for the inevitable next move.

Postwar life in Magrath turned out to be a sparser version of the ghettoization that had characterized the years immediately after the bombing of Pearl Harbor. Mary, her siblings, and her parents worked for white people, but they socialized almost exclusively with family members, other dispossessed former residents of the Gulf Islands, and a handful of Nikkei from elsewhere in British Columbia. The children played games with white classmates at school, but they never brought anyone home to the Murakamis' shack.[140] In fact, the only person who brought visitors, Alice, did so out of necessity. Even in church, their marginalized status remained painfully legible—for instance, in the disdain with which a fellow parishioner once regarded the impoverished family's donations.[141]

Moving to Cardston brought an important but complicated change of circumstance. Mary now found herself literally in the heart of a mid-century Canadian small town, with all its claims of cohesiveness, egalitarianism, and economic opportunity. But the slippages between those claims and the reality of daily existence would have weighed increasingly heavily on a young woman whose life had been so thoroughly shaped by racialization. From the moment she stepped out of the house until the moment she got home, Mary continued to live in an enclave, but this time one to which she did not belong.

For one thing, the Murakamis and Okanos were not Mormon. Cardston was home to several denominations of Christianity, including the Anglican Church, which was especially active on the neighboring Kainai Reserve.[142] Nonetheless, the Latter-day Saints were massively predominant, so much so that Mary recalls that she and one other student would be left essentially alone in the classroom when their cohort left to attend Seminary, a daily period of religious instruction that was designed into the school day.[143] Begun as an experiment in 1912, Seminary rapidly became a pillar of the faith, providing children with instruction in Mormon doctrine from an early age. No less important, it also placed religious practice at the heart of education. Students might leave school to attend the day's instruction, but they never had to travel far, and Seminary itself often occurs in the midst of the day's lessons—that is, students would leave school for Seminary and then return for the rest of their coursework.[144] Thus, although Mary was not a practitioner, Mormonism loomed large in her life, while the Anglican Church became remote. In fact, Mary's most notable memory of Anglicanism in Cardston is of a 1951 visit by the Reverend Nakayama, who readers may recall made a practice of looking in on Nikkei families scattered throughout the province. Nakayama stayed with the family for a night or two before going on his way.[145]

Further complicating the situation was the fact that the Murakamis and Okanos were not longtime residents of Cardston. Membership in the Chamber of Commerce and in the Rod and Gun Club must have helped, as did the kids' participation in extracurricular activities. But those activities could hardly have put them in the same position as longtime residents, some of whose ancestors had helped found the town. Furthermore, the Murakamis and Okanos started off as renters, and when they did eventually move into a space they owned, it was the addition Katsuyori and James had built off the back of the Du-Eet Cafe. This would have had the biggest impact on the children. New in town, governed by the demands of the restaurant, and never durable members of any single neighborhood, they spent much of their time in Cardston repeatedly settling into new circumstances.

Last, but not least, the Murakamis and Okanos were not white. And while citizens of Cardston as a group seem never to have expressed the sort of virulent anti-Japanese racism that dominated politics in British Columbia, difference haunted every aspect of the families' lives. We can see traces of that haunting in local publications from the time. For instance, when the

Cardston News reported Kumanosuke Okano's death in November 1949, it provided a fairly accurate account of his life, including when he and Riyo each arrived from Japan, the fact that he "was one of the biggest farmers on the Salt Spring Islands," and the fact that expulsion from British Columbia (which it called "evacuation") had brought them to the province. But it also referred to him as "Kumanosuki" and spelled the Murakamis' last name as "Mirakami."[146] To be fair, many papers in southern Alberta in the early twentieth century exhibited wildly uneven copy editing. And, over time, the track record of the *Cardston News* improved, at least with respect to the Murakamis. Even so, it must be noted that people with a clearer place in the community and more common last names, such as Blackmore, Bradshaw, Lundrigan, Trelease, or Willmott, were less subject to variable spelling.

Nikkei had lived in southern Alberta for decades, and they had become a much more noticeable presence after their expulsion from British Columbia.[147] But for most Albertans, people of Japanese ancestry still fell outside the conventional categories of British, Francophone, "immigrant" (i.e., Central European), or First Nations. Consequently, the Murakamis, like other Nikkei, became subject to ad hoc sorts of perception, which come through in innumerable little discontinuities, such as those misspellings or the suggestion in a 1948 issue of the *Lethbridge Herald* that the Du-Eet Cafe as "the only Japanese"—as opposed to Japanese Canadian—"business in Cardston at present."[148] The primary documents show a culture of whiteness grappling with people whose non-whiteness seemed inseparable from traits it recognized and valued, such as athletic capability, studiousness, or business acumen. A telling example is Mary's inclusion in the "Dream Girl" roster for her 1951–1952 high school yearbook. Alongside candidates for Hair, Eyes, Smile, Figure, Legs, Personality, Most Likely to Succeed, and Athletic(ism), she won in the curious category of Hands.[149]

Such indecipherability, perhaps more than anything else, might have been what made postwar Nikkei life on Main Street so peculiar for Mary. Every sidewalk she traveled, every room she entered, every conversation she had required at least a measure of translation, confirming the awareness of a new kind of isolation. Sitting alone in the classroom with the only other non-Mormon student her age was an experience she and Sylvia Widmer shared, but Sylvia Widmer was white, and her family had not been criminalized, forced from their home, and dispossessed. As a result, any such sharing would always necessarily be of a limited sort. Going places with family members would only have sharpened the sensation. To attend a dance at the Social Centre with Rose meant that Mary was now half of the non-white people in the room. The boys with whom she danced may have appreciated her academic commitment, enjoyed watching her play basketball, or admired her hands.[150] Nonetheless, white, mostly Mormon, and male, they remained worlds away.

But for a young Nikkei Canadian woman emerging from a childhood fractured by inland exile, a sense of alienation was beginning to take shape not only with respect to her own family but also with respect to others. She noticed, for instance, that although First Nations people would regularly dine in the Du-Eet Cafe, their teenaged children never attended the dances at the Social Centre.[151] She also noticed Treaty Day, which came every summer and soon raised ethical challenges for her. When local members of the Kainai Nation would receive their Treaty Day annuity—$5, a sum that has not increased since 1875—they would come into town. Some would spend their money on a meal at the Du-Eet or one of its competitors, while others would shop.[152] Consequently, Treaty Day represented an important economic as well as political moment in the local business calendar. But the responses to that moment could vary widely, as Mary found out. For example, the mother of a classmate owned a shop that sold knickknacks alongside its other goods. On Treaty Day, this woman would swap out part of her inventory.[153] "This mother would bring out all these junky trinkets and [also] perfume in these tiny, tiny vials. . . . And she would say, 'Oh, this is for the Indians.' "[154] Observing the change in inventory and hearing the dismissive rationalization, Mary began to recognize the contours of marginalization. "I didn't like that at all."[155]

Attitudes toward First Nations peoples varied widely in southern Alberta in the late 1940s and early 1950s. As Keith Regular has observed, early in its history the Kainai Nation became an integral part of the regional economy and, thus, an important presence in the region's political life.[156] But being a presence is not the same as being equal, let alone being in control. The Kainai people were constantly having to fend off incursions by local ranchers and farmers, to chase lessees for late payment, and to lobby local officials to honor agreements. As a result, the Kainai people were undeniably part and parcel of the local economy, and they formed all manner of complex relationships with their white neighbors. But such relationships were always marked by friction and were always unequal.

Mary's experience of difference in postwar southern Alberta was necessarily idiosyncratic and fragmentary, as were the relationships available to her. After nearly ten years in the company of mostly Nikkei, she was now awash in a sea of almost exclusively white people. To be sure, First Nations customers came to the Du-Eet, and the family had at least some contact with Indigenous people outside of work. Alice also seems to have gone on a few dates with a young Kainai man before marrying Ted Tanaka.[157] But the family's connection with First Nations was at best attenuated, filtered largely through newspaper reports and snippets of conversation overheard. Consequently, Mary's memory of postwar Indigeneity is fragmentary, knit together from fleeting presences and jarring statements that over the intervening years became a nagging absence that eventually drove her to learn more about the Kainai Nation and its history.

In this way, Mary's experience of Indigeneity became a critical factor in her political awakening, one that developed over time and drew on important moments of discontinuity in Cardston's wider claims of mid-century idealism. Kainai students were rare at Cardston High School; members of the community who attended school on the southern part of the reserve had long done so at the religious institutions set up there, one Catholic and one Anglican.[158] In the early 1950s, though, two did attend Cardston High. As the only other non-white students, they stood out for Mary. She recalls, for instance, Evelyn Eagle Speaker (later Evelyn Locker), who was one of the earliest First Nations students to attend Cardston's public schools.[159] Eagle Speaker had attended St. Paul's Catholic school on the reserve, but she and her family saw equal access to education as critical both for the survival of Kainai Nation and for reshaping public perception of its people. With that in mind, she got permission from the Indian Affairs Department and the Alberta Board of Education to attend Cardston High School, from which she graduated in 1953 before going on to study at Henderson Business College in Calgary.

Mary knew none of this at the time, though. For her, Eagle Speaker was an enigma: "She would come just as the bell rang, and . . . she sat down, she took notes, never said a word, and soon as the bell rang, she would just fold her books and disappear."[160] The two never had the chance to connect socially because, like most other members of the Kainai Nation, Eagle Speaker came into Cardston with a narrow purpose. For her, as for the citizenry of Cardston, the place of Indigeneity in town was tightly constrained. There were, for instance, restrictions on how often and where a member of the Kanai might venture off the reserve. There also were restrictions on what they might buy. One Cardstonian noted in 1962:

> Recreation for the Blood Indians in the town ranges from roaming the streets and collecting in the cafes to frequenting the pool halls, bowling alley, and local cinemas. One other activity which may be classed as recreation, requiring both time and money on the part of the Blood Indian, involves the American town of Babb some ten miles [1.6 km] from the international boundary into the State of Montana. According to the Alberta provincial laws, the Blood Indians cannot purchase any alcoholic beverages in the province of Alberta and as a direct result, many carloads of Blood Indians motor to the small town of Babb for this specific purpose.[161]

Mary lived the life of an outsider, but her daily life was still centered on Cardston. As a result, she was struck by Eagle Speaker's quick departure. There were no afternoon sprints to the library for this classmate, no dances at the Social Centre, and certainly no riding around town on the handlebars of a friend's bike.

Mary sensed something remarkable in Eagle Speaker's presence, but she could make little sense of the woman at the time because even in class she revealed little if anything: "She was very quiet."[162] Eagle Speaker's laconic presence in the classroom became, for Mary, a point around which ideas of difference began to crystallize. Imagine, then, what a shock it was when Mary spotted her former classmate in the summer of 1954: "When we were having one of those mini-stampedes in Cardston, here [*gasps*] on the float is *Evelyn*! Queen of the [Calgary] Stampede! And I thought, 'Holy cow!'"[163] Founded in 1886, the Calgary Stampede eventually became an annual rodeo and exhibition. Beginning in 1946, the festivities included the selection of a Stampede Queen and two Ladies in Waiting, who, much in the manner of a traditional beauty queen, were expected to give speeches, attend public events, sit for newspaper interviews, and otherwise promote the Stampede. In addition to the memory of her enigmatic presence in the classroom, what made Eagle Speaker's appearance so remarkable was the fact that until that year the title of Queen had always gone to a white woman. Now, however, here was Mary's former classmate, standing on a parade float, smiling and waving at the crowd—in essence, doing the last possible things Mary could have imagined a non-white woman doing.

Mary was not alone. The previous spring, Eagle Speaker had secured the sponsorship of the Calgary Elks Club, who backed her candidacy for the role of Stampede Queen. For the Elks, it was an opportunity to promote their organization as a progressive force supporting what it presented as an exemplary First Nations individual. To quote the *Lethbridge Herald*, "This is a distinct honor for Queen Evelyn and her people and we feel sure she will conduct herself with the grace and dignity that goes with the office."[164] Almost immediately, however, a problem arose. Mindful of the visibility being Stampede Queen would bring, Eagle Speaker's mother had fashioned a traditional outfit for her daughter to wear. However, a number of voices had arisen in protest, insisting that the Queen should wear "conventional cowgirl garb"—that is, a nostalgia-driven, implicitly white outfit that had become standard fare by that time.[165] The various parties overseeing the Stampede eventually came to an agreement that allowed Eagle Speaker to wear traditional Kainai clothing on two occasions and to wear "the regulation 'Hollywood Cowboy' dress" for the remainder of her public events.[166]

When, decades later, Mary finally got the chance to speak with her former classmate, the mechanics of her selection became clear. Chuckling, Mary recalls that, "I asked her how in the heck she became Calgary Stampede Queen, and she said, 'We sold the most tickets.'"[167] Although the competition deployed the standard beauty-contest criteria, selection of the Queen was indeed based on ticket sales: buying a twenty-five-cent ticket in a candidate's name brought that candidate twenty-five votes, with the proceeds going to local charities.[168] Recognizing the importance of this opportunity to address the regional public, Eagle Speaker's family mounted a winning campaign. Their aim and hers was not to be radical but simply to make Kainai people legible *as people*. Indeed, Eagle Speaker had already been pursuing broader acceptance both for herself and for members of her community. She had, for instance, won prizes for her writing as early as 1948, writing in which she addressed the question of how white people interpreted Kainai ways of life.[169]

It would be years before Mary fully realized that her time in Cardston had been another lesson in the mechanics of whiteness. It was whiteness of a more polite sort than she had encountered before, and her family was no longer officially under government supervision. But in her relative isolation and in her dawning sensitivity to the impoverishment and dispossession of other non-white peoples lay the seeds of a political engagement that would blossom later in life.

FOUR

College and the Beginnings of Political Self-Awareness

At first glance, Mary's life from the mid-1950s through the early 1980s looks straightforward. She departed the small town in southern Alberta where she had spent her later teens, helped her parents move to British Columbia, attended the University of Toronto, spent summers helping work her parents' land, moved back to Vancouver after graduation, met and then married someone she loves, and then settled into a quiet neighborhood outside the city, where the couple raised two children. In fact, to the casual, especially non-Nikkei observer, the life thus described seems remarkably unremarkable, especially for someone who had survived nearly fifteen years of state-sponsored violence and dispossession. But to frame Mary's life this way—as a quintessential late twentieth-century economic success story—not only flirts with the "model minority" myth; it also misses a critical point. Like those of her parents and siblings, Mary's life has been one of increasing resistance to wartime injustice and its aftermath. It is therefore meaningless to ask when Mary became politically engaged. The real question is how that engagement came into focus for her over time, how it metamorphosed from intuitive, atomized, and relatively isolated efforts into increasingly programmatic and cooperative action. Indeed, we would do well to think of her entire life from 1942 onward as encompassing what Tetsuden Kashima, referring to Nikkei in the United States, once called a "crisis of readjustment."[1]

Starting Over Yet Again

By 1954, the Murakamis had finally regained economic stability. The Du-Eet Cafe was thriving; they owned both the building that housed it and, having expanded off the back of that building, their home. They had not been able to move in 1949, when Ottawa rescinded its wartime policy and allowed Nikkei to return to the west coast of British Columbia. By 1954, however, they had managed to earn enough money to consider leaving southern Alberta. In this respect, they exemplified the dry observation by Forrest La Violette in 1948 that "evacuation has given the savings account a new importance."[2] For Kimiko, that account meant seemingly limitless possibilities were finally available. For Katsuyori, it meant that the family could finally reclaim its place on Salt Spring Island, and eventually he convinced Kimiko. He hoped to repurchase the original plot on Sharp Road. Barring that, he would try to recoup one of the farms the Custodian of Enemy Property had sold out from under the Okanos. In the likely event that plan also failed, he would buy a new parcel of land.

Katsuyori's aim was unusual among Nikkei who had lived on Salt Spring Island. According to one white neighbor, a scant three Japanese Canadian families attempted to return after 1949. Katsuyori's focus and determination were also unusual: of those three families, only the Murakamis remained on the island permanently.[3] As reserved but warm as he had been toward his neighbors and customers in Cardston, Katsuyori was above all a man of conviction. He had built a life on the island, and he would rebuild that life despite persecution. So, once the family had socked away enough money, Kimiko and Katsuyori set his plan in motion.

They knew from one of Kimiko's brothers that the challenges would extend beyond money or logistics. Having gotten governmental permission to move due to his wife's poor health, Victor Okano had returned to the island with his family around 1948, well ahead of the March 1949 date when restrictions finally expired.[4] Upon arriving, they quickly realized that their wartime mistreatment had not been purely a government initiative; it permeated every level of provincial society, with only a handful of people expressing overt support for their return. As Mary later recalled, the majority of white islanders closed ranks in an attempt to deny the Okanos a foothold. Recognizing the family's predicament, "this one lady who had this big farm took pity on them and said, 'You could live in our barn.' [But] then, some people heard about this, and they told this lady that if they let Victor and his family live in the barn, they're going to burn it down while [the family is] sleeping." The Okanos then moved into a small hut that drew less attention, put their son and daughter in school, and began rebuilding their lives.[5]

As for the Murakamis, their 1954 return would happen in three stages. First, Katsuyori would travel to Salt Spring Island and find a place for the family. Second, they would sell the Du-Eet Cafe. The third stage of the move involved selling the building that housed the Du-Eet. Initially they would retain ownership of the building to ensure rental income during the transition, but once the farm was self-sustaining, they would sell the Cardston property. With that in mind, they placed ads in southern Alberta newspapers offering the business for sale. A Chinese Canadian family by the name of Yip contacted them, and the two families negotiated the transaction.[6] The Murakamis then bought a car for James, who built a trailer to pull behind it. After that, they mapped out the route for two long drives between Cardston and southern Vancouver. On the first trip, Katsuyori brought Rose, Richard, and Bruce so that they would arrive in time to start school. (Rose would graduate the following year as valedictorian of her class.) They also could help their father and uncle unload the trailer and set up house. Meanwhile, Kimiko, Violet, and Mary stayed in Cardston to run the Du-Eet Cafe and to take care of Riyo Okano.[7] When James returned, the sisters and their mother loaded up the trailer one last time, wished the Yips and their former neighbors well, and finally went home.[8]

The family's return has been documented well by Brian Smallshaw,[9] among others, but parts of the story merit renewed consideration. For instance, Katsuyori first tried to recover land that the Custodian of Enemy Property had sold without the families' consent. He approached each occupant with an offer, and each declined.[10] This result could not possibly have come as a surprise. He was approaching owners who had acquired productive, well-prepared land for what even the Bird Commission had determined were unduly low prices. Even if the Murakamis paid full market value, any move the white farmers might make would necessitate buying a plot that was more expensive once inflation and the labor that land would require were taken into account. As someone who had spent years building his agricultural business, followed by more years spent rescuing a restaurant and building it into a successful local attraction, Katsuyori would have understood the financial situation. But he sought to buy the land not simply because it was well prepared and familiar, but also because that was the only way it could become *his* once again—even if everyone knew that no one would sell. The very act of approaching those other farmers was a reassertion of his and his family's right to exist in white Canada.

Still, that family had to eat, and so Katsuyori eventually moved on, finding a landowner, Gus Galbus, who was willing to sell.[11] Galbus sold Katsuyori an unimproved plot on Rainbow Road, just a third of a mile (half a kilometer) south of the Sharp Road properties where he and the Okanos had first worked so hard to build a life for themselves. The plot was in a good location, placing the Murakamis in the middle of a thriving agricultural zone with well-developed transportation infrastructure. The site itself, however, was a forbidding prospect. Salt Spring Islander Don Cunningham was a young boy at the time, and he remembers the place being wild. "It was land that nobody else wanted," he recalled, essentially a dense thicket of broom mined with cedar stumps and interwoven with blackberries and gorse—"you name it, it was in there." Undaunted, "the Murakamis went in, they basically cleared the land as best they could by hand." After this, they hired Galbus to break the land with his tractor and plow, enabling them to begin farming once again.[12] In his account, Cunningham echoes a long-standing assertion about Nikkei in North America: "It was just a case of they were prepared to do the work that nobody else was prepared to do."[13] There is a very important reason for that preparedness: having returned to an inhospitable culture, the Murakamis had no other option if they were to survive.

But the Murakamis had *chosen* to return to that culture, and not because of financial necessity. In fact, leaving Cardston for British Columbia entailed significant economic and well as personal risk. After years of backbreaking labor, Katsuyori and Kimiko finally enjoyed a steady income from the Du-Eet Cafe, and they had built up significant savings. The motivation for returning to British Columbia, to Salt Spring Island, to the land they had cleared and lived on and farmed was never strictly economic. The decision to undertake these risks late in life, especially to approach the people living on what was rightfully their land, was instead a counterpart to the repeated legal challenges Torazo Iwasaki pursued in his effort to recover what racists and economic opportunists had stolen.[14] But Iwasaki insisted on working through the Canadian legal system, and on revealing its myriad failings. In the wake of the Bird Commission's meagre recommendations, the Murakamis recognized that such efforts would likely achieve little. Better to buy new land and demonstrate the many failures of racist hysteria while also getting on with the business of living.

To get on with the business of living did not mean ignoring past wrongs, though, let alone trying to fit in. That is why, after Katsuyori found the plot, he and Kimiko paid for it using a bag filled with cash. A check would have sufficed for the transaction, but something more was at stake. Gavin Mouat brokered the deal and attended the closing, and his presence allowed the Murakamis to engage in a localized, private protest. Laying that cash out on the table, they demonstrated not only that they had survived despite betrayal at the hands of white islanders, including Mouat himself, but also that racists on the island would not keep them from rejoining a community they had helped build.

Angered by the Murakamis' perseverance, some islanders sought to drive them from their home. Mary recalls, "We got all kinds of threatening phone calls, or people walking down the . . . the main road in front of our house, you know, shouting at us."[15] And after Kimiko took her children to the Anglican church, the minister once again came to the house and informed her they were unwelcome in the house of worship they and their relatives had helped build.[16] This seems to have been the last straw for Mary, who, despite remaining a spiritual person, never returned to the fold. The impact was intergenerational, too. When her own children were born, she sent them not to an Anglican church, but to a Baptist one with a strong investment in social justice.[17]

To be sure, there were a few differences with respect to the family's return to Salt Spring Island. For instance, while the island's adult population still had a vocal and aggressive racist contingent, Rose, Richard, and Bruce seem to have encountered little trouble from their schoolmates.[18] In addition, a number of white neighbors welcomed the family back. Nonetheless, a significant part of the island's population maintained the British Columbian tradition of anti-Asian bigotry.[19] Undaunted, the Murakamis set about improving not only their own plot but also the island's shared spaces. For instance, when the family first visited the grave of baby Ryoichi upon their return, they found the markers overturned and defaced, trash piled everywhere. To honor both their son and members of the island's former Nikkei community, the family cleaned up the cemetery, and Katsuyori restored the markers as best he could. With efforts such as these, it increasingly became clear the Murakamis were there to stay.

It would be hard to overstate the importance of such insistent visibility. Local bigotry was both virulent and sustained; it also could be systematic. Not long after the Murakamis returned, neighbors told them someone had called a town meeting after hearing that Katsuyori was on his way back. We have no record of who attended, but Mary has summed up the predominant feeling as "'We don't want any Japs back on the island.'"[20] Rumor became the order of the day. Word had spread about how the Murakamis had paid cash for their property, and the news led to rampant speculation about how the family could possibly have accumulated such a sum, one that they had been so bold as to expend in hard currency. Echoing an old stereotype about the supposed untrustworthiness of Asian immigrants, at least one islander even enlisted government help. Mary later recalled,

> Somebody phones the Revenue Canada, you know, "How did the Murakamis get that money?," you know, as if we stole it. And so, one day this guy from the Revenue Canada comes to see my mum and says, . . . "*Concerned people of Salt Spring Island would like to know where you got this money.*" So my mum said, "Go and contact my lawyer in Lethbridge, Alberta. He will tell you how we got that money."[21]

Briant W. Stringham, an attorney who had worked for the Murakamis when they lived in Cardston, once again came through.[22] Chuckling at the memory, Mary notes that the Revenue Canada official never darkened her family's doorstep again.[23] By simply living on the island, as fully and visibly as possible in the face of bigotry, Katsuyori and Kimiko engaged in a decades-long demonstration of their right to exist as Nikkei in Canada (figure 11).

At the heart of that demonstration lay their farm, to which they immediately turned their attention. After clearing their new land and reestablishing their farming operation, the Murakamis slowly began to get a foothold on the island. Times were tough in the early days, but the family could still rely on income from the building that housed the Du-Eet Cafe until the business began to turn a consistent profit. Restaurants in Victoria, delighted at the return of their prized berries, soon began buying up whatever the farm could produce. Finally able to rely on the farm for their living, the Murakamis eventually sold the building in Cardston and bid a

FIGURE 11. The Murakami house on Rainbow Road, Salt Spring Island, 1950s. Photo courtesy of the Salt Spring Island Archives.

final farewell to southern Alberta.[24] In 1959, the family achieved symbolic parity with their pre-war success, once again selling strawberries to the Empress Hotel for a visit by English royalty—this time, Queen Elizabeth and Prince Phillip.[25] Of course, that milestone would not have been possible without the support of those islanders who broke with racist sentiment and patronized the family in its earliest days. More important, though, it would not have been possible without Katsuyori's and, eventually, Kimiko's determination to reestablish their family in the province that had systematically set about dispersing, dispossessing, and impoverishing them—and that still harbored many of the same tendencies that it had nursed over the previous seventy-five years.

Other changes were also under way. Alice had married and moved to the United States; Rose was about to finish high school and was planning to attend university; Richard and Bruce were just a few years away from following her. It was a time for other departures as well. Having been on the island for several years, Victor and Evelyn Okano decided to relocate their family to Victoria. Victor had found work there, for one thing. He also had grown distant from his mother. Always a difficult person to get along with, Riyo had become more challenging and less forgiving with age.[26] Living in the same house as her daughter and her son-in-law mitigated the situation, but Victor still felt he and his family had to move. As for James, he had helped the Murakamis during their first year back on the island, but in 1955 he moved to Vancouver, where he eventually founded a successful car-repair service.[27] Once he had established himself, he hired a go-between who introduced him to his future wife, Mary Nakano, with whom he raised three children—two daughters and a son.[28] Even as Katsuyori, Kimiko, and Violet once again put down roots on Salt Spring Island, the family began to disperse.

For Mary, it was time to head east. During the first year back, her parents had encouraged her to pursue a college education—something her uncles and older sister had been denied due to the deprivations of forced dispersal and inland exile. Rather than apply to schools in British Columbia, Mary made a bold choice. She applied to and was accepted by the University of Toronto, where she would become a student in Trinity College. Mary has identified Trinity's Anglican affiliation as a motivating factor, but the prospect of living in a wholly new city entirely of her own choosing seems to have played a bigger role: "Maybe in the back of my head I was thinking that I wanted to test myself, you know. Can I do it on my own? I mean, I grew up everywhere that I didn't . . . want to be."[29] Having been forced from her childhood home, having been shunted into livestock stalls, and having spent more than a decade moving through a series of camps, toiling on sugar beet farms, and living on the margins of a small-town community in southern Alberta, Mary finally got the chance to blaze her own trail.[30] And so, as her parents, siblings, uncles, and aunts were doing in British Columbia, she made a claim for herself. Having helped her parents re-establish themselves on the island, she said farewell to her family, boarded a train, and set off for Ontario.

Going East

Mary was initially caught off guard by the sheer scale of Metropolitan Toronto.[31] She had passed her high school days in a town that was home to fewer than three thousand people on a busy day, and since the majority of her activities had taken place within a few blocks of the Du-Eet Cafe, she had traveled largely on foot. By contrast, in 1954 the population of greater Toronto had surpassed a million people distributed over a considerably larger area. And as the city had grown, its public transportation system had struggled to keep pace. Even something as basic as getting around would be a challenge.

To ease the transition into big-city life, Mary's parents reached out to friends and acquaintances in the area. Having employed a number of Nikkei immigrants, the Murakamis were able to draw on those connections. Two families with whom they remained in regular contact had been forced eastward by wartime expulsion, joining the exodus of Nikkei who were able to move themselves to either Toronto or Montreal.[32] To be sure, those contacts could only do so much, since Nikkei arriving in Toronto had been under intense pressure not to form a visible community.[33] Nonetheless, the family would have known these people could help Mary get her bearings. It is also not unreasonable to suspect they hoped she might be able to make inroads among other Nikkei there, for, as Keibo Oiwa has argued regarding Montreal, Nikkei forced from British Columbia might have been "invisible from an outsider's point of view, but not necessarily from that of the community members."[34] Kinship, generational, religious, and socioeconomic networks continued to link individuals and groups scattered throughout their new hometowns. Newspapers did so, too, providing another important binding medium for a population that had been scattered far and wide. (To read a paper like *The New Canadian* or even the *Montreal News Bulletin* is often to observe that project set explicitly in motion.[35]) We can therefore see in the Murakamis' efforts a dependency on that fragile low-profile continuity.

The first family Mary stayed with was that of Itoku Murakami, who had emigrated from the area around Hiroshima. As Mary recalls, the man may have been a distant relative, which would help explain the family's ability to ask for his help.[36] According to government documents, Murakami was a fisherman with a share in the River Fish Company who supplemented his income, as many Nikkei did, with small-scale farming. He grew loganberries, strawberries, and peas on two small Steveston lots that the Custodian of Enemy Property eventually sold out from under him.[37] Murakami, his wife, and their seven children initially lived in Clarkson, then a small town southwest of Toronto. Eventually, they moved into the city proper, ultimately landing near the Riverdale neighborhood, which put them about three miles (five kilometers) east of the university. It was there that Mary stayed for her first few months in Ontario.

Following this, Mary's parents arranged for her to stay with Ruth Hirano, who by then went by the married name Tsujimura. After being expelled from University of British Columbia in his fourth year of studying chemical engineering, her husband, Koichi, was also sent to Slocan, which may have been where they met. The young couple had three children, and they lived in a very small house in the southern part of Etobicoke, but Mrs. Tsujimura wanted to lend Mary a hand, given the help her family had received from both the Okanos and the Murakamis. Readers may recall that Kumanosuke and Riyo allowed the Hiranos to build on their property. The memory of that accommodation, of the fact that Mary's father helped build her family's home, and also of mutual support the families likely provided one another in Slocan, seem to have loomed large. "And so, she felt kind of obligated to maybe do something for me."[38]

In the end, though, while she was back on Salt Spring Island helping her parents the following summer, Mary decided to move yet again. She had several reasons. First, she did not want to impose on the Tsujimuras, whose home was already full almost to bursting. Second, the commute from Etobicoke to campus involved an extremely long bus ride.[39] (The neighborhood, which was a township at the time, runs northward from Lake Ontario between Toronto and Mississauga.) Third, waiting for that bus in wintertime meant additional exposure to the elements. And so, at the forefront of Mary's mind was the question of how she might find a place that brought her closer to campus without being prohibitively expensive.

She found a partial answer in a newspaper ad she answered soon after returning to Toronto at the end of the summer. A woman by the name of Thompson, who lived in Old Toronto, was interviewing prospective nannies to care for her two-year-old son. Mary called the woman, who hired her without so much as conducting an in-person interview.[40] In return for the work Mary performed, Mrs. Thompson would provide room and board plus $10 per month.[41] The commute offered little or no improvement on what Mary had navigated in 1954 and 1955. Living in a wealthy neighborhood, the Thompsons were located well north and to the east of the university. The result was a still lengthy ride on public transport:

> Toronto only had one subway, which was north-south, and it didn't stop at very many places because it wasn't that long a subway. And I think it took me over half an hour, between the subway and the bus that I had to take. I had to take the streetcar from the university to the subway, and from the subway I would go up to where I had to get off at the end of the line, and then I would . . . hop on the bus to where I had to get off.[42]

Nonetheless, Mrs. Thompson was kind—no minor concern for a young Nikkei woman in the 1950s—and the prospect of a decent salary in addition to room and board was too appealing to pass up.[43] So, Mary moved once again, this time to a place where she would stay through graduation.

School Days

Trinity College was a very different place in 1954 than it is today, and Mary realized almost immediately that she did not fit in. For one thing, the college's Anglican affiliation was far more pronounced. While no longer primarily a training ground for missionaries and church officials, it nonetheless retained some of the stern ethos of its founder, John Strachan.[44] Unsurprisingly, perhaps, many of the college's students and faculty sought to reaffirm what one early student called the college's "strict domestic—almost monastic—discipline" as the institution entered its second century.[45] Perhaps the most infamous example of this is a society called Episkopon that was founded to identify and punish behaviors deemed unseemly or immoral.[46] A 1952 centennial history of Trinity cheerily summarized the group's activities this way:

> There was a place the sanctity of which no female feet were permitted to invade. [Women first officially attended Trinity in 1888.] This was the Recreation Room, beneath Strachan Hall. . . . It was in the dimness of that

candle-lit room that men hung their heads in shame as the Venerable Father Episkopon poured forth through the medium of his Scribe his awful condemnations and exhortations. The soph-frosh smoker forsook the underground nature of its downtown haunts, and came up in the Recreation Room happier and healthier for its proximity to fresh air.[47]

Episkopon may have been an extreme example of Trinity's religious character, but its motto—*notandi sunt tibi mores* (your behaviors will be noted)—could in many respects sum up the character of the institution during Mary's time there. Hence the imperfect fit; Mary's family still belonged to the church, but they had drifted somewhat over the years, particularly after repeated racist outbursts by the Anglican minister on Salt Spring Island.

Mary found her studies to be a mixed bag, too. Some of her experience likely boiled down to the usual vagaries of undergraduate education. Her course on food chemistry was a hit, while circumstances conspired to make Sociology unremarkable. In some cases, though, racialization played a direct role. Home Economics, for instance, was run by a deeply passive-aggressive instructor: "This professor, this woman, kept deliberately mispronouncing my name. . . . It doesn't matter how many times I corrected her; she would say that. She would say 'mer-ACK-a-me' instead of Murakami." Even Mary's classmates noticed the problem, though they too failed to change the instructor's behavior: "Some of the girls would holler in class, 'It's Mura-KA-mi!' And she would continue to say 'mer-ACK-a-me.'"[48]

Anthropology also raised problems, though in a different way and to varying extents. Both of the classes Mary took in that department discussed interactions between white and Indigenous peoples, but they did so in dramatically different ways. In one course, Mary objected to the professor's discussion of First Nations, feeling that his account expressed the sort of racism and ethnocentrism she had noticed in parts of the Cardston community. By contrast, the anthropology course she took with Edmund Snow Carpenter did more than treat its topic respectfully; it resounded with a sense of cultural vibrancy: "He *related* really well with First Nations and Inuit people." That quality of relating to a group, not just relaying thoughts about them, won Mary over: "It was really interesting; I really enjoyed his class."[49]

The student population presented its own challenges. Above all, Mary noticed that her cohort was not only overwhelmingly white, but also wealthy. As a result, she found no common ground with almost anyone she met at Trinity: "I was brought up not knowing anything about how to socialize with a bigger society, and all of these kids—about 95 percent or more of these students—came from privileged families; they all came from private schools. I had nothing in common with them, you know."[50] It is worth emphasizing, though, that Mary attributes that bad fit not only to economic and racial differences but also to the fallout of her wartime and Cardston years. Having never been exposed to a population such as she now encountered, she had no idea how to navigate her social circumstances.

Still, Mary seems to have received invitations to join the larger University of Toronto community, including other Nikkei students. She went bowling with other Japanese Canadians a few times, and she attended several events set up by the Nisei Students' Club, a group for young Japanese Canadians at the university.[51] Neither of these opportunities fired Mary's imagination enough to warrant the time and money it would take to participate, though. Her parents were stretching themselves to pay for her tuition, and she lived at a considerable distance from campus in an expensive city. Better, she decided, to concentrate on her studies and on her work for the Thompsons. Her life would be spare—so spare, in fact, that it is unrepresentative of Nikkei life in mid-century Toronto—but it would be purposeful and it would be free of the unjust constraints she had endured from 1942 onward.

Mary's life in Toronto was even so spare that it seems to have worried her employer.[52] Laughing to herself, Mary now recalls, "I had a couple of times where my host mother, Mrs. Thompson, *insisted* that I go and do something, and she would, you know, loan me her fur coat and things like that."[53] As a result, Mary also went on a couple of dates with young Nikkei men, one an aspiring doctor from Montreal and the other a student planning to become an engineer.[54] In the end, though, recreation of the sort Mrs. Thompson had in mind was a privilege Mary could ill afford: "My goal was to get a university degree; that was my main goal to be there, and there was no way I was going to disappoint my parents. That was very important because they were sacrificing so much for me."[55] Although she was finally choosing her own path, that path was still sharply limited by the financial hardships forced dispersal and dispossession had visited upon her family as well as by the threat of racist aggression her parents continued to face.

There was, however, one regular pleasure Mary did allow herself: annual travel to the United States, where she would see her sister over the Christmas holiday. The trips began toward the end of the Murakamis' time in Cardston, and during the first trip, Richard came along. The two took a train to Seattle and then transferred from there to Chicago.[56] In subsequent years, though, Mary traveled alone. Alice and her husband were busy, too, so most of Mary's time was spent riding the El and wandering through the city's various neighborhoods.[57] Still, the visits gave her a brief respite from homework and her off-campus job, and the evenings provided her with an opportunity to catch up with Alice, who had always been a vibrant and forceful presence in the Murakami house.[58]

Something else that leavened Mary's life in Toronto was her discovery of another Japanese Canadian student at Trinity College. The two met purely by happenstance, but their paths crossed just as Mary's doubts about her academic home were beginning to crystallize. "Lucky for me, there was another Nikkei student that registered the same year." Both Mary and this other woman, Katherine Miwa (now Suzuki), were required to enroll in a course called Religious Knowledge, which is where they met. They hit it off immediately. They were, after all, two of the handful of non-white students in the college: "Yeah, you know, she was the only one that looked like me."[59] More important, they had a shared history: "She had the same experience, right? She was incarcerated and had all her family's possessions taken away. So, we bonded quite well because we had so much in common."[60]

Out of necessity, the pair socialized mainly on campus. Katherine lived in Toronto proper, which was a lengthy bus ride from the Thompsons' house, and the cost of that round trip would have added up quickly. "For me, $10 [per month, her income as a nanny] was a huge amount of money. You know, when you have nothing, $10 is a lot of money." Consequently, she was scrupulous about every last expenditure: "I used to budget one cup of coffee once a week, and that was ten cents."[61] Such were Mary's financial circumstances that at some point Katherine's younger sister, who was in high school at the time, started buying bus tickets for Mary at the youth rate.[62] Otherwise, Mary would have had to pay the full adult fare. As a result, once in a while, Mary was able to splurge. For instance, she once took the nearly two-hour bus ride up to Hamilton, where she met Katherine's mother and two of Katherine's sisters.[63] Such instances were rare, though. Between the expense of living in Toronto and the need to save up for her summertime trips back to Vancouver, Mary's budget simply could not sustain regular large expenses.

Postwar Nikkei Political Awarenesses

Mary was right to wonder whether she should have enrolled in a division like University College (UC) rather than Trinity. First and foremost, UC boasted a more diverse population. It was home to a majority of members in the West Indian Students' Association (WISA).[64] Free of any sectarian affiliation, University College also had become home to the university's Jewish population. Well before Mary arrived, that population had begun working to shore up its social and cultural presence on campus, for instance through the establishment and expansion of the B'nai B'rith Hillel Foundation. WISA and Hillel are especially noteworthy because their public profiles and stated missions ranged more broadly and were at times more overtly political than the aims of organizations such as the Nisei Students' Club or the Chinese Student Christian Association, which was also active during Mary's time on campus. (As we will see in a moment, Nikkei were politically active in Toronto, most notably in the case of the Japanese Canadian Committee for Democracy, but the Nisei Students' Club seems not to have engaged in such action directly or programmatically.)

Founded in 1954, WISA initially served mainly as a place for its members to maintain their sense of community while living and working far from home. By 1957, though, the organization's outreach efforts were becoming more prominent: "The more general aims of the Association include the desire to foster on the campus an awareness of and interest in the West Indian cultural heritage and way of life."[65] To that end, members had organized public presentations as well as dances, among other things. As part of their efforts, they also made participation in the group broadly available: "Associate membership, which is open to anyone interested in the Association, permits full participation in the Association's activities."[66]

In addition to promoting an understanding of Jewish scripture, the B'nai B'rith Hillel Foundation also saw itself as a means for improving relations with people of other faiths. As it declared in the opening remarks for its 1955 yearbook statement, the group, "promotes inter-religious understanding and is vitally interested in inter-group relations. Cultural and social programs on the broadest possible basis serve this aim."[67] The challenge of "inter-religious understanding" was far from abstract in a city and province that were marked by profound anti-Semitism.[68]

By the mid-1950s, that same recognition of commonality had helped transform a number of labor organizations, which began to pursue muscularly anti-racist legislative and legal action.[69] A historical event involving the town of Dresden provides a prime example. Located on the Sydenham River about four hours southwest of Toronto, the rural hamlet of Dresden is perhaps best known today as the burial place of Josiah Henson (1789–1883). In 1830, Henson had escaped slavery in Maryland and, accompanied by his wife and two children, fled north to what was then Upper Canada.[70] The family had chosen their destination with care. After 1793, Upper Canada's policy barring the importation of new slaves effectively made any Black person arriving in the region free by default. In 1834, Henson founded the Dawn Settlement, a community of freedom seekers who settled just west of what would become Dresden. At its peak, the community boasted roughly five hundred members.

By the mid-1950s, however, Dresden had become infamous as a hotbed of white supremacy—so much so that a 1954 episode of the documentary television series *On the Spot* referred to the situation as simply the "Dresden Story."[71] A number of local restaurants became notorious for refusing to serve non-white customers, despite the fact that Black residents made up roughly 20 percent of the population of the area and despite the fact that federal law prohibited such bias.[72] Starting in 1943, Kay's Cafe, which had become known as an especially stalwart defender of white supremacy, became a central site in the mid-century Canadian fight for equity and social justice. Led by Hugh Burnett, a World War II veteran and business owner, Black citizens in the Dresden area formed the National Unity Association (NUA), which pressed unsuccessfully for local anti-discrimination statues.[73] A turning point came when the NUA joined forces with provincial labor organizations.

The history of labor unions is in no small measure also a history of racism. In Canada, for instance, many unions were governed by explicitly racist policies well into the 1940s. Toward the end of World War II, however, many Jewish labor organizations changed their priorities to address both anti-Semitism and other kinds of bigotry, which they saw as interlinked forms of exploitation. The Canadian Jewish Labour Committee (CJLC) declared in a 1947 report, "Anti-Semitism, anti-Negroism, anti-Catholicism, anti-French or anti-English [beliefs] . . . and union-smashing are all part of a single reactionary crusade of hatred and destruction."[74] Driven by this belief, Sid Blum, the leader of the CJLC in the 1950s, joined forces with the

NAU and the Toronto Association of Civil Liberties to root out Dresden's white supremacism, using Kay's Cafe as their prime example.

Working through the Committee on Group Relations, which Blum and his collaborators had founded, the coalition orchestrated a series of tests beginning in 1949.[75] An aggressive cat-and-mouse game ensued over the next six years. The committee would send Black customers into selected restaurants, followed by white customers. Sometimes servers would simply ignore the Black customers; sometimes the testers would find the restaurant supposedly closed during business hours; on several occasions, the restaurant closed abruptly after the testers arrived. Several University of Toronto students even volunteered to serve as testers.[76]

One of the students was Ruth Lor (later Malloy), a Chinese Canadian graduate from Victoria College (1954) who participated in a test with Hugh Burnett and Bromley Armstrong, a Black financial officer of the CIO-UAW. Lor then wrote about her experience in the *Varsity*, the University of Toronto's student paper.[77] Her essay was not the highest-profile account of Dresden's white supremacists—*MacLean's*, the *Toronto Star*, and the *Toronto Telegram* reached wider audiences—but it helped demonstrate that injustice elsewhere in Ontario was very much the business of students at the University of Toronto. Finally, after years of evading Canada's 1954 Fair Accommodation Practices Act (which the CJLC and its allies had helped advance), in the fall of 1956 the owner of Kay's yielded, demonstrating the potential legal and social cost of bigotry to the larger Dresden community.[78]

Action by Jewish workers and business owners was not restricted to legislative and legal efforts. Having experienced the corrosiveness of Canadian anti-Semitism at length, the Jewish population in Toronto also provided an early and crucial welcome for Nikkei forced eastward by British Columbia's racism. Many of the jobs Nikkei initially found upon moving to Ontario were with Jewish employers, who moved quickly to help their newly dispossessed neighbors. Herbert Tanaka, a Nisei, wrote to his wife in 1945, "The Jews are kicked around a lot in Eastern Canada and realize our situation more than you can imagine. Most of the Japanese here work for a Jewish firm, for they are the only ones fair-minded to employ us."[79]

Nikkei, for their part, recognized this commonality. As the longtime activist Roger Obata has written, Nikkei who moved to Toronto after 1942 quickly came to recognize parallels between the bigotry they experienced and the mistreatment of their neighbors:

In the early 1940s, Toronto was still known as a Waspish town with very few visible minorities. Racial bigotry was right out in the open, especially against Jews. It was not uncommon to see prominent signs reading "Gentiles Only" and "No Jews Allowed" at some of the summer resorts like Jackson's Point on Lake Simcoe or at some of the posh golf and country clubs in and around Toronto. This flagrant anti-Semitism was something that the Japanese Canadians could easily relate to, not just from recent memories of the expulsion and internment, but going back much earlier to days in Vancouver when some movie theatres and swimming pools excluded Asians.[80]

As was the case with anti-Semitism, there were exceptions to anti-Japanese action in Ontario. There was, for example, the Reverend James Finlay of the Carlton Street United Church in Toronto. First, he took in the family of Muriel Kitagawa and her husband, housing them for the better part of a year while they found stable financial footing and a place to live. After that, he established a social center for the large number of Nisei who had landed in Ontario following expulsion from the west coast. Some of the wealthier members of his community objected, but Finlay put the matter to a vote by the whole congregation, who decisively countered the naysayers.[81]

Such efforts by members of the Jewish community and of the United Church were important. Ontario had initially maintained a policy of barring any Nikkei moving from British Columbia. In addition, as Forrest La Violette observed in 1948, it was "difficult to rent houses due to wartime congestion and informal discrimination, and the only way to secure adequate living accommodation in wartime-crowded cities was by purchasing a home—which was virtually prohibited by the government."[82] Furthermore, local councils repeatedly stymied efforts by Nikkei to set up their own businesses.[83] At every turn, institutionalized white supremacy made life in the province difficult. In fact, although informal after the revocation of provincial laws that forbade Nikkei from British Columbia to settle in Ontario, exclusionary action was so widespread and virulent that by 1948, it had become known in some quarters as the "Toronto problem."[84]

Nonetheless, by the early 1950s, Toronto was becoming known informally as New Niseiville, in a nod to the fact that members of the second generation were some of the first to move there and had subsequently set about recruiting family members and friends to join them.[85] Those "pioneers" were far more successful than anyone initially would have predicted.

Ontario had been home to no more than about three hundred people of Japanese ancestry before the war. By the time of Mary's arrival, however, Toronto alone boasted a Nikkei population of some seven thousand people, the largest such concentration in Canada.[86]

Furthermore, that population had become increasingly activist, not least because key Nisei had rekindled their political efforts as life began approaching normalcy in the later 1940s. For many of these people, the memory of growing pre-war agency remained strong. In 1936, for instance, the Japanese Canadian Citizens' League (JCCL) had formed under the leadership of a Nisei named Harry Naganobu. Their decision to pursue the franchise for all Nikkei, not just veterans, was driven primarily by the younger generation's intense awareness of the double standard they endured as citizens. That sense of being Canadian, and yet somehow not fully so, led to an alliance with the Co-operative Commonwealth Federation (CCF), which helped arrange for a Nikkei delegation to present their case before the Special Committee on Elections and Franchise Acts. Although—perhaps more accurately in part because—they had the support of the CCF, the JCCL's effort came to naught.[87] Nonetheless, it had demonstrated the potential for collective Nikkei action. Now that Canadians more broadly had begun to engage with the topic of universal human rights, the time seemed ripe for renewed engagement.

A number of leading figures in the JCCL were involved in the founding of the Toronto-based Japanese Canadian Committee for Democracy (JCCD), which began as a Nisei-driven group formed to protect the Nikkei community from further depredation as well as to fight for political and economic equity.[88] Continuing its members' earlier efforts at securing the franchise, the group waged an important battle against 1944 legislation that denied the vote to "any person whose racial origin is that of a country at war with Canada."[89] The JCCD worked with the Cooperative Committee for Japanese Canadians, which proved an important ally in the fight against deportation, the fight to ease restrictions on Nikkei property ownership, and in the establishment of the Bird Commission. It is worth noting that, despite the group's assimilationist aims and its support for a policy of distributing Nikkei as widely and inconspicuously as possible, the Cooperative Committee also spearheaded the publicity campaign that helped turn popular opinion not only against deportation but also against British Columbian efforts to continue excluding Nikkei from the province.

Unfortunately for Mary, the Nikkei social structure she encountered during her time in Toronto was indelibly marked by wartime injustice in ways that, combined with her own postwar challenges, made it difficult for her to become part of that community. In addition to economic, legal, and cultural obstacles stemming from dispossession, most people of Japanese ancestry in Toronto in the later 1940s and 1950s also faced conflicting pressures within their own community. Many of the most politically engaged Nisei were older than Mary. And those with whom she was closest in age came from extremely diverse economic, religious, social, and cultural backgrounds. Some had grown up in tight-knit Nikkei communities with strong religious and historical ties, while others had grown up virtually cut off from others of Japanese ancestry. Experiences and thus cultural and political traits could vary wildly. A girl who was the oldest child of an impoverished family coming of age in Steveston during the 1930s would have lived a very different life from the son of an established agricultural family entering his senior year of high school in the fall of 1941.[90] Some Nisei might have spent their young lives exclusively in the company of white neighbors and classmates, while others might still recall the shock of their first day in an English-language elementary school dominated by white children.

Such variability meant that New Niseiville was simultaneously far-flung, wildly diverse, and strangely close-knit. It was far-flung not only because of expense and infrastructure, but also because of the way wartime conditions continued to reverberate. The federal government's policy of dispersal loomed large, especially when backed by the memory of the loyalty survey and its threat of deportation. Adding to this was the widespread belief, held not only by racists but also by many Nikkei, including JCCD members, and their non-Nikkei defenders in groups such as the CCJC, that living in anything like a visible community would render them too easy a target. For instance, in 1943, when presented with the chance to form a group that might lobby on their behalf, Nisei in Montreal voted the idea down. An article in *The New Canadian* observed: "The majority of the young people gave their opinion that the formation of a Nisei group would attract undue and unfavorable attention, give rise to misunderstanding and actually hinder the process of assimilation."[91] They might be proud of the Standing Committee Nikkei had formed to protect their community from racists and economic opportunists, but they were disinclined to expose that community to what seemed like excessive risk. Rather than court a repetition of what they had suffered during and after the war, Nikkei who moved eastward after their expulsion from British Columbia therefore struggled to navigate the expectation that they ought to keep as low a public profile as they could and that they be seen mixing as harmoniously as possible with their white neighbors, even as they worked for greater economic and political equity. And yet, the fact that this question reached the point where it merited a formal vote shows that an important part of the community was beginning to work toward greater and, perhaps more important, unapologetic agency.[92]

As fractured and fractious as it was, though, the Toronto Nikkei community in the 1950s possessed an important sense of itself. It was, after all, largely the result of wartime expulsion and dispossession, the memory of which loomed large enough that Mary recalls it being an undercurrent in the Nisei Students' Club: "I did interact with other Japanese Canadian students, and we did talk about it then. There was a group [the Nisei Students' Club] . . . but we didn't really go into the details that we do right now, like today."[93] Indeed, the fact that Nisei established a club for themselves at the University of Toronto tells us something vitally important. Following on the success of that social center James Finlay had established during the war, the existence of the Nisei Students Club demonstrates that Nikkei students, no less than the West Indian, Jewish, and Chinese Christian populations, recognized and met the need to connect with one another. The fact that members of that group and of the Nikkei bowling group sought to recruit both Mary and Katherine tells us that they also recognized the value of actively engaging with others who might otherwise not act on that need.

For Mary, though, the challenges were more than financial. For one thing, after a decade spent moving from place to place, never settling for more than a year or two, she had difficulty forming close relationships with other people her age. That difficulty came through in the way Mary closed herself off from other children during the early years of inland exile. (Recall, for instance, her decision in Slocan and Extension never to form close emotional bonds with people her own age.) While that strategy might have saved her the pain of repeated farewells, it now compounded the economic and logistical obstacles to having a social life, to forming relationships with other Nikkei, and thus to focusing that sense of right and wrong that Mary had begun to develop in Cardston.

To some extent, one might link her experience to that of pre-war Nisei who had grown up without a sizable Nikkei cohort. As Midge Ayukawa has noted, life among other people of Japanese ancestry could be surprisingly challenging for members of the second generation who grew up in predominantly white communities.[94] But the way Mary describes her initial landing at Trinity suggests an additional layer to the problem. Recall her declaration that "I was brought up not knowing anything about how to socialize with a bigger society." That statement does not refer to an unhealthy family dynamic; on the contrary, Mary has repeatedly spoken of how warm and socially rich her domestic circumstances were. Her parents were supportive of their children, all of whom—boys as well as girls—they had hoped might graduate from university. Dinners were marked by vigorous, wide-ranging conversation, and everyone was expected to participate.[95] Rather, Mary seems to be describing a remnant of her years of internal exile, a reluctance to form bonds that stemmed from her conviction that the only emotional bonds that forced displacement could not disrupt were those of her immediate family. As a result, looking back on Mary's time in Toronto, it is difficult not to think of that period as an extension of paradoxically claustrophobic isolation that Forrest La Violette first identified as a characteristic of wartime Nikkei existence in the interior ghost towns and government camps.[96] Mary's life in Toronto marked the beginnings of her own resistance to forced dispersal and dispossession, but it also prolonged her relative isolation from other Nikkei.

Most important, Mary's immediate family had returned to a place that, despite their history there, continued to bear an unmistakable hostility toward them. As for Mary herself, the move to Toronto was something she undertook only partly to test herself. It also was meant to provide skills she could then use to help her family back in British Columbia. She had moved east specifically to move westward later. It is particularly remarkable, therefore, that she formed a firm and long-standing friendship with Katherine Miwa, for that friendship was destined to weather yet another departure (figure 12). Nonetheless, that friendship awakened something in Mary, something that would blossom only gradually in the decades still to come.

Its contours were perhaps visible at the time, though. While they had a shared history, Mary and Katherine talked about wartime life only intermittently during their time at university and rarely in detail. Mary has chalked this up to necessity: "Right now I would bring it forth right away, but at that time, I think I was just trying to survive." Still, the sense of a shared past and present helped Mary forge her first solid friendship since

FIGURE 12. Mary Murakami graduating from the University of Toronto, 1958. Photo courtesy of Mary and Tosh Kitagawa.

the family had been forced from Salt Spring Island. Although she cannot recall when the two of them first discussed their wartime experiences, those experiences were a critical part of their bond: "We knew that we had something in common."[97]

FIVE

Transformational Relationships

Given the accolades and press coverage she has received in recent years, Mary might strike readers as someone whose activism must always have looked as it does now. In truth, though, her many achievements chronicle an important transformation from intuitive, atomized resistance to increasingly programmatic and shared political engagement. The first outwardly recognizable sign of that transformation came with her participation in the redress movement, initially as an early-1980s recruit to the cause and then as one of many Nikkei who worked tirelessly at ground level liaising with non-Nikkei. That transformation accelerated with her work as a member of the Vancouver Human Rights Committee of the Japanese Canadian Citizens Association and as a fundraiser for the Powell Street Festival in the later 1980s through the early 2000s. It became even more fully legible in her successful efforts to prevent the naming of a government building after a virulent white supremacist and to secure diplomas for Nikkei wrongly expelled from the University of British Columbia. Last but definitely not least, it took on a strongly interpersonal component when, in concert with her husband, Tosh, Mary became a surrogate parent for many of the students in the Asian Canadian and Asian Migration Studies program at University of British Columbia.[1]

It can be difficult to reconcile such vigorous and deeply social activism with the largely solitary woman of those wartime, Cardston, and Toronto years. In that earlier period, shaped by the repeated assaults of wartime injustice and deprived of so many opportunities, Mary sought to keep her life emotionally, financially, and socially spare so that she might always be prepared for the next move, the next catastrophe. She had decided in her formative years to live almost exclusively within the orbit of her family. How, then, did she wind up so thoroughly enmeshed with other people, so firmly entangled in so many communities, and such a vocally committed anti-racist?

To answer this question, it helps to know something about how the history of Nikkei in Canada shaped her husband, Tosh (Toshiaki). Tosh's father, Yosokichi, emigrated from Shiga Prefecture in 1907 at the age of fourteen, having been brought over by his father, Takejiro. Takejiro had finally established a toehold in British Columbia after well over a decade of hard toil in the timber industry.² In 1918, he bought a five-acre plot in Mission City, some nine miles (fifteen kilometers) east of Vancouver, and began the berry-farming operation that would become his family's primary source of income.³ After Takejiro's death in 1921, Yosokichi took over the farm, which he expanded in 1930 with the purchase of an additional five acres.⁴ It was on this farm that Tosh and his five siblings were born.⁵ Tosh was four when, in 1936, his mother, Sada, died during the birth of her sixth child, Yukio. A young caretaker named Nobuko Yamaura moved in with the family and, a few years later, married Yosokichi.

Aside from the death of his biological mother, Tosh recalls the family's pre-war years as a protracted idyll. These were not easy times, but they were largely happy ones spent in a close-knit Nikkei agricultural community that expulsion and dispossession destroyed.⁶ Criminalized, shipped to Diamond City, Alberta, to work on sugar beet farms, and systematically impoverished by the Canadian government, Tosh's father, stepmother, and the majority of their children never resettled in British Columbia. The family did, however, eventually reestablish economic independence and, over time, managed to build up modest savings. Having achieved this milestone, in 1948 Yosokichi moved everyone to Lethbridge. He did this prior to Ottawa officially easing restrictions on the movement of Nikkei. Tosh observed, "Many people started migrating away [from where they had lived during inland exile] in '48. . . . That's how we left the farm: no one stopped us." In Lethbridge, Yosokichi bought a piece of land and, with the help of his three eldest sons, built a house.⁷ Once the house was finished, Yosokichi and Nobuko settled in permanently, raising not only Tosh's original siblings but also a new clutch of half-siblings. Of the Kitagawa children, most remained in southern Alberta, though some did eventually return to British Columbia.[8] The story of the Kitagawa family is important, and this thumbnail does not do it justice. It will have to suffice, though, because if we want to get a sense for how the history of Nikkei in Canada shaped Tosh, we should focus on his decision to move from Lethbridge back to British Columbia in the early 1950s.

A Nisei in Vancouver

We still know relatively little about the return of Nikkei to the Vancouver area after the last restrictions expired in April 1949. Nonetheless, a few common denominators mark the stories that have been recorded to date: discriminatory hiring practices, apartments that were available to rent only if the person calling "sounded white," and occasionally the support of a few non-Nikkei individuals and political organizations.[9] But common denominators do not mean uniformity of experience. Someone returning in April 1949 to a tragically diminished Powell Street navigated very different conditions from those the Murakamis faced on Salt Spring Island in 1954.[10] In both cases, the hazards included economic and social exclusion, intimidation, vandalism, and even violence. And yet, each place in each moment differed, as did the individual circumstances of the people asserting their right to exist in British Columbia. The most common denominator was that, if you decided to return to British Columbia in the later 1940s or 1950s, you needed to be determined and resourceful.

Tosh is a case in point, having learned early how to make his own way. After being expelled from British Columbia and put to work on sugar beet farms, his family had their farm sold out from under them by the Canadian government to pay for their expulsion. As a result, Tosh's father and stepmother could not afford to send him to university. Instead, from his early teens onward, he had had to earn a wage. He took on his first paid work around the age of eleven, and even in those early days his mix of wit and resolve proved critical. The family had landed on a farm run by a couple named Ken and Mary Russell, for whom young Tosh quickly became an important hand:

> The farmer whose land we were supposed to look after, he kind of liked me, too, and he allowed me to drive the tractors and things, and then he

actually hired me. . . . He would say, "Go over there and till this piece of property . . . ," and I would get on the tractor and do it after school and on the weekends. And I did this, oh, all the way up until I was about sixteen. He just entrusted me, and I was like a hired hand, a twelve-year-old hired hand.[11]

Tosh earned more than the Russells' trust; he also earned a degree of their affection: "I think he thought I was very clever, and so, he took a shine to me. And he didn't have any children yet, and I was kind of new to him because he was only a newlywed himself. . . . I remember that when he finally did get a family, a boy and a girl, I used to babysit them also. So, I was like a son to him in many ways. . . . We got along great, and he treated me like an adult."[12] The resulting bond was strong and amicable enough that, in 1962, when Mary was pregnant with their son Landon, the Kitagawas visited the Russells on their farm.[13]

Do not let the warmth of that relationship fool you, though. Like the Murakamis, the Kitagawas had struggled to survive in Alberta. And as it had from Mary, it also exacted a toll from Tosh: "I didn't really play with kids that much because as soon as school was over, I was out working, and that was in between working in the beet fields. . . . [The Russells] would feed me. After school, I would eat there, and then I would walk home in the dark, more or less."[14] Tosh was quick-witted and charming, but his character was shaped by necessity and governed by an iron will. Anything less would have jeopardized his and the family's survival.

The 1948 move to Lethbridge put an end to farm work, allowing Tosh a measure of normality during his high school years—though only a measure, since he commuted to Diamond City in order to stay with his classmates.[15] Tosh was active in sports, and he now claims to have "goofed around more than anything" during that time.[16] This claim is at odds with virtually every aspect of life Tosh has described regarding his Diamond City and Lethbridge years, though. The Kitagawa boys had to help their father build the family's home, and, because that home cost a lot relative to their modest income, they also still had to earn wages.[17] And so, after graduation, Tosh got a job in the sales division of International Harvester. Later on, he spent time selling cookware door to door.[18] The work was constant and the labor was hard, but those lean years provided an important foundation that was more than just economic. It also was emotional, sparking in him the desire for a life different from the one that forced dispersal had imposed on him. And so, in the early 1950s, having helped his family get back on stable financial ground, Tosh came back to Vancouver equipped with little more than a knack for working with complex machinery, a quick wit, and the clothes on his back.[19]

But if you ask Tosh why he left Lethbridge, he will probably tell you something like this: "I got restless being in a small town. And so, I think I was maybe around twenty when I decided to come back to the coast. So, I just got on the bus and came out to the coast and started to look around, found a job."[20] The simplicity of Tosh's statement belies the complexity of the circumstance. In 1952, Vancouver was home to just over two thousand Nikkei—less than 10 percent of the population had been before expulsion[21]—all of whom had struggled to find housing and work. It was a situation *The New Canadian* had predicted as early as 1947:

> When viewed in cold reason, the advantages in returning to the coast are imagined rather than real, sentimental rather than concrete. The coast offers the advantage of a milder climate and certain familiar fields of employment as in gardening, fishing, berry-farming, etc. But the coast also retains its deep-rooted discrimination in the broad field of economic activity, which older Niseis and Isseis will remember. B.C. also has its wage differentials in the forest industries (although the wartime manpower shortage has prevented its operation in the interior), its fishing licence limitations for Japanese. Socially, too, returning to the coast will not be like "going home."[22]

Nikkei were all too aware of the risks postwar life in British Columbia would entail. Plus, the vast majority of them were unable to afford a move—a situation that many recognized was not only widespread but also part of the government's plan all along.[23] Consequently, when the ban finally did expire, the rate of return was so slow that *The New Canadian* published a wry article by a "special correspondent" recounting the rude awakening of a white real estate agent. Having taken a stack of listings to greet the anticipated flood of returnees at the train station, the agent encountered a single Nikkei couple. The article ends with the agent realizing his mistake as he notes that the ban's expiry fell on April Fool's Day.[24]

Despite the occasional joke about self-defeating racism or lighthearted statement about being "restless," a return to the coast was not something you undertook lightly. Even *The New Canadian*, which had speculated that most returnees would be "those who feel their destiny tied to their old home towns [sic]," recognized that the act of moving back to British Columbia was more than just a sentimental decision. It was also a form of resistance, pushing back against what the paper described in 1945 as a "shameful curtailment of civil liberties."[25] For any Nikkei who returned to British Columbia in the late 1940s through the late 1950s, pulling up stakes and heading back to the province that had actively persecuted them, their relatives, and their community was a complex and multifaceted move. Rather than foreground the cultural, political, or even emotional aspects of his experience though, Tosh presents this moment of intuitive resistance as little more than an economically risky whim.

Tosh was a young, resourceful, and unusually independent man, and as a result he was willing to take greater risks than many. That willingness helps us understand why he chose his destination first and then sorted how he would survive second. And sort it he did. Although Tosh dismisses his early housing in Vancouver as what he now calls the "Bum of the Month Club," he had in fact laid the groundwork for his move ahead of time.[26] He arranged to stay at the home of a married couple with whom he had sold cookware in Lethbridge.[27] And upon arrival, he immediately started looking for jobs that played to his skills. Eventually, he found work in a tire shop, rented an apartment, and began settling into the city.

After working his way up to a managerial position at the tire shop, he got a job on a road-construction crew and then, later, in a home-furnishing store. Slowly, steadily, he built a life for himself. He also made a number of friends. One in particular stands out:

> I met a guy in construction. He was going to university, and he came to work . . . a summer job while he was going to university. And he was green as grass, so I kind of showed him the ropes of construction because the construction guys treat new people like dirt. And so, I kind of looked after and mentored him.[28]

There is a lot in this statement. All of Tosh's co-workers at the time were white, and so were all his local friends. Given that he had at one point been the "new kid" on that crew and given that this was British Columbia in the 1950s, we should recognize that he found himself in precisely the same sort of position he had encountered repeatedly during his time in Alberta: moving by necessity into a white-dominated space that he would have to navigate carefully. Honed by experience, his wits undoubtedly served him well, but there were other skills he also had developed. In this case, one that stands out is his empathy for the underdog, whom he describes with characteristic humor, but whom he also treated with respect. It should come as no surprise, then, that Tosh and his new co-worker struck up a friendship that persisted after the young man went back to school.[29]

Nikkei readers might recognize Tosh's communication style. He may crack more jokes than some men of his age and background, but his elisions, his shorthand references, and, above all, his reluctance to disclose emotional content are noteworthy features of communication among people of Japanese ancestry who lived through wartime expulsion and dispossession. And yet, his observations about the history of British Columbia racism are unequivocal. Recounting the measures implemented against Nikkei in the 1930s, for instance, he has rightly observed that the bombing of Pearl Harbor was not a cause of anti-Japanese activity but instead "a very convenient mechanism to get rid of the Japanese Canadians."[30] Similarly, he can cite crucial details of inland exile: how many Nikkei were in Alberta and how many in Manitoba; the primary towns where they landed; details of the government's efforts to populate labor camps; the demands of beet farming and, by implication, the full value of the labor Nikkei were forced to provide; and the pitiful compensation they actually received versus the cost of living at that time.[31]

Taking command of his past and presenting it on his terms, Tosh approaches history itself not simply as a cluster of facts to be regurgitated but as an *instrument* with which to move his listener. And with that instrument, omission is at least as important as inclusion. The gaps and silences, the evasions and self-deprecating remarks all implicitly acknowledge, as Mona Oikawa has demonstrated, unrecoverable moments, indelible yet incommunicable memories, singular experiences that cannot be conveyed but, in their insistent presence, challenge the attentive listener to act.[32] Unless we understand this, we have little chance of understanding how Mary's own elisions, silences, and refusals to disclose are inseparable from her vigorous, tireless, and deeply social activism. For it is at least partly in that sense of lived historical injustice, implicit in one moment and explicit in the next, that Mary and Tosh seem to have found each other.

Mary's Return to British Columbia

After she graduated from the University of Toronto in 1959, Mary returned to Vancouver so that she could be near her parents and help them whenever the need might arise. While their situation had improved somewhat since the mid-1950s, Katsuyori and Kimiko continued to endure informal assaults ranging from petty vandalism to the theft of crops.[33] Plus, money was still tight. Richard had begun his undergraduate work at the University of British Columbia (UBC); Rose had only recently completed her training to become a nurse; and Mary had enrolled in a one-year teaching-certification program. Consequently, everyone had to economize as best they could. With that in mind, Mary and Rose looked for a place they and their brother could share. Just as *The New Canadian* had predicted, even in the later 1950s this was a difficult task. Mary recalls that

> it took us a long, long time to find a place. . . . We would have masses of marking on a newspaper, you know, the ads, and we'd go to every one of them. And Rose and I would knock on these doors, . . . [and people would say,] "Oh, we just rented it out." And so, one time, Rose and I went across the street and phoned that same number, and the lady said, "Oh, yes! Come on over!" And so, we said, "Well, we were just there," and she hung up on us.[34]

Eventually, their luck turned. They found a landlord willing to rent to the three of them and moved into an apartment near the university. Their room was on the third floor of a grand old house that had been subdivided, with students crammed into every available space, including rooms that were not suited for the task. Mary recalls, for instance, an impoverished student who lived in an adjacent space that did not even have so much as a hotplate. After hearing that he subsisted on two raw eggs and a handful of ready-to-eat items every day, she and her siblings started passing along their leftovers to him.[35]

In 1960, after receiving her teaching certificate from UBC, Mary got a job at Kitsilano Secondary School.[36] It was not her first choice. "I wanted to go back to Salt Spring to teach at the school, you know, so I could help my mum and dad the same way that Rose wanted to help them. But then, when I went to the school board, the fellow said, 'No Jap is going to teach any of our kids.'"[37] Nonetheless, she needed to help pay for her sister's and her brother's tuition, so there was little choice.³⁸ Fortunately, over time, she and her colleagues at the school became friendly. One of them even told her about a young man he was convinced she should meet. He had gotten to know this guy when he spent a summer working on a road crew, and he insisted that the two were an absolutely perfect match. Chuckling at the memory, Mary recalls resisting what seemed like an eternity of her colleague's badgering. Becoming serious, she adds: "I didn't want to get connected to anybody at that time because I was helping my sister and brother through university."³⁹

This brings us to why an understanding of Tosh's history can help us better grasp the impact of Mary's. As had been the case during Mary's time in Cardston and at the University of Toronto, the sole constant in her life in Vancouver, the sole stable entity she had known for nearly two decades, was her immediate family. And while her parents might have managed to rebuild a customer base and achieve a measure of economic stability, the specter of anti-Japanese sentiment was never out of mind. Mary had experienced it herself both in the early threats and insults directed at the Murakamis upon their return to Salt Spring as well as in her interaction with the island's school board.

Rose, too, found that anti-Asian exclusion remained the order of the day among key authorities. As Mary tells it, "She wanted to come back to the island to be near my mum and dad and work at the hospital that was on the island. But . . . when she went to apply for a job there [in 1962], they told her that she wasn't qualified. And yet, she was a top student that graduated from Vancouver General."⁴⁰ Recognizing the futility of the situation, Rose returned to Vancouver and took a job at the hospital where she had trained.⁴¹ Far more than a ghost from the sisters' formative years, racism remained an active presence in their lives. Ever attentive to that presence, both Mary and Rose felt obligated to continually prepare for the worst, just as their parents had been forced to do repeatedly after the bombing of Pearl Harbor.

In light of this need for preparedness, dating some friend of a friend was, Mary felt, at best, a luxury she could ill afford; at worst, it could divert her from the task of survival. For his part, Tosh was in no hurry either: "This friend of mine that I worked with . . . kept telling Mary that she should date me. And he would say the same thing to me. . . . So this went on, and Mary said no, she doesn't go on blind dates, and I said no, I don't go on blind dates. But he was very persistent, and finally both of us, to get him off our backs, we agreed to go on a blind date." Persistence turned out to be critical for all involved, because that first date did not go well. Tosh took Mary to a Stan Kenton concert, where the music was so loud it drowned out any attempt at conversation.[42] Tosh continues: "Anyway, I think I asked her for another date, and I think she turned me down. But I persisted."

MARY: Yeah, I remember that. Because when I first met him, I thought he was kind of a showoff, a bit arrogant, so I didn't want anything to do with him.

How did Tosh prevail?

MARY: Well, you know, he's a salesman.

TOSH: I sweet-talked her!

What was the date?

MARY [*chuckling*]: I don't remember . . . because I think it was just this constant, constant, you know, asking, asking, and then, I guess like the first time, where I said yes, I'll go out with him on a blind date, same thing. It got to the place where, "*OK!*"

As both of them laugh, Tosh once again deflects attention from his hard-won skills by pretending to be tragically self-absorbed: "That's not true, Mary. She said, '*Whoa!* Jesus, what a hunk!'"[43] Still, there is no disguising the role those skills played. In the same way that he talked his way into the Russells' household in Alberta, a job at an International Harvester dealership in Lethbridge, a strong sales record for WearEver, and a leadership position on that road crew, he talked his way into a relationship that has proven transformative for both him and Mary.

Wartime expulsion and dispossession had shattered Mary's social world, small though that had been on Salt Spring Island, and driven her into a kind of self-imposed isolation:

> It's painful to say goodbye to friends, and then I don't know if I'm ever going to see them again, you know, because we were moved ten times. And so, psychologically, I decided, "I'm not going to make friends that would be my lifetime pals." . . . I [knew] a lot of people, but I never got attached to them.[44]

This is a critical part of what Mary has in mind when she says of her university years that she had little understanding "about how to socialize with a bigger society." She had spent her teenage years in rural and small-town circumstances, and even in these contexts, she lived a relatively isolated life. No less important, though, she maintained that relative isolation, having learned that even Nikkei in similar straits—whether in the beet fields, in Slocan and Extension, or just passing through Cardston—were always on the move. Only her family remained stable, so it was only to her family that she would dedicate herself. "Sweet-talking" his way into this particular life was a Herculean task that required that Tosh deploy the skills and the iron will that wartime expulsion had sharpened in him. But it also awakened in Mary an appreciation of traits she had long considered extraneous. What seemed like arrogance or showing off in the context of basic survival turned out to be the prelude to extraordinary warmth, generosity, and eventual political transformation.

Tosh has always been sharp-witted, and at least some of his siblings seem to have shared that trait. His earliest memories of life in Mission City are peppered with mischief. On one occasion,

> my older brother stole a can of tobacco from my dad. . . . And he had the papers, and he was able to roll cigarettes. And I remember . . . that our garage was built on an incline, so the back portion of the garage was supported by posts, and so there was, like, a hollow underneath the garage. And we used to go there and have a smoke after school and then climb the cherry tree to eat the cherries to disguise our breath.[45]

But his astuteness and the charm it animates also proved crucial for the family's and Tosh's own survival. Those qualities enabled Tosh to find all-important paid work during his formative years; they helped him get by as one of barely a handful of Nikkei in his schools; they opened up new work opportunities in Lethbridge; they gave him the confidence and the means to move back to British Columbia when Nikkei life in the province was tenuous at best; and, eventually, they enabled him to work his way into Mary's heart.

In this last case, though, there had to be a shared foundation on which Tosh's wit and charm could build. That foundation seems to have been the experience of forced dispersal, inland exile, dispossession, and the subsequent hard scrap necessary to regain financial stability. Although neither Mary nor Tosh has identified wartime injustice explicitly as a major factor in their early relationship, it is inconceivable that their shared experiences did not contribute to the bond that formed between them. After all, it had been an important, if understated, factor in the formation of Mary's friendship with Katherine Miwa in Toronto. At a time when substantial numbers of Nikkei were intermarrying with their non-Nikkei neighbors, co-workers, and classmates, these two gravitated toward one another. They were bucking a trend so marked that it became a point of debate in both *The New Canadian* and, in the United States, the *Pacific Citizen*. The matter was far from an abstraction, especially in Tosh's case. Says Mary, "When we got engaged, Tosh phoned his dad. And the first thing he said was 'Is she Japanese?' . . . He didn't want his children to marry outside of the Nikkei community."[46]

Charm and persistence were undoubtedly also factors, but they would have gotten someone only so far. Then, as now, persistent men were a dime a dozen. A few of them might even have rivaled Tosh's dashing looks and quick wit. But none in Mary's orbit shared the history of wartime expulsion, displacement, dispossession, impoverishment, and ethnic cleansing. And none had braved the continued racism of British Columbia the way he had, the way she had, or the way her family had. As was the case with Katherine Miwa, implicit shared understanding—laconically mentioning certain events or places or critical experiences while also being keenly aware of them, even braced for their repetition—circumvented the guard Mary had put up against virtually anyone outside her immediate family. That shared understanding allowed the two of them to engage in an extraordinarily eloquent form of communication, freighted with all manner of emotional, social, economic, and political resonances.

Expanding Family

Within a few months, Mary and Tosh were a couple. Tosh had quit the road crew and was working at a furniture store. The new job kept him busy, but he somehow still became a regular around dinnertime at the apartment where Mary, Rose, and Richard lived. He recalls, "Instead of dinner for three, she was always cooking dinner for four." (Mary disagrees: "For six! For six!"[47]) Eventually, things became serious enough that Mary took Tosh to Salt Spring Island to meet her family. The dynamic was unlike anything Tosh had encountered in his childhood home. Coming just a few years after the death of his mother, expulsion from British Columbia completely disrupted domestic life for the Kitagawas: "There was very little communication; unlike Mary's side of the family, our side of the family are not very close. In other words, there was very little conversation because, I think, essentially my dad and mum had to work so hard—you know, from dawn till dusk—and just trying to put food on the table and clothe us was just a full-time job. So, there was very little dialogue, as I recall, growing up."[48] It is not that the Kitagawas were unaware of their mistreatment. Rather, there was no social mechanism in place for them to address it as a family. In fact, when asked what his father thought about topics like wartime injustice or interracial marriage among Nikkei, Tosh observed that "Mary talked to my dad more than I did because she would talk about things like that with him."[49]

The difference in family life proved as transformative for Tosh as Tosh's attachment to Mary did for her. Dinner in the Murakami household was characterized by wide-ranging conversation in which everyone was expected to participate. Joining in the conversations, Tosh found a sense of belonging he had not felt in decades, perhaps ever. The result, according to Mary, was striking.

> When Tosh married into our family—rather than me marrying into *his* family—he, you know, he adored my father, and he tried to be like him. And so, he is more like my dad, now, after we got married, to the point where his friends thought *my* parents were *his* parents. Because he would say, "my mum," "my dad," and so one day I had to straighten him out because they said to me, "Where do your parents live?" They said, "Oh, I know where *Tosh's* parents live. They live on Salt Spring Island." So, I said, "Excuse me. They're *my* parents."

Chuckling, she adds, "He adopted my parents."[50]

This anecdote is as instructive as it is sweet, showing us the beginnings of a pattern that became more pronounced in the later trajectory of Mary's and Tosh's lives. Having honed their survival skills under the burden of racism and state-sponsored violence, each of them created new opportunities neither of them could have imagined. But those opportunities could arise only under very specific conditions that were as much emotional and social as they were legislative, geographical, economic, or political; they could arise only through the right relationships. Forming a friendship with Katherine Miwa awakened Mary to the potential for stable and rewarding bonds outside her family. That awakening enabled Mary to see the potential of a bond with Tosh—potential that was economic, yes, but also emotional and social. And Mary, along with her siblings and her parents, awakened in Tosh a sense of the foundation that high-level, intimate communication could provide.

After Mary and Tosh got married on August 5, 1961 (figure 13), they lived briefly in an apartment on 14th and Main in Vancouver.[51] Their son Landon was born in 1962, and soon afterward they moved to a house in Richmond. One of Tosh's customers had bought the place as a retirement destination, but in the interim he wanted to rent it out to someone he could trust. After about a year, the Kitagawas moved into their own home in another Richmond subdivision. It was there, in 1964, that their daughter

FIGURE 13. Wedding portrait of Mary and Tosh Kitagawa, August 5, 1961. Photo courtesy of Mary and Tosh Kitagawa.

Karen was born. Soon after, Tosh started his own furniture and appliance business. Finally, each of them felt like they were in a place to contemplate setting down permanent roots.

One day in 1968, while driving through a new development in Delta, they spotted a sign nailed to a tree. It had a telephone number and nothing more. Feeling bold, Tosh declared, "'You know, a guy should buy some property out here because some day it's going to be really valuable, it'll be a good investment.' And it was just sort of man talk, you know, all-talk-no-action sort of thing."[52] Never one for "all talk," Mary jotted down the number and called the property owner the next day. Within six months, they had begun construction on the lot. Tosh would work at his store during the day, swing by the family's place for dinner, and then drive to the lot where, continuing the Kitagawa tradition, he built much of the house himself. After selling their Richmond home, the family moved in at the beginning of January 1969, and soon afterward the house had its first working bathroom. Mary cooked and washed dishes there until the kitchen was finished, toward the end of 1970.

Mary's supervisors, in keeping with sexist practice at the time, had required that she resign her teaching post after becoming pregnant with the Kitagawas' first child.[53] However, Tosh's business was doing well. Now that the family was on solid financial ground and living in a home they had no plans to leave, the pressures that had dogged Mary and Tosh for so long began to recede. And so, they settled into a seemingly unremarkable middle-class suburban British Columbia life: coaching or almost as often founding and *then* coaching their children's sports teams; moving through a series of social groups based on their children's activities; helping the children with homework; and so forth. As the children grew, Mary's and Tosh's lives shifted accordingly. For instance, as Landon and Karen approached high school age, Mary started taking elective courses at UBC.[54] Political activism must have seemed like the furthest thing from anyone's mind in the Kitagawa household.

The Past in the Present

Centered on Powell Street, the postwar Nikkei Canadian community in British Columbia had begun reconstituting itself, driven primarily by Sansei (third-generation Japanese Canadians) and Shin-Issei (postwar immigrants from Japan).⁵⁵ In the later 1960s, a cluster of students formed the Wakayama group, after the Japanese city from which many Steveston Nikkei had emigrated. Working with Chinese Canadian students, the group assembled a slide show on the history of Asian migrants in Canada.⁵⁶ Veterans of this effort went on to collaborate with other Sansei to edit the *Powell Street Review*, whose single 1972 issue remains a touchstone for discussions of Japanese Canadian history and identity. In 1975, a group of Sansei and Shin-Issei founded Tonari Gumi, the Japanese Community Volunteers Association, which was designed to help Issei who had resettled in Vancouver but lacked the language skills, money, or political connections to navigate the area's challenges on their own.⁵⁷ The association's drop-in center, first on Powell Street and later on Hastings, subsequently became a center of gravity for still more activists and volunteers. These efforts led to a watershed moment in 1977, which brought both the founding of the Powell Street Festival and the culmination of the Japanese Canadian Centennial Project in an exhibition about migrants from Japan, *A Dream of Riches*.⁵⁸ Like many other Nikkei of their generation, Mary and Tosh found themselves connecting to the larger Japanese Canadian community through these events. For instance, they attended the *Dream of Riches* exhibition, which both of them describe as almost a kind of pilgrimage: "It was a huge gathering; everybody came from across Canada."⁵⁹

Another important bridge to the larger community was the fight for redress.⁶⁰ The National Association of Japanese Canadians (NAJC) had been pressing for government action since the later 1970s. After years of labor, the organization began negotiating with Ottawa, and as discussions continued, both sides eyed developments in the United States, where Japanese Americans eventually secured an official apology from the U.S. government as well as $20,000 for each surviving victim of forced dispersal. Armed with this precedent, the NAJC was able to negotiate a formal apology from the Canadian government and $21,000 for each surviving Nikkei Canadian who had been expelled from British Columbia and dispossessed—the additional $1,000 serving to acknowledge, among other things, state-sponsored postwar ethnic cleansing—as well as pardons for those imprisoned for violating orders-in-council associated with expulsion, a fund of $12 million for rebuilding community infrastructure, Canadian citizenship for those who had been unjustly deported after the loyalty survey, and a promised $24 million for a Canadian Race Relations Foundation (made a Crown corporation in 1996) dedicated to safeguarding human rights in Canada.⁶¹

Achieving that result took immense effort, and not only because of governmental intransigence. The struggle for redress also took place within the Nikkei community itself. A significant number of Japanese Canadians felt the effort raked needlessly over old ground, exposing what was left of the community to further bigotry. Others believed the NAJC's work would fail and that its resources were better directed elsewhere. They might have been forgiven for thinking so, too, at key points in the negotiation process. In 1984, for example, the government offered a symbolic sum of $6 million, which the NAJC refused. There was no way the Canadian government could fully compensate Nikkei for the impacts of wartime injustice. However, this sum was so small that accepting it risked looking like yet another opportunistic government-imposed arrangement, rather than a conclusion that demonstrated the agency, the history, and above all the rights of Nikkei Canadians. And yet, although little more than a token gesture, the government's offer indicated potential for success. It also demonstrated the need for clear and consistent messaging about the true scope of Nikkei losses during and after expulsion from British Columbia. Who better to provide that messaging than the people who had endured those losses?

To that end, redress activists began to set up small gatherings in peoples' homes.[62] In 1984, one of the organizers reached out to ask if the Kitagawas wanted to participate. Tosh recalls it as very much a grassroots effort: "You know, someone would invite three or four Japanese Canadian families, and they would discuss the redress movement and how it was going, how it was progressing, and how everyone could help. So, we went to one of these parties in Surrey, and Mary and I then got involved."[63] The meetings were relatively informal, their purpose being to connect Nikkei in the area. Actively bringing people together was necessary, too, for Tosh's and Mary's experience of relative isolation after returning to British Columbia was typical, with the majority of returnees and their families scattered throughout greater Vancouver.

There was something more, though. To some extent, these house meetings also were designed to gather, reshape, and amplify forms of resistance that had thus far been intuitive and largely isolated. Simply exercising the rights associated with citizenship—acting on freedom of movement, expecting equal employment opportunities, or demanding fair housing—was, as Nikkei knew all too well, a political act. But, for people impoverished by dispossession, the professional and economic aspects of such resistance could potentially get lost amid the pressures as well as the comforts of pursuing economic stability. Transforming that intuitive resistance into a shared, programmatic effort, the redress movement's house meetings were designed not to reconstitute a long-lost Nikkei voice but rather to bolster a Nikkei voice that was becoming all the more powerful for racist efforts to fragment and silence it.

With that in mind, the meetings encouraged an unusual kind of disclosure. Mary recalls, "I think the first meeting we went to, the people who were organizing these wanted to know the stories of your experience, that we *did* experience this incarceration, forced uprooting. . . . These are the stories that they wanted to hear, that we *did* suffer and that we deserved redress."[64] The aim was not to record those stories for people outside the community but rather to allow Nikkei to voice an experience that many, like Tosh and Mary, had long allowed to remain largely implicit. Making that shared experience explicit enabled the participants in the house meetings to begin taking fuller command of their histories and to reshape their political engagements from something intuitive, implicit, and isolated into something focused, explicit, and above all shared.

There is a commonality here with the kind of transformation Tosh and Mary had initiated in one another. Those house meetings, like Tosh's entry into the Murakami fold, provided a supportive environment for a fractured and dispersed people. To be sure, the redress movement was itself fractious; its work and workings remain subjects of often profound disagreement to this day.[65] As Mary's entry into activism demonstrates, though, those meetings helped initiate the outpouring of political energy that have marked her life in the years since. That outpouring, however, took a form that previously had been alien to her.

Focused, Purposeful Disclosure

Mary recently remarked that although she initially had difficulty disclosing her experience of wartime injustice, the cathartic aspects of that practice have gradually come forward as she has continued to recount her history: "When I first started to tell it, I was so emotional; my voice was always shaking. But now . . . I'm fine because I've . . . told the story so many times."[66] How does someone who was forced by circumstance to be so guarded about her personal life become so eloquent when voicing the *experience* of wartime injustice? Some things are perhaps better left unsaid, especially for people raised with the expectation that you should carry yourself with restraint, that you should avoid complaining, and that you should guard your privacy—an expectation confirmed not only by Japanese cultural traditions, not only by mid-century prairie and small-town Canadian cultural traditions, but also by the relentless pillorying of Nikkei in the Canadian press and in person during Mary's early years.

Those house meetings certainly went some way toward changing how Mary and Tosh discussed their experiences. First and foremost, they effected a shift away from mainly talking *around* certain topics toward engaging with people *through* them. Tosh describes the transformation this way:

> By and large, everyone was just going about doing their business and raising a family and sort of integrating into the white community and didn't talk about the incarceration period. It was just sort of locked in, deep inside them. And what this movement did is, once we started having the meetings, and, all these group meetings and things, all of a sudden, they became emboldened and wanted to talk about it. And that was the whole idea, so the concept that they had really worked because many, many Japanese Canadians of our age group, which were the Nisei, basically had integrated into the mainstream and then put that, that part of history in the back of their minds. And what the redress committee did is bring that out into the forefront again.[67]

The process did not begin from scratch but rather with Nikkei who had undergone similar transformations. Mary recalls a larger meeting at the Vancouver Japanese Language School, where "more or less people who were vocal before and those people who were organizing these house meetings—they were all there on the, on the stage there."[68] Having discussed both the broad contours of wartime injustice and the day-to-day experience of it, they set discussion in motion, thereby helping to shape the voices of more reticent Nikkei.

While these early discussions were a means for Nikkei Canadians to engage with one another, they were designed to be expansive as well as inclusive. The inclusiveness came across in the decision by Nikkei activists to form alliances with other marginalized groups. A number of the Redress Committee's meetings, for instance, featured First Nations people among their speakers.[69] Such presentations testified to the sheer scale of state-sponsored violence; they also marked the formation of an important alliance between marginalized groups: by 1985, the National Association of Japanese Canadians, to which the Redress Committee belonged, was voicing support for the Stoney Point band, which was working to reclaim land taken from it by the Canadian government during World War II.[70] Later, the organization offered a series of proposals for how Ottawa could address the historical injustices experienced by First Nations peoples.[71]

As for expansiveness, the early house meetings also shifted Nikkei away from talking mainly with one another and increasingly toward talking with people who did not necessarily share their sense of historical injustice. During the fight for redress, for instance, Mary sat for several radio interviews not because her interviewers were always sympathetic—on the contrary, at least one started out a skeptic—but because she had come to understand that voicing her experience of injustice could help others comprehend the scale of suffering Nikkei Canadians had endured. In the course of winning over that doubtful interviewer, she caught the attention of other listeners, including a reporter who telephoned Mary out of the blue with questions about her story. "So, I said, 'You know, I wrote an essay at the University of British Columbia that tells a story of our experience. Would you like to read it?' . . . She said, 'Oh, yes.' She was, you know, willing to learn. So, I sent her my essay, she read it, and she published the story of our family in the *Vancouver Sun*, and she became my advocate." Although disinclined to talk about her experiences, Mary realized that doing so could have immense political power: "One person at a time we had to convince in order to . . . come on our train."[72]

Where did that essay come from? It was not a product of the house meetings, which had involved conversation rather than writing. The answer brings us to another factor in Mary's transformation, one we might easily miss: her studies at UBC after Landon and Karen reached high school age. In 1982, she took a course in the Asian Studies Department. Taught by René Goldman (b. 1934), it was a general history of China and Japan and, as Mary has emphasized, *not* the history of Chinese or Japanese immigrants in Canada. As the course got under way, Professor Goldman laid out five possible topics for his students' research papers, but then he took Mary aside and gave her a very different assignment. Mary recalls, "He came to me and said, 'I don't want you to write any of those [topics].' He says, 'I want to know about . . . what happened to Japanese Canadians during the war.'"⁷³ The assignment caught Mary off guard—she had barely even begun to engage in that sort of disclosure with other Nikkei outside her family. Nonetheless, she pursued the project at Goldman's urging.⁷⁴

Professor Goldman, it turned out, was a Holocaust survivor whose parents, along with many members of his extended family, were murdered in the Shoah. Born in Luxembourg, he and his family fled to Brussels in 1940 to escape implementation of the Nuremberg Race Laws. Established in 1935, these laws performed two functions. First, they deprived Jews of full German citizenship, thereby also depriving them of political rights. Second, the Nuremberg Race Laws banned intermarriage, defining it as a form of *Rassenschande* (racial defilement). In 1942, the Goldmans fled to southern France, where they hoped to catch a boat to freedom. While in a small town near the Swiss border, Goldman and his mother were arrested. Goldman's aunt managed to help the boy escape the authorities, but he witnessed his mother being dragged aboard the train that carried her to Auschwitz and, the following autumn, her death. Goldman spent the next two years moving from refuge to refuge before being briefly reunited with his father, who had evaded capture and joined the French resistance. Although it would be nearly twenty years before he learned this, his father eventually died during a death march from Auschwitz to Landsberg in early 1945. Upon receiving his high school education in Poland, Goldman participated in an exchange program with China. Spurred on by that experience, he earned his doctorate in Chinese history from Columbia University before joining the department of Asian Studies at UBC in 1963.⁷⁵

There is a great deal to unpack regarding Mary's interactions with Goldman. For now, we should focus on that assignment, which not only departed from the official content of the course but also required that Mary depart from her own past practice. Before this time, she had spoken about wartime injustice almost exclusively with her family, which meant there were all sorts of shorthand that needed no explication, no historicization. Discussions in Toronto had been similarly brief and infrequent, even with Katherine Miwa, and Mary and Tosh almost never discussed the matter in the first decade or so of their marriage. Here, though, was a Euro-Canadian professor at UBC asking that she delve into that history, *her* history, and he was doing so in a course dedicated to an entirely different topic.

The assignment was transformative in two ways. First, it helped Mary realize that her history merited formal study and explicit discussion. Second, and perhaps more important, it forged a bond between her and her professor. Although from dramatically different backgrounds and subject to very different forms of injustice, they nonetheless found a kind of common ground in conversation about their backgrounds, their experiences: "I used to go with him to his office almost after every class. . . . So, I used to, you know, we used to talk a lot at his office. He used to invite me after class, and we used to weep and [*chuckles, a little embarrassed*] weep on each side of the desk, you know. Like, he would tell me his story, and I would tell him my story."[76]

The result was reciprocal transformation, for both Mary and Goldman came out of their conversations changed. Their disclosures, their reckonings with the past were mutually reinforcing. Here were two people made to feel keenly aware of their difference on an almost continuous basis.[77] It is as if the same kind of mutual recognition that animated Mary's friendship with Katherine Miwa expressed in a dramatically new way, partly because of the differences in their backgrounds and partly because, by this time, scholarship, political action, and personal experience had become intertwined in substantially new ways. The result was a kind of allyship that is legible not only in Goldman's assignment to Mary but also in her summary of their bond: "He was a Jewish professor who lost his parents in the Holocaust, and he was the same age as me. 1934 he was born. And the last image he has of his mother was the [collaborationist gendarme] dragging his mother away."[78] Even as she describes the basis of his efforts on her behalf, she acknowledges that their experiences were only analogous, never equivalent.

Analogy formed a crucial point of contact for Mary and Goldman, bringing together two people who had long recognized but had not necessarily known how to articulate their experiences of persecution. In this way, it set the stage for a crucial development in Mary's activism: her willingness to talk about the *experience*—not just the legislative, juridical, economic, and demographic facts—of wartime injustice. Encountering a person whose experience led him to inquire about her own, Mary finally came face to face with someone who could grasp that history, even though he did not share it directly. Goldman's inquiries and his support awakened in her an awareness that others, outside of her family and perhaps even outside of the Nikkei community, might be willing and able to hear the truth of her history. He was, in fact, the first non-Nikkei with whom Mary talked about her experience in any real detail.[79]

From Intuitive Resistance to Programmatic Action

As we have seen, Mary's life prior to the advent of redress was one primarily of intuitive, localized resistance—*returning* to British Columbia, *choosing* Toronto as her college home, *supporting* her parents after graduation. Even closing herself off from other children constituted an effort to offset the damage done by wartime injustice. Eventually, intuitive action ceased to be sufficient. Time was a primary factor not only because it provided opportunities for reflection and for Mary to take command of her history, but also because it redistributed opportunities to define herself by bringing her into contact with transformative people at critical moments. Having finally chosen a destination all her own, Mary was able to engage with that destination on terms at least partly of her own devising, a circumstance that enabled her to connect with Katherine Miwa. Having found paying work and settled in Vancouver for the long term, she was in a position to entertain the prospect of dating a brash, young Nisei possessed of striking warmth and generosity. Having reached a point where her family life afforded her the opportunity to take classes at UBC, she was able to pursue a course that brought her into contact with René Goldman. Each relationship helped make the next possible, as relationship-driven changes cascaded gradually through her life. And this cascade of changes helped put her in a position to pursue those house meetings in the run-up to redress. The trajectory at issue is one of incrementally greater and more explicit re-engagement with the question of what it means to be Nikkei in Canada.

A Call to Action Close to Home

It all began when Richard set up an automobile repair service on a plot west of Ganges on Salt Spring Island. Many islanders worked on cars in their yards, sometimes with multiple cars in various states of disrepair. Richard, however, found himself the sole target of critics, most notably from an organization called the Islands Trust. The trust was set up to protect Gulf Islands heritage structures and wildlife areas, but someone had decided to use it as an instrument for hobbling economic competition and expressing their racist views. Mindful of the trust's criticisms, Richard, Rose, and Kimiko attended a 1989 meeting of the trustees. (Katsuyori had died in 1988.) When they got home, they received an irate phone call from one of the trustees, who informed them that the organization would drive "you Japs" from the island.[80] That promise proved hollow, but the pressure did not let up. Members of the RCMP involved themselves, issuing threats to the family, and at one point a cluster of No Parking signs suddenly appeared in front of and to either side of Richard's business.

Finally, Richard could not stand it any longer and reached out to Mary. Transformed by those earlier contacts and now recognizing the potential of collective effort, she contacted the Human Rights Committee of the Japanese Canadian Citizens' Association of Greater Vancouver (GVJCCA).[81] The committee, along with help from the GVJCCA and involvement of the national office of the RCMP, helped resolve the matter on the island. In addition, though, the committee helped reshape Richard's approach to the situation. Mary recalls, "They ran a workshop for us . . . and they gathered a *lot* of people at that workshop. And they taught us how to deal with racism; they had a social worker there, and we told our story. And from then on, it gave Richard . . . [an] idea of how to speak to . . . these racists. And so, he was able to deal better with the situation he was suffering." Even so, Richard still needed help, though now the task was more manageable. "When we were there in the summer, we started to advocate for Richard, too, whenever we heard anybody speaking badly to Richard [because] he was a very gentle person; he wasn't like the women of the family. He was a kind and gentle person. . . . He'll turn the other cheek instead of fighting back."[82] The business of fighting back proved contagious, as local allies started pulling down the No Parking signs; some even became active advocates for Richard and his family.[83]

In addition to reshaping Richard, the episode also further changed Mary. She became a member of the Human Rights Committee, with Tosh driving her to their regular meetings on Powell Street. He was proud of her, but it seems to have been more than he was prepared to undertake, at least initially: "I used to sit in the other room while they were talking about human rights issues because," he adds, laughing self-deprecatingly, "I wasn't very human rights–oriented at that particular time."[84] He soon would be, though, thanks in large part to Mary. He recalls that during one meeting, someone on the Human Rights Committee asked what someone who was not on the committee might think about a particular issue. Mary mentioned that her husband was waiting outside, so they invited Tosh in to offer his opinion.[85] Downplaying his strengths as usual, he says, "I started voicing my opinion, and . . . once I did that, I was doomed."[86]

But when the topic of the Powell Street Festival comes up, Tosh changes tack. Although he is quick to say that his contribution had nothing to do with the Human Rights Committee, he is unmistakably proud of the support he has provided the Nikkei community in Vancouver. After becoming active in the GVJCCA along with Mary, in the later 1990s Tosh began to attend other meetings. One in particular stands out: a planning meeting for the Powell Street Festival. By this time, the festival was beginning to suffer from its own success. Attendees were plentiful, including non-Nikkei populations, but volunteers and contributors were suffering high rates of burnout. Fundraising was also a major challenge. "There is never enough money," the Powell Street Festival Society Board stated in its 2000 call for help published in the *JCCA Bulletin*. "The Festival runs on an extremely tight budget. Currently, there are not enough people with experience or time to do a lot of fundraising over and above the bare-bones costs of running the Society and the Festival."[87] This situation, they noted, was aggravating the problems of burnout and a diminishing pool of volunteers.[88]

For Tosh, the answer was clear. Bake sales and the like would not suffice. There needed to be something that would attract a larger number of customers and entice them to spend more money. Initially, he arranged for a friend who ran several commercial greenhouses to provide fresh fruit and vegetables. During the first year, Mary and Tosh increased the revenue nearly twentyfold, bringing in well over $2,000. Subsequent years saw that figure continue to increase, but the arrangement was not sustainable. It required people to haul crate after crate of produce to the festival, a labor that became less enjoyable with each passing year. Around 2008, Mary suggested to Tosh that they come up with an alternative, and he raised the issue at the next planning meeting. "So they said, 'What are we going to do?' . . . You know, it's fate. Someone from Hawai'i, one of my friends got back from Hawai'i in the previous few days, and he was raving about this Spam sushi. So, I went back to the meeting and said, 'Well, why don't we sell Spam sushi?' And they all laughed, and they said, 'What the heck is that?' And so, they sort of had a great chuckle about that fund-raising idea."[89]

Undaunted, Tosh went home and looked up Hormel, the maker of Spam. Never one for half measures, he phoned the company's Toronto headquarters and asked to speak with their marketing manager. Astonishingly, the operator put him through. "And so, I gave her the two-minute spiel of who I was and what we were planning. And she said, 'Jeez, that sounds like a great idea.' She says, 'How can we help you?' And I says, 'I have no idea.'" Laughing incredulously, he adds, "She said, 'Leave it with me,' and I hung up the phone. And about two weeks later—it was about two weeks, I guess—a big truck pulls up, and he's got a whole pallet-load of Spam and hats and T-shirts and aprons, everything. So, we went down to the Powell Street grounds on the festival day and we started selling Spam sushi, and we've been doing it ever since."[90]

Such efforts may indeed not be directly related to the work of the Human Rights Committee or its sister organizations in Canada and the United States. Furthermore, they would never have borne fruit without the hard work of many other people who have been committed to the long-term success of the Powell Street Festival. Nonetheless, Tosh's efforts grew out of his relationship with the committee. They became possible because of the transformations his life with Mary have wrought, and they repay a kind of support the reconstituted Nikkei community has provided the Kitagawas over nearly five decades.

It bears repetition: Tosh's work is inseparable from the work of others who have built, nurtured, and expanded the Powell Street Festival. His work also is inseparable from Mary's. Most obviously, she helped him haul vegetables, coordinate the groups making Spam rolls, and so forth. But she also helped bring him into a larger shared discussion of Nikkei life and history in Canada, reciprocating the emotional and social awakening he had initiated in her. To be sure, there was a degree of cultural self-awareness internal to the Kitagawa family, but it was lived rather than discussed, intuitive rather than programmatic, implicit rather than vocalized.[91] As Tosh grew up, much of his sense of self had arisen through contact with people outside his family. During his first seven years, that meant close involvement with other Nikkei, but with the destruction of the Mission City community, he lost a critical means of self-definition.

Tosh did gradually establish a sense of himself amid his peers, but the demands of school and work still meant that his was a relatively solitary Nikkei existence alongside white families whose shared experience of poverty gave them a common ground.[92] From expulsion to survival to re-establishment in Lethbridge, Nikkei life for Tosh thus was informed in large part by his father's reticence. Of the train ride east, for instance, he says "We were a little excited because it was sort of like a new adventure, more or less, because my father never told us, you know, about the war or what was happening or anything else." Barely ten years old, Tosh was unequipped to sort the situation, and so he hung onto the few details that were available to him. "It was almost like we were going to have a holiday, because all of a sudden, we were riding the train—we never rode in the train. And we're being sent to a place called Diamond City, and we thought that was like New York because it was so much bigger—we thought that just from the name that it had to be a major metropolitan area. And in essence, it was three grain elevators and a post office."[93]

But as Mary began to reclaim the fuller political significance of her experience, she provided an example for Tosh. She also has provided an example for others. Take, for instance, her decision to pursue honorary diplomas for students unjustly expelled from UBC in 1942.[94] Her inspiration was the 2008 decision by universities on the West Coast of the United States to award such diplomas to students they had wrongly expelled after the bombing of Pearl Harbor. Mary had never met any of those former students—she was only six when Order-in-Council P.C. 1486 took effect—but she understood in deeply personal ways the importance of education. Not only had it transformed her, especially in recent years, but it also had been a central feature of life for the Murakamis during and after expulsion. For Richard, whose time in Cardston was especially painful, it was something to push against socially, even as he strove academically. Alice, though deprived of access to higher education by wartime injustice, nonetheless long cherished the kindness and support of Mildred Fahrni, later remarking: "I think it's ironic how years go by and you finally really understand what your mentors have meant to you. For me, I feel deeply indebted to her. . . . [She] made me become a free thinker."[95] Rose made school an athletic, intellectual, and social hub. And for Mary, it was a ticket out of southern Alberta and into a life of her own making. Surely it would have been similarly important for those Nikkei students whose lives were thrown into chaos and whose future prospects were irremediably damaged by wartime injustice.

Mary contacted the president of UBC, who referred the matter to the Senate Tributes Committee, a body tasked with selecting recipients for honorary degrees. The chair of the committee wrote Mary to say that the former Nikkei students, along with Nikkei faculty and staff (of which in fact there had been none), had left UBC of their own accord and that the university was therefore not in a position to award degrees. What was more, the committee stated that Mary's request fell outside their brief, which was to award degrees for lifetime achievement rather than undergraduate academic performance. After further back-and-forth, Mary decided to change her course of action. She had form: in 2007, she read about the decision to name a government building in Vancouver after the racist politician Howard Charles Green. She immediately recognized the name of the man who had been instrumental both in the forced dispersal of Nikkei from British Columbia and in the unjust sale of their property by the Custodian for Enemy Property. Rather than simply lament the decision, she mounted a successful campaign to have the building renamed in honor Douglas Jung (1924–2002), the first Chinese Canadian member of Parliament. The change became official in 2008; more important, though, Mary and Tosh became friends with some of Green's descendants in the process.

Mary applied the lessons she had learned in 2007–2008 to her dealings with UBC. She not only enlisted fellow Nikkei, in particular the GVJCCA and other organizations that had been involved in redress, but she also made a broader appeal. She began giving public talks and sitting for interviews, and she enlisted others to do the same, most notably Mits Sumiya, one of the former students. She also continued writing to the Senate Tributes Committee, and she initiated a nationwide letter-writing campaign and set up an online petition. For someone as private and reserved as Mary had long been, taking both the experience and the history of wartime injustice public in this way marked a new sort of personal exposure. But, having knit herself into a community founded on the interpersonal recuperation of that experience, she was able to count on widespread support and understanding, even in the face of pushback by opponents.

Mary's campaign, bolstered by Tosh's meticulous research to find and contact surviving former students, yielded extraordinary results (figure 14). UBC agreed to award honorary diplomas, but it also funded the establishment of an academic program dedicated to the broader history of Asian migrants in Canada. Although UBC was slow to implement their plan beyond the diplomas, further pressure from Mary and Tosh helped bring it to fruition.[96] Subsequently titled Asian Canadian and Asian Migration Studies, the resulting academic program brings together faculty and students from across a wide range of disciplines. As part of her efforts, in 2017

Mary co-designed and taught a course on the history of Nikkei in Canada with Dr. John Price, now Professor Emeritus of Pacific and Asian Canadian History at the University of Victoria. It is worth noting that, while the impact of the work with UBC has been academic, it also bears a strong interpersonal component. Mary and Tosh's work at the university and their close involvement with ACAM from its early days have created a kind of extended family with a revolving group of informal relatives who, except during the pandemic, regularly visit their surrogate grandparents. It should perhaps come as no surprise, then, that she received an honorary doctorate from UBC in 2020.

To understand how the history of Nikkei in Canada shaped Mary, you really should understand how it shaped Tosh. Meeting him initiated a series of emotional, political, and social transformations that had been potential but needed the right circumstances, the right relationships—the right opportunities—to bring them forward. It all started at the family dinner table. "During that conversation at the table," Mary recalls, "We talked

FIGURE 14. Tosh Kitagawa with degree recipients Henry Okada (standing) and Roy Oshiro at the University of British Columbia ceremony, 2012. University of British Columbia Archives, photo by Don Erhardt [UBC 35.1/998].

politics and all kinds of things. And that's where I learned about what we had experienced, and we were experiencing."[97] While these conversations started at a very early age for her, the destruction of a stable Nikkei community meant that for a long time they would begin and end at that table. And yet, looking back over her life, we can in retrospect see them grow outward with increasing vigor and confidence in Mary's friendships with Katherine Miwa, with Tosh, with René Goldman, and with a Nikkei community reshaping itself. Tosh's impact on Mary occurred partly because of their implicit shared experience but also partly because of the explicit charm and wit and humor that experience had demanded of him. She responded in kind, producing an impact that extended from her family's impact on her. Those dinnertime conversations in Magrath, in the Extension, in Cardston, and back on Salt Spring Island had laid a foundation for the expansion that René Goldman and the redress house meetings set in motion in the 1980s. That expansion took Mary's conversations outward, initially toward others who shared her experience. And as those conversations sharpened her skills and reinforced her resolve, she found a voice to speak with those who were unaware of or doubted her experience or those who push back against the change she advocates.

Afterword

How could someone survive all that Mary, Tosh, and their families—like the other 22,000 Nikkei who were forced from British Columbia, set to work in beet fields or locked away in inland ghost towns, or those lucky ones who had enough money to move eastward on their own—have had to contend with? Part of the answer lies in the educational and economic foundations early Japanese migrants managed to build in the later nineteenth and early twentieth centuries. Part of the answer lies in entangled Nikkei traditions, Canadian frontier and prairie cultures, and mid-century aspirational liberalism. And part of the answer lies in the non-Nikkei allies—Mildred Fahrni, for instance, or members of the Cooperative Committee on Japanese Canadians—who extended a helping hand to Nikkei soon after expulsion and later became important political allies in the fight for equitable political representation and for compensation for economic losses due to dispossession.

But the most important part of the answer lies in the people themselves. It lies in how they, as people, strove to connect with and support one another. It lies in how they took the survival strategies they had been forced to develop during inland exile and redeployed them to increasingly vocal and programmatic ends over time. It necessarily also lies in those non-Nikkei—especially the pioneers like Ann Gomer Sunhara and Roger Daniels—who have worked to shed light on the profound wrongs done to Nikkei in North America. In short, it lies in how people alive to injustice have pursued deeply human, coalitional bonds with one another.

Those bonds are difficult to form for many reasons, the most important of which has to do with those of us who want to learn about the past, as opposed to those who experienced it and would speak (or not speak) of that experience. No proper accounting for historical injustice can occur without the participation of those who suffered, but the burden of that accounting falls decreasingly, if still disproportionately, on the original targets of injustice, their children, and their grandchildren. It is now increasingly the job of those whose families did not experience dispossession, inland exile, and ethnic cleansing—readers, listeners, and onlookers who are even further separated by that shared history. For these people, understanding the history of Nikkei in Canada, like that of Nikkei in the United States, is difficult because it requires rigorous comparison of the behavior of these countries and their citizens with the claims they constantly advance about freedom and equality. Doing that is difficult because it necessitates that we speak honestly about the unequal distribution of opportunities—privilege, yes, but also the fragilities that privilege breeds. And it is difficult because

FIGURE 15. Mary and Tosh Kitagawa with Landon Kitagawa and Karen (Kitagawa) Bennett at Mary's appointment to the Order of British Columbia, 2018. Photo courtesy of Mary and Tosh Kitagawa.

so much of that history is bound up with legislation and jurisprudence. The dry language of government denatures, even denies the violence of what actually happened. Although important, such historical focus also risks giving the impression that what actually happened was a discrete cluster of episodes. But anyone who wants to truly remember that history—not just memorize some terms, dates, locations, and events—must first remember that the loss involved was profound, that it built on precedent, that it was continuous, that it has been durable, and that it is inseparable from other forms of historical injustice.

Most important, the history of wartime injustice also was and still is a *lived experience* both for survivors and for their families (figure 15). But that lived experience is difficult to apprehend. Remembering loss does not entitle others to access the experience of that loss; it therefore also does not require that the targets of injustice voice their experiences in terms that are recognizable to others.[1] Awareness of that experience is vitally important, but so is the ultimate inaccessibility of that experience.[2] The most important reasons for this have to do with the agency of the individual and with our capacity for respecting that agency. Those who have lived through injustice have the *right* to choose whether, how, when, and why they might disclose. Respecting that agency allows us to work against the durable—in so many ways *continuing*—deprivation at the hands of white nationalists and economic opportunists. Respecting that agency also reminds us that even the details of loss themselves are fragile, equally at risk of loss. In this respect, the fragility of history should motivate us, provided we relate to that fragility with compassion.

Take, for instance, a moment from the Murakamis' time in Cardston. Readers may recall a brief 1951 visit by the Anglican Reverend Goichi Gordon Nakayama. They may also recall that Mary's brother Richard started suffering from night terrors around that time. Only in 1997 did Mary and her sister Rose learn that the two events were connected.[3] As we saw in chapters 2 and 3, Nakayama had made himself an important figure among Nikkei in southern Alberta, traveling among isolated families, ministering to them, performing missionary work, and reporting on labor conditions. His work did not end with the war itself. Still barred from returning to British Columbia after the cessation of hostilities, he settled in Coaldale, where he founded the Anglican Church of the Ascension. A pedophile, he also spent those years grooming and terrorizing ever more children. He had long been the subject of rumors, but rumor moves idiosyncratically, and its reach is therefore necessarily restricted. Consequently, only decades later did it become clear that Nakayama had used that peripatetic life to identify and pursue vulnerable members of the community.[4] Covered up by senior members of the Anglican Church in Canada, his crimes did not become public until 2014—nearly twenty years after he died—and no one knows the full extent of the harm he did, though his victims likely number in the hundreds.

As important as the complicity of church authorities was, though, forced dispersal also played a direct and material role in this tragedy, just as it did in innumerable others. The fragmentation and dispersal of the Nikkei community after the bombing of Pearl Harbor aided and abetted Nakayama. Government-sanctioned racism fueled widespread mistrust of white law enforcement, especially the RCMP, which was a direct, visible, and often malign presence during the long period of inland exile—and in Richard's case, well into the 1990s. Expulsion from British Columbia and subsequent outbursts of racism there and elsewhere in Canada further stoked the fear that any negative press would only worsen conditions for everyone of Japanese ancestry. And of course, the dispersal of British Columbia's Nikkei community across Alberta, Quebec, Manitoba, and Ontario fractured normal channels of communication by breaking up communities and scattering their constituents far and wide.[5] Dictated by the government's postwar policy of ethnic cleansing, dissolution of the Nikkei community did more than intensify the need for contact with someone—anyone—who shared the community's historical, cultural, linguistic, and religious background. It also drove and damaged the rumor mill, which otherwise might have thrown up more robust obstacles to Nakayama. In sum, a sexual predator benefitted directly from the forced dispersal, dispossession, and systematic alienation of Nikkei. That alienation enabled Nakayama to travel without hindrance from isolated, demoralized, economically desperate family to isolated, demoralized, economically desperate family.

Only Richard knows the full extent of what happened in Cardston, but he has discussed it with his sisters. More importantly, he has always treated the topic with an eye toward the well-being of others, including the decades when he did not discuss it at all. Not wanting to cause his mother grief, he kept the matter to himself until Kimiko died in 1997.[6] Soon after, though, Richard related part of his experience to Mary, but his account was laconic and focused mainly on the welfare of his younger brother, who had been seven years old at the time. As Richard recalled it, the old man chased the boys around the house insisting, "I need a kiss for Jesus! I need a kiss for Jesus!" Richard took Bruce by the hand and ran outside, spiriting the two of them to safety. That is as much as he has ever been willing to discuss.

To respect Richard's privacy is, in some small measure, to work against the grain of racism and economic opportunism, since these continually deny the agency of colonized and marginalized people. It is also to recognize that all such disclosures necessarily entail omission, withholding, and obliqueness because they are motivated by the desire to shape relationships and, therefore, are themselves shaped. For instance, Richard's decision to disclose Nakayama's criminal activity in Cardston arose out of the need to explain elements of the family's history to his sisters, and his decision to give Mary permission to discuss that disclosure arose from his wish to support the claims of others whom Nakayama had abused.[7] Nonetheless, the full extent of his suffering will never be knowable. We can only imagine it, and in so doing begin to grasp the scale of the losses—local and intense on the one hand but also so vast as to be almost immeasurable on the other—suffered by Nikkei Canadians both during wartime and in the decades after. Richard is only one of the people on whom Nakayama preyed, and the particular losses those people have experienced are part of the larger losses they and their families experienced as targets of white nationalism. Furthermore, their losses are but a fraction of the losses that 22,000 Nikkei suffered directly and that countless more have suffered indirectly in the decades since. So much has been lost, even aspects of loss itself. But knowing this, we can hold fast those fragments that remain and, more important, relate them to others. Attunement to fragments of the past drives the project, as when Mary eventually sought out Evelyn Eagle Speaker (by then Evelyn Locker). Haunted by the memory of that elusive, bookish presence, her aim was to gain at least some modest understanding of how the only other non-white student she saw in her classes might have found life in southern Alberta and to use that understanding to expand from her own experience outward.

Historical Entanglement

As a Yonsei (fourth-generation Nikkei) American descended from families incarcerated by the U.S. government during the war, my touchstones differ from Mary's. Some of the differences are due to age. My parents were born around the same time as she was, and they were targets of state-sponsored violence for being of Japanese ancestry. Some of the differences are due to geographical and political disparities. My parents were imprisoned by the U.S. government and, as a result, endured different sorts of injustice. Some of the differences are cultural, borne of our respective faiths or our social networks. And yet, the commonalities are undeniable. Some of these are also historical. Mary's and my parents' respective injustices shared roots in white nationalism and racial capitalism. Furthermore, Canadian wartime policies were frequently modeled on American precedent, albeit revised to fit the structure of a parliamentary democracy. Some of the commonalities are cultural, but these commonalities always bear the unmistakable mark of difference. I may recognize a particular term or cadence in something Mary says, but I will just as often misrecognize a term or cadence or touchstone, my error coming into focus as she explains her point. Hers is a *Nikkei Canadian* life, and our relationship is enriched by the fact that we are almost as much separated as we are bound by a shared history. To study her part of that history is to have the invaluable opportunity to observe a rigorous mind, fully in motion, continually meeting the world. It is to see thoughtful adaptation in the face of repeated insults and injuries as well as intermittent successes. And it is also a chance to see part of that shared history change across space and over time.

Tetsuden Kashima summed up the phenomenon in his observation that the history of Nikkei in the United States "consists of a series of alterations and adaptations occurring in response to events faced by individuals, regional groups, and in certain cases, by all group members."[8] The same must be said of Nikkei in Canada, who are sometimes depicted as having simply ventured into a new land, suffered a single discrete disruption, and then made a life for themselves nonetheless. The truth is far more sobering. Having been propelled to Canada by economic necessity and social upheaval in Japan, Nikkei have continually had to navigate an unlevel playing field. Thus, their stories do not follow a convenient, for some perhaps even a comforting trajectory from hardship through old-timey racism to middle-class success. That trajectory is merely a story people tell themselves to avoid recognizing that history and thus historical injustice live in the present. It is legible in our presumptions and stereotypes, in our laws, even in the physical, political, and social infrastructures by which we move through the world.[9] Just ask the Saanich people, on whose ancestral land the Canadian laws governing preemption encouraged the Okanos, Murakamis, Iwasakis, and other Nikkei as well as many immigrants of African ancestry to settle.

These histories—of First Nations peoples, of colonization, of immigration, preemption, dispossession, and ethnic cleansing; of sugar beet farms and residential schools; of Doukhobors and Chinese immigrants and southern Alberta Mormons; of high school sports, provincial stampedes, the regulation of diners, hunting, and land rights—are entangled. The recognition of that entanglement is something else that drove Mary to connect with Evelyn Locker in later years. Connection led to an expanded sense of how resistance to white nationalism and state-sponsored violence might look, and that expanded sense shed further light on how non-white peoples of various backgrounds have done far more than simply carry forward inherited traits; they have engaged in a kind of synthesis, constantly formulating and reformulating their identities in relation both to dominant forms of cultural production—"whiteness," broadly conceived—and to other modes of existence—financial, linguistic, religious, sexual, and so forth. To connect with her enigmatic former classmate enabled Mary to gain a fuller sense of what identity might be and how the weight of history continually reshapes it.

Living History

Identities are relational. We tell each other who we are, but we also tell ourselves who we are in relation to the people and institutions around us. This is the case even when those around us ignore or deny who we are, where we have come from, and what we have experienced. For Nikkei, repeated struggles to reestablish themselves economically, socially, politically, and culturally in the wake of wartime injustice destroyed old relations and established dramatically new and often ephemeral ones. Dispersed across Canada by government fiat, they found themselves awash in predominantly white cultures. The relationships that formed as they went about reconstituting their lives were thus determined in large part by the dictates of whiteness, and for most people who classed themselves as white, wartime injustice either did not exist or was a regrettable necessity. For many, that is still the case. For instance, think of Mary and Tosh's 1962 visit to the Russells in Diamond City. Not a word was spoken about expulsion from western British Columbia or the forced sale of Nikkei property. For the Russells, who had felt quite warmly toward Tosh, those events had no place in the conversation, even though those events are what brought Tosh and the Russells together. It is tempting to categorize this as erasure and stop at that, but erasure itself is relational. Whatever reasons the Russells had for not addressing the matter—and malice does not seem to have numbered among them—their silence helped normalize the supposedly apolitical reticence that, for some Nikkei, seemed like it was simply part of postwar life. Tosh has made this observation about his own political awakening:

> I think I was no different than many, many Japanese Canadians at my age group. By and large, everyone was just going about doing their business and raising a family and sort of integrating into the white community and didn't talk about the incarceration period. It was just sort of locked in, deep inside them. And what [the redress] movement did is, once we started having the meetings, . . . all of a sudden, they became emboldened and wanted to talk about it. And that was the whole idea, so the concept that they had really worked because many, many Japanese Canadians of our age group, which were the Nisei, basically had integrated into the mainstream and then put that, that part of history in the back of their minds. And what the redress committee did is bring that out into the forefront again.[10]

Constrained by the postwar relationships ethnic cleansing made possible, Nikkei were enmeshed in that erasure.[11]

To be enmeshed in that erasure was not to approve of it or even to be apolitical, though.[12] If we do not always recognize, say, the Murakamis' return to Salt Spring Island as a form of resistance, it is likely because that resistance does not immediately match the benchmarks of the predominantly judicial, political, and historical frameworks that shape our expectations. For instance, Torazo Iwasaki's repeated attempts to reclaim the land and money that white nationalists stole from him may not have been radical, operating as they did within the frameworks of Canadian jurisprudence, but they were sufficiently explicit that they became clearly legible as political action. That arguably was one of Iwasaki's goals: to establish an explicit claim that would flag the difference between what the law supposedly stood for and what it actually accomplished.

Important though his protest was, though, Iwasaki also wanted his land and some semblance of his pre-war life back. In the end, he achieved neither of these goals. The Murakamis made a different decision, opting to reclaim their lives and an approximation of their land on the island rather than put Canadian jurisprudence to the test. In this respect, their actions were a measure not of resignation but of dismissal. Gavin Mouat and others on the island had already demonstrated what white people were willing to do, law or no law, so why bother butting heads with them? Better to beat them at their own game: show up with a bag full of cash and buy *from them* a property they had spent years expecting to place in white hands. (They took this action, we should recall, after they had approached each person who bought the Okanos' and Murakamis' original properties.) For Katsuyori and Kimiko, actions like these allowed them to express political conviction while also being hard-nosed about the sort of relationships 1950s British Columbia would allow Nikkei to pursue. This is not to suggest that either approach to dispossession was superior. It is simply to recognize that both—unambiguously vocal protest and seeming resignation—were relational forms of resistance.

Voice and Change

Nikkei Canadian forms of resistance, like those of Nikkei Americans, have evolved as different relationships, different opportunities have arisen. Mary, for instance, found herself increasingly cut off from other Nikkei, first because of the family's repeated moves and later because of their relative isolation in Cardston. Shaped by that isolation, the model for social and political discourse outside her family gradually became white, middle class, and distinctly small-town in its frameworks. To be sure, the Nikkei Canadians she met in Toronto shared her general history and, in their own ways, her experience. But the majority of them belonged to a community that had already begun to consolidate its regional and cultural identity as early as the mid-1940s. Dispersed throughout Toronto they may have been, but they also enjoyed a relatively coherent sense of group identity and were anchored by a predominantly urban life that they, their families, and local allies had built over the previous decade. Financially and culturally, Mary found herself once again largely isolated. And when she eventually returned to British Columbia permanently, her existence became once again one dictated by predominantly white colleagues, neighbors, and friends. Within the resulting networks, there were relatively few opportunities to sharpen her sense of history and of injustice beyond the intuitive. And yet, we can see resistance in her day-to-day actions: moving to Toronto, calling that landlord who claimed her apartment had been rented, and supporting her parents' decision not just to settle back on Salt Spring Island but to buy a new property from the very person who, as representative of the Custodian for Enemy Property, had mismanaged their property and then profited from its sale.

The political agency of Nikkei Canadians has in fact been evident since their earliest days in the country, when they conducted strikes and formed unions and civic organizations. Wartime and postwar injustice constrained that agency by severely disrupting relationships and restricting opportunities. It is unsurprising, then, that this agency would once again take overt forms as those disruptions and restrictions receded—and that this agency would overtly engage with the disruptions and restrictions that shaped it. We see an example of that trajectory in Mary. She now possesses and exercises a voice that most clearly came into its own in the later 1980s and early 1990s. Prior to her contact with Sansei and Shin-Issei activists, she still exercised resistance to wartime injustice and white nationalism, but that resistance—shaped by *white nationalist* silences about injustice, *white nationalist* erasures of history, and *white nationalist* refusals to acknowledge reality—was necessarily intuitive, something she had essentially to create on her own. Family life had taught her the difference between just and unjust action, but it also had taught her a specific range of mechanisms for pushing back against injustice. Her voice might be raised at the dinner table or in the company of trusted others (a small group indeed, after years of inland exile), but there was no framework of relations in which she could pursue what most readers would now recognize as political action until conversations with René Goldman brought her experience directly and explicitly into view, and until the redress movement drew her and Tosh into its orbit. What we see in her case, then, is not a trajectory from silence to voice to action, but rather a trajectory from relatively isolated, intuitive action toward the shared, programmatic expression of political power. We also see a trajectory that, in the context of a longer history of Nikkei in Canada, restores and extends earlier forms of political engagement.

This is where the long history of Mary's family—in truth, her families—takes on perhaps its greatest importance. Tough as nails, Riyo Kimura landed in British Columbia, joining a husband she had never met, and did what she had to do to survive. She was not a terribly warm or kind person, but she built a family in tandem with Kumanosuke Okano, even as their survival remained an open question for her entire life. In the process, she fought and struggled and scrapped, but she also raised an extraordinary daughter, Kimiko, who married an extraordinary man, Katsuyori Murakami. Together, they raised a tight-knit family in which exercising a thoughtful, considerate voice—especially, Mary has noted, a woman's voice—was among the highest values. And from that family came five extraordinary siblings, all of whom have profoundly impacted the lives of those around them. In this respect, too, Mary is both unusual—in the public profile and the sweep of her activism—and representative—in her generosity, her conviction, and her desire to help even the people who oppose her by listening to them, weighing their position, and then exercising that thoughtful voice. If we learn nothing else from the history of Mary Kitagawa and her family, then, let it be that political work begins and is repeatedly reimagined in conversation.

Notes

Introduction

1. On Green's statement and the larger anti-Japanese context in which it circulated, see Patricia E. Roy, *The Triumph of Citizenship: The Japanese and Chinese in Canada, 1941–1967* (Vancouver: University of British Columbia Press, 2007), ch. 3, esp. 142–144.

2. I draw here on the model presented by Michael Omi and Howard Winant in *Racial Formation in the United States: the 1960s to the 1980s*, 3rd ed. (New York: Routledge, 2015). Of particular importance is their recognition that, while racial formation operates at every scale, it is "always and necessarily a social and historical process" (110). Accordingly, racialization is determined by historical factors, but it continually reconstitutes and reshapes itself through interactions among individuals, groups, and institutions. Hence the importance of attending to non-Nikkei groups at key points in this book. To do otherwise would be to omit crucial factors governing both how Mary's mind met the world and how the world, or at least one part of it, met that mind. See also Natalia Molina, Daniel Martinez HoSang, and Ramón Guttiérrez, eds., *Relational Formations of Race: Theory, Method, and Practice* (Berkeley: University of California Press, 2019), especially Daniel Martinez HoSang and Natalia Molina, "Introduction: Toward a Relational Consciousness of Race" (1–18), and George Lipsitz, George J. Sánchez, and Kelly Lytle Hernández, with Daniel Martinez HoSang and Natalia Molina, "Race as a Relational Theory: A Roundtable Discussion" (22–42).

3. This term was current in Mary's family for as long as she can recall. Unlike some Nikkei, her parents never resorted to pejorative terms. Karen M. Inouye, interview with Mary Kitagawa, December 2, 2023.

Regarding Nikkei responses to, and engagement with, North American discourses of race, see Andrea Geiger, *Subverting Exclusion: Transpacific Encounters with Race, Caste, and Borders, 1885–1928* (New Haven, CT: Yale University Press, 2011), ch, 1, esp. 78–83; Andrea Geiger-Adams, "Reframing Race and Place: Locating Japanese Immigrants in Relation to Indigenous Peoples in the North American West, 1880–1940," *Southern California Quarterly* 96:3 (2014): 253–270; Janice Matsumura, "More or Less Intelligent: Nikkei IQ and Racial/Ethnic Hierarchies in British Columbia and Imperial Japan," *BC Studies* 192 (Winter 2016–2017): 51–69.

4. See in particular Stephanie Bangarth, *Voices Raised in Protest: Defending North American Citizens of Japanese Ancestry, 1942–1949* (Vancouver: University of British Columbia Press, 2008).

5. E. P. Thompson, *Witness against the Beast: William Blake and the Moral Law* (New York: New Press, 1993), xix.

6. On the importance of memory in Nikkei activism, see Alice Yang Murray, *Historical Memories of the Japanese American Internment and the Struggle for Redress* (Stanford, CA: Stanford University Press, 2007); Todd Stewart and Karen J. Leong, with John Tateishi and Natasha Egan, *Placing Memory: A Photographic Exploration of Japanese American Internment* (Norman: University of Oklahoma Press, 2008); Karen M. Inouye, *The Long Afterlife of Nikkei Wartime Incarceration* (Stanford, CA: Stanford University Press, 2016).

7. See, for instance, the first-person accounts published in *Nikkei Images* by, among others, Michiko Midge Ayukawa ("Lemon Creek Memories," 17:1 (2012): 11–16), Tamiko Haraga ("My Experiences during the Second World War," 7:3 (2002): 18–19), and Frances Kuniko Nakagawa ("Reminiscences of My Stay in the Livestock Building," 18:2 (2013): 4–5), as well as indispensable book-length work by the survivors of wartime injustice, including William T. Hashizume, *Japanese Community in Mission: A Brief History, 1904–1942* (Scarborough ON: self-published, 2002), and Yon Shimizu, *The Exiles: An Archival History of the World War II Japanese Road Camps in British Columbia and Ontario* (Wallaceburg, ON: self-published, 1993).

8. On this point, I follow the argument laid out with respect to Japanese Americans in Tetsuden Kashima, "Japanese American Internees Return, 1945 to 1955: Readjustment and Social Amnesia," *Phylon* 41:2 (1980): 107–115.

9. Rose Murakami, *Ganbaru: The Murakami Family of Salt Spring Island* (Ganges, BC: Japanese Garden Society of Salt Spring Island, 2005), 31–37, provides a short summary of what the family has had to withstand.

10. Murakami, *Ganbaru*, 37.

11. Diploma recipients carried photographs of their deceased classmates as part of the ceremony.

12. Concerning the legislative and juridical aspects of wartime injustice in Canada, see Ken Adachi, *The Enemy That Never Was: A History of the Japanese Canadians* (Toronto: McClelland and Stewart, 1976); Ann Gomer Sunahara, *The Politics of Racism: The Uprooting of Japanese Canadians during the Second World War*, rev. ed. (Burnaby, BC: Nikkei National Museum, 2020); and Mona Oikawa, "'Driven to Scatter Far and Wide': The Forced Resettlement of Japanese Canadians to Southern Ontario, 1944–1949," (MA thesis, University of Toronto, 1986). See also Jordan Stanger-Ross, ed., *Landscapes of Injustice: A New Perspective on the Internment and Dispossession of Japanese Canadians* (Montréal–Kingston: McGill–Queen's University Press, 2020); and, for the broader North American context, Greg Robinson, *A Tragedy of Democracy: Japanese Confinement in North America* (New York: Columbia University Press, 2009). See also Mona Oikawa, *Cartographies of Violence: Japanese Canadian Women, Memory, and the Subjects of the Internment* (Toronto: University of Toronto Press, 2012); Jordan Stanger-Ross and Pamela Sugiman, eds., *Witness to Loss: Race, Culpability, and Memory in the Dispossession of Japanese Canadians* (Montréal–Kingston: McGill-Queen's University Press, 2017). All include important bibliography.

13. Roger Daniels, "Words Do Matter: A Note in Inappropriate Terminology and the Incarceration of Japanese Americans," in Louis Fiset and Gail M. Nomura, eds., *Nikkei in the Pacific Northwest: Japanese Americans and Japanese Canadians in the Twentieth Century* (Seattle: University of Washington Press, 2005), 190–214; Roy Miki, *Redress: Inside the Japanese Canadian Call for Justice* (Vancouver: Raincoast Books, 2004), esp. 50–55.

Chapter 1

1. Brian Smallshaw, "The Murakami Women of Saltspring Island," *BC Studies* 204 (Winter 2019–2020), 187, also notes this similarity.

2. Tomoko Makabe, *Picture Brides: Japanese Women in Canada* (North York: Multicultural History Society of Ontario, 1995); Michiko Midge Ayukawa, *Hiroshima Immigrants in Canada, 1891–1941* (Vancouver: University of British Columbia Press, 2008).

3. Kornel Chang, *Pacific Connections: The Making of the U.S.-Canadian Borderlands* (Berkeley: University of California Press, 2012), esp. chs. 3 and 5.

4. Geiger, *Subverting Exclusion*, 100–104.

5. While the amendment included a small procedural refinement regarding how violators would be struck from the voters' rolls, its primary function was to replace a key paragraph in the 1875 act with an expanded definition of those not eligible to vote: "No Chinaman, Japanese, or Indian shall have his name placed on the Register of Voters for any Electoral District, or be entitled to vote at any election of a Member to serve in the Legislative Assembly of this Province. Any Collector of any Electoral

District, or Polling Division thereof, who shall insert the name of any Chinaman, Japanese, or Indian in any such Register, shall, upon conviction thereof before any Justice of the Peace, be liable to be punished by a fine not exceeding fifty dollars, or to be imprisoned for any period not exceeding one month." "An Act to Amend the Provincial Voters Act," February 21, 1895 (C.A. 1888, ca. 38), https://www.bclaws.gov.bc.ca/civix/document/id/hstats/hstats/1789119422.

For more on the history of racist legislative efforts at the time, see James W. St. G. Walker, *"Race," Rights and the Law in the Supreme Court of Canada: Historical Case Studies* (Waterloo: Wilfred Laurier University Press, 1997); Renisa Mawani, *Colonial Proximities: Crossracial Encounters and Juridical Truths in British Columbia, 1871–1921* (Vancouver: University of British Columbia Press, 2009).

6. Adachi, *The Enemy That Never Was*, 46–50, 57–61, and 63.

7. For more on this, see Peter Ward, *White Canada Forever: Popular Attiudes and Public Policy toward Orientals in British Columbia*, 3rd ed. (Montréal-Kingston: McGill University Press, 2014); Roy, *The Triumph of Citizenship*.

8. For a summary of these and related efforts, along with bibliography, see Masumi Izumi, "The Japanese Canadian Movement: Migration and Activism before and after World War II," *Amerasia Journal* 33:2 (2007), esp. 49–57.

9. For another approach to the terminology of Japanese ancestry and generations, cf. Andrea Geiger, "Reframing *Nikkei* Histories: Complicating Existing Narratives," *BC Studies* 192 (Winter 2016–2017), 13, n. 1.

10. This account is based on Andrea Geiger-Adams, "Writing Racial Barriers into Law: Upholding B.C.'s Denial of the Vote to Its Japanese Canadian Citizens, Homma v. Cunningham, 1902," in Fiset and Nomura, eds., *Nikkei in the Pacific Northwest*, 20–43.

11. The chief judge of the Vancouver County Court found in Homma's favor, noting that provincial law created two classes of citizen. The decision was affirmed at the level of the BC Supreme Court but overturned at the level of the Privy Council in London, which in 1902 disingenuously cited American legal precedent in support of the province's defense. See Geiger-Adams, "Writing Racial Barriers into Law," 29–31.

12. Audrey Lynne Kobayashi, "Emigration from Kaideima, Japan, 1885–1950: An Analysis of Community and Landscape Change" (PhD dissertation, University of California, Los Angeles, 1983). Cf. the emigration of Nikkei from North America in the 1930s discussed by Andrea Geiger, *Converging Empires: Citizens and Subjects in the North Pacific Borderlands, 1867–1945* (Chapel Hill: University of North Carolina Press, 2022), 174–177.

13. Andrea Geiger, *Subverting Exclusion*, 72–78, notes that for some, North America also represented freedom from the social and cultural constraints at which they chafed in Japan, though at a cost.

14. Rumiko Kanesaka and Brian Smallshaw, eds., *Island Forest Embers: The Japanese Canadian Charcoal Kilns of the Southern Gulf Islands* (Ganges, BC: Japanese Garden Society of Salt Spring Island, 2018); Mitsuo Yesaki, *Sutebusuton: A Japanese Village on the British Columbia Coast* (Vancouver: Peninsula Publishing, 2003), esp. 14, 19–25.

15. Mitsuo Yesaki, Harold Steves, and Kathy Steves, *Steveston Cannery Row: An Illustrated History*, rev. ed. (Vancouver: Peninsula Publishing, 2005), esp. 22–23; Yesaki, *Sutebusuton*, 20–21; Daphne Marlatt, ed., *Steveston Recollected: A Japanese-Canadian History* (Vancouver: Provincial Archives of British Columbia, 1975), 21. Yesaki, *Sutebusuton*, 6, notes that different boat-building designs and skills intermingled in the third quarter of the nineteenth century.

16. See in particular the account provided by Paul M. Nagano in Goichi Gordon Nakayama, *Issei: Stories of Japanese Canadian Pioneers* (Toronto: NC Press, 1984).

17. Ayukawa, *Hiroshima Immigrants in Canada*, esp. 18–19.

18. See, for instance, Audrey Kobayashi, "Camp Road," in Daniel J. Keyes and Luis L.M. Aguiar, eds., *White Space: Race, Privilege, and Cultural Economies of the Okanagan Valley* (Vancouver: University of British Columbia Press, 2021), 118.

19. Yesaki, *Sutebusuton*, 10. The two Nikkei-owned businesses were the Fisherman's Hospital and a boat works run by George Isomura. The third, a Chinese-owned business, was the Hong Wo General Store, which had opened in 1905. Yesaki suggests this register underestimated the number of businesses by a significant margin. By 1911, twenty-three white-owned businesses were recorded alongside thirteen Nikkei-owned and nine Chinese-owned enterprises (ibid., 43), though again this number almost certainly errs on the low side.

20. Okano, who had previously been married as well, had children by his first wife. Karen M. Inouye, correspondence with Mary Kitagawa, January 26–27, 2024.

21. Kobayashi, "Emigration," 117. The interested reader should consult Kobayashi's larger discussion of the matter (ibid., 117–124). Kinship networks readily adapted to circumstances such as Riyo Okano's. As Kobayashi (120) has noted, "In the case of a divorce, the woman was expected to dissociate herself completely from the [family unit into which she had married], usually by returning to her original family, who would then seek another affinal position for her."

22. Yesaki, Steves, and Steves, *Steveston Cannery Row*, 13–15, 28, 45, 50–51; Yesaki, *Sutebusuton*, 33–34, 62–63, and 66–70; William T. Hashizume, *Japanese Community in Mission*, esp. 18–20. On the connection with educational values in Japan, see Yesaki, *Sutebusuton*, esp. 9.

23. Ayukawa, *Hiroshima Immigrants in Canada*, 6.

24. Ibid., 7.

25. Ibid., 8.
26. Ibid., 9.
27. Ibid., 8.
28. This figure was exceeded only by Okinawa, which saw nearly 10 percent of its people leave, and Kumamoto, about 5 percent. The average for Japan as a whole was closer to 1 percent. Ayukawa, *Hiroshima Immigrants in Canada*, 9–10.
29. Ibid., 10–11.
30. Yesaki, *Sutebusuton*, 17.
31. For more on this, see Chris Friday, *Organizing Asian American Labor: The Pacific Coast Canned-Salmon Industry, 1870–1942* (Philadelphia: Temple University Press, 1994), ch. 5, esp. 116–124, regarding the impact of this success on gender relations in Steveston proper.
32. Rose Murakami, *Ganbaru*, 1, suggests that Kimiko was the first Japanese Canadian baby born in Steveston.
33. The moral fiber of the community seems to have been almost as pressing a concern. See, for instance, Stan Fukawa, "Rescuing Wayward Men and Raising the Status of the Japanese in Canada: Early Goals for a Chapel/Hospital," *Nikkei Images* 17:2 (2012): 14–16; cf. Yesaki, *Sebutusuton*, 31, who also says that the mission was converted into a hospital only after a typhus outbreak. For a point of comparison, see Masako Fukawa, "Lifting the Veil on Nanaimo's Nikkei Community: From Settlement to Return," *BC Studies* 204 (Winter 2019–2020), 151–161.
34. Yesaki, Steves, and Steves, *Steveston Cannery Row*, 43–46; Marlatt, ed., *Steveston Recollected*, 29–30 and 35–38. See also Helen Elizabeth Ruth Vandenberg, "Race, Hospital Development, and the Power of Community: Chinese and Japanese Hospitals in British Columbia, 1880–1920" (PhD dissertation, University of British Columbia, 2015).
35. Marlatt, ed., *Steveston Recollected*, 11. Murakami married in 1906.
36. Ibid., 24.
37. Yesaki, *Sutebusuton*, 11, cites a 1901 census, according to which Steveston's Japantown had a population of 396 men, 46 women (all but one married), and 23 children under the age of sixteen. On racialized discourses of gender and sexual morality with respect to Nikkei women in North America, see Geiger, *Subverting Exclusion*, 82–90.
38. See Friday, *Organizing Asian American Labor*, esp. 116–124.
39. See, for instance, Patricia E. Roy, *A White Man's Province: White Politicians and Chinese and Japanese Immigrants, 1858–1914* (Vancouver: University of British Columbia Press, 1989), 207–13; Geiger, *Subverting Exclusion*, 119–123.
40. Marlatt, ed., *Steveston Recollected*, 19.
41. Ibid., 19. See also Ayukawa, *Hiroshima Immigrants in Canada*, 14.

42. Karen M. Inouye, correspondence with Mary Kitagawa, January 26–27, 2024.

43. Inouye, correspondence with Mary Kitagawa, May 5, 2022.

44. This paragraph builds on Rebecca Salas, interview with Mary Kitagawa, June 17, 2017, and Inouye, correspondence with Mary Kitagawa, May 5, 2022.

45. Cf. the common practice of hiring help discussed in Yesaki, *Sutebusuton*, 14–16.

46. On housing, see the reminiscences in Marlatt, ed., *Steveston Recollected*, 12–18.

47. Inouye, correspondence with Mary Kitagawa, May 5, 2022. Cf. Geiger, *Converging Empires*, 76–79, regarding the derogatory attitude expressed by some Nikkei concerning First Nations people, whom they associated with the Ainu people of Japan.

48. Mary has suggested that the family was already on Salt Spring Island before the 1907 Vancouver race riots (Inouye, correspondence with Mary Kitagawa, May 5, 2022). Cf. Murakami, *Ganbaru*, 9, who gives a date of 1909. Sayoko's 1908 birth took place in Ganges rather than Steveston, which suggests the family was already on the island by that time. See Brian Smallshaw, *As If They Were the Enemy: The Dispossession of Japanese Canadians on Saltspring Island* (Victoria: University of Victoria Press, 2020), 49.

49. For those in a position to make such a move, though, the rewards could be considerable, as several Nikkei immigrants argued at the time. See, for instance, Michiko Midge Ayukawa, "Yasutaro Yamaga: Fraser Valley Berry Farmer, Community Leader, and Strategist," in Fiset and Nomura, eds., *Nikkei in the Pacific Northwest*, 71–94.

50. Inouye, correspondence with Mary Kitagawa, May 5, 2022.

51. See Howard Hiroshi Sugimoto, *Japanese Immigration, the Vancouver Riots, and Canadian Diplomacy* (New York: Arno Press, 1978).

52. For the range of non-Nikkei views regarding the riots as well as the rights of immigrants in Canada, see Greg Robinson, "Quebec Newspaper Reactions to the 1907 Vancouver Riots: Humanitarianism, Nationalism, and Internationalism," *BC Studies* 192 (Winter 2016–17): 25–49.

53. On the discrepancy between myths of the gentleman farmer and life on the ground, see Ruth W. Sandwell, *Contesting Rural Space: Land Policy and Practices of Resetttlement on Saltspring Island, 1859–1891* (Montréal–Kingston: McGill University Press, 2005), esp. ch. 1.

54. On the general disregard of BC politicians and corporations for Indigenous land rights, see Geiger, *Converging Empires*, ch. 2, esp. 58–62.

55. Sandwell, *Contesting Rural Space*, 29. For more on preemption, see Robert

E. Cail, *Land, Man and the Law: The Disposal of Crown Lands in British Columbia, 1871–1913* (Vancouver: University of British Columbia Press, 1974).

56. Oikawa, *Cartographies of Violence*, 12–13.

57. Sandwell, *Contesting Rural Space*, esp. 61–84 and 106–113.

58. Inouye, correspondence with Mary Kitagawa, May 5, 2022.

59. The murders of several Black islanders in the later nineteenth century demonstrate in tragic microcosm the complexities of Gulf Island racialization and its fallout. Sandwell, *Contesting Rural Space*, 159–192. On Black settlers of the Gulf Islands, see Charles B. Irby, "The Black Settlers on Salt Spring Island in the Nineteenth Century," *Phylon* 35:4 (1974): 368–74; Crawford Kilian, *Go Do Some Great Thing: The Black Pioneers of British Columbia*, 3rd ed. (Madeira Park, BC: Harbour Publishing, 2020), esp. 127–151.

60. On preemptor marriages to First Nations women, for instance, see Sandwell, *Contesting Rural Space*, esp. 179–180, 193–194, and 210–213.

61. Marie Elliott, *Mayne Island & the Outer Gulf Islands: A History* (Mayne Island, BC: Gulf Islands Press, 1984), esp. 39–45, 55–57, and 65–73; Charles Kahn, *Saltspring: The Story of an Island* (Vancouver: Harbour Publishing, 1998), 207–208 and ch. 14. See also Smallshaw, "The Murakami Women of Saltspring Island," 199.

62. Inouye, correspondence with Mary Kitagawa, May 5, 2022.

63. Ibid. For biographical information concerning the Tasaka family, see Ted Ohashi and Yvonne Wakabayashi, *Tasaka* (North Vancouver: self-published, 2005).

64. Cited in Kanesaka and Smallshaw, eds., *Island Forest Embers*.

65. Inouye, correspondence with Mary Kitagawa, May 5, 2022. The kiln in question was located just west of the town of Ganges and a little over a half mile (roughly one kilometer) from where the Okanos eventually bought land.

66. Smallshaw, *As If They Were the Enemy*, 67. Cf. Murakami, *Ganbaru*, 1.

67. See Kanesaka and Smallshaw, eds., *Island Forest Embers*.

68. Inouye, correspondence with Mary Kitagawa, May 5, 2022.

69. Smallshaw, *As If They Were the Enemy*, 44–45; Kahn, *Saltspring*, 254.

70. Inouye, correspondence with Mary Kitagawa, May 5, 2022.

71. Murakami, *Ganbaru*, 5.

72. Sandwell, *Contesting Rural Space*, 52–60, 125–128, and 152–157.

73. John Endo Greenaway, "Kimiko Murakami: A Portrait of Strength," *The Bulletin* (December 2005), 3. Mary recalls only salmon fishing, which the family gave up in 1920 (Inouye, correspondence with Mary Kitagawa, May 5, 2022).

74. Sandwell, *Contesting Rural Space*, esp. 137–138 and 150–152.

75. Inouye, correspondence with Mary Kitagawa, May 5, 2022.

76. Greenaway, "Kimiko Murakami," 3.

77. Ibid.

78. Marlatt, ed., *Steveston Recollected*, esp. 53–56; Yaseki, Steves, and Steves, *Steveston Cannery Row*, esp. 14–15, 52, 61–62, and 66; Yesaki, *Sutebusuton*, 13–16 and 39–42; Ward, *White Canada Forever*, 119–123.

79. Andrea Geiger, "Disentangling Law and History: Nikkei Challenges to Race-Based Exclusion from British Columbia's Coastal Fisheries, 1920–2007," *Southern California Quarterly* 100:3 (2018): 263–296. Regarding the efforts of Yasutaro Yamaga, a Fraser Valley community leader, to help his fellow farmers avoid stirring up resentment among their white competitors, see Ayukawa, "Yasutaro Yamaga."

80. Inouye, correspondence with Mary Kitagawa, May 5, 2022.

81. Greenaway, "Kimiko Murakami," 3. Cf. Inouye, correspondence with Mary Kitagawa, May 5, 2022.

82. Inouye, correspondence with Mary Kitagawa, May 5, 2022.

83. Ibid.

84. Dorothy G. Bell, "Are Canadian Salmon Doomed?," *Maclean's*, January 21, 1923.

85. Yesaki, *Sutebusuton*, 13–14, 28, and 46.

86. On labor organization among Nikkei fishers, see Masako Fukawa with Stan Fukawa and the Nikkei Fishermen's History Book Committee, *Spirit of the Nikkei Fleet: BC's Japanese Canadian Fishermen* (Madeira Park, BC: Harbour Publishing, 2009). Regarding conflict among the unions and the cannery owners, see Timothy Mark Stielow, "No Quarter Required: Japanese Experiences and Media Distortions in the Steveston Fishers' Strike of 1900" (MA thesis, Simon Fraser University, 2012). Cf. alliances that formed among different groups and unions in the U.S., as documented in Friday, *Organizing Asian American Labor*, esp. chs. 7 and 8.

87. Yesaki, Steves, and Steves, *Steveston Cannery Row*, 61–64; Ward, *White Canada Forever*, 120–121.

88. Ward, *White Canada Forever*, 119.

89. Ibid., 120.

90. Geiger, *Converging Empires*, ch. 3.

91. See, for instance, Marlatt, ed., *Steveston Recollected*, 53–56; Yesaki, *Sutebusuton*, 34–36, 55–56, and 60–82.

92. Ward, *White Canada Forever*, 122.

93. Murakami, *Ganbaru*, 9.

94. See, for instance, L. J. P. van Vliet, A. J. Green, and E. A. Kenney, *Soils of the Gulf Islands of British Columbia*, vol. 1: *Soils of Saltspring Island* (Victoria: Ministry of the Environment, 1987).

95. Smallshaw, *As If They Were the Enemy*, 188.

96. Kahn, *Saltspring*, 253.

97. This paragraph builds on Inouye, correspondence with Mary Kitagawa, May 5, 2022.

98. In this instance, the critical relationship was not only within a given family, but also between two families. On this, see Kobayashi, "Emigration," 124–128.

99. According to Mary, Kimiko likely did not travel to Japan with thoughts of marriage. Inouye, correspondence with Mary Kitagawa, May 5, 2022.

100. Howard Hiroshi Sugimoto, *Japanese Immigration, the Vancouver Riots, and Canadian Diplomacy* (New York: Arno Press, 1978), 263. Hashizume, *Japanese Community in Mission*, 101–105, provides examples of the almost psychotic amount of documentation required.

101. Karen M. Inouye, correspondence with Mary Kitagawa, January 26–27, 2024.

102. Contracts could be terminated if the sponsor failed or was otherwise unable to meet these terms. As Ayukawa has noted (e.g., *Hiroshima Immigrants in Canada*, 76), many yobiyose eventually became *yoshi*, or men adopted as husbands by their sponsoring families, but that most commonly happened over time. Also, these men frequently took on the sponsoring family's name. Katsuyori did not.

103. Murakami, *Ganbaru*, 9.

104. Inouye, correspondence with Mary Kitagawa, January 26–27, 2024.

105. Calculated from the map and statistics provided by Smallshaw, *As If They Were the Enemy*, 50–52.

106. Inouye, interview with Mary Kitagawa, October 9, 2020.

107. Murakami, *Ganbaru*, 11.

108. Inouye, interview with Mary Kitagawa, October 9, 2020.

109. Ibid.

110. Inouye, interview with Mary Kitagawa, September 1, 2022.

111. Kahn, *Saltspring*, 253; Greenaway, "Kimiko Murakami," 4.

112. Inouye, interview with Mary Kitagawa, October 9, 2020.

113. Sandwell, *Contesting Rural Space*, 137.

114. Inouye, correspondence with Mary Kitagawa, May 5, 2022

115. Ibid.

116. Inouye, interview with Mary Kitagawa, October 9, 2020.

117. Inouye, correspondence with Mary Kitagawa, May 5, 2022. For more on Black families on Salt Spring Island, see Irby, "Black Settlers on Salt Spring Island"; Kilian, *Go Do Some Great Thing*.

118. Inouye, correspondence with Mary Kitagawa, May 5, 2022.

Chapter 2

1. Order-in-Council P.C. 365 (January 27, 1942) authorized the expulsion of all Japanese nationals aged 18–45. Forty-three years old, Katsuyori fell just inside the span. For the relationship between specific acts of physical violence and the larger

project of state-sponsored anti-Nikkei aggression, see Kirsten Emiko McAllister, *Terrain of Memory: A Japanese Canadian Memorial Project* (Vancouver: University of British Columbia Press, 2010), esp. 12–15.

2. This account builds on Rebecca Salas, interview with Mary Kitagawa, June 17, 2017.

3. Inouye, interview with Mary Kitagawa, June 28, 2022.

4. Salas, interview with Mary Kitagawa, June 17, 2017.

5. On the politics of such a claim, see Oikawa, *Cartographies of Violence*, esp. ch. 1.

6. McAllister, *Terrain of Memory*, 12–13.

7. See, for instance, Ken Adachi, *The Enemy That Never Was: A History of the Japanese Canadians* (Toronto: McClelland and Stewart, 1976), ch. 5.

8. Adachi, *The Enemy That Never Was*, 189–192.

9. On the use of legislation as a rhetorical gesture to fan xenophobic sentiment, see Erika Lee, *At America's Gates: Chinese Immigration during the Exclusion Era, 1882–1943* (Chapel Hill: University of North Carolina Press, 2003), esp. 19–79.

10. On this point, it is worth considering the view many Canadians had of the situation after the bombing of Pearl Harbor: "In 1942, virtually all Canadians saw [expulsion from western BC] as a necessary evil, justifiable in terms of national security, a defense against the possibility of anti-Japanese mob violence, and a way of solving the 'Japanese problem' by helping them to disperse and assimilate." Ross Lambertson, *Repression and Resistance: Canadian Human Rights Activists, 1930–1960* (Toronto: University of Toronto Press, 2005), 102.

11. Regarding the seizure of fishing vessels, see Sunahara, *The Politics of Racism*, 68–69. For historical background on this effort, see Geiger, *Converging Empires*, esp. 162–182. Regarding the impact of the seizure, see Marlatt, ed., *Steveston Recollected*, 58–59. On the committee that oversaw the seizure, see Stanger-Ross and Sugiman, eds., *Witness to Loss*.

12. "Keep Cool and Keep Calm," *The New Canadian* 5:6 (January 14, 1942): 1.

13. "Many Questions Asked: Worried People Await Details of New Orders," *The New Canadian* 5:7 (January 16, 1942): 1.

14. Forrest La Violette, *The Canadian Japanese and World War II: A Sociological and Psychological Account* (Toronto: University of Toronto Press, 1948), esp. 156–158. The classic study remains Tamotsu Shibutani, *Improvised News: A Sociological Study of Rumor* (Indianapolis: Bobbs-Merrill, 1966), which includes extensive discussion of how rumor became a perversely binding social medium for the Japanese Americans during their wartime incarceration.

15. See, for instance, "Worried People Await Details of New Orders" and "Reasonable Enforcement of New Regulations Expected," *The New Canadian* 5:8 (January 19, 1942): 1.

16. "Fabrication," *The New Canadian* 5:9 (January 21, 1942): 1. Relying on government assurances that there would be a distinction between Japanese nationals and Nikkei possessing Canadian citizenship, the article opened by stating: "No confirmation from any reliable source could be found today for an Ottawa dispatch to a Vancouver newspaper, declaring that all British Columbia's Japanese population would be moved from the coast. It is felt that the story is only a 'kite in the wind,' written to support the policy of the paper."

17. "Storms Brewing in the U.S.," *The New Canadian* 5:13 (January 30, 1942): 1; "April 1st Deadline for Removal of Nationals," *The New Canadian* 5:17 (February 9, 1942): 1, which carried the subheading "18–45 Group Affected—RCMP in Charge—Work Camp West of Jasper Likely"; and "Alien Removal by Labor Dept. Soon," *The New Canadian* 5:20 (February 16, 1942): 1, which also noted that Nikkei naturalized before 1932 would be exempt from expulsion.

18. "Move All Japanese Ultimate Govt. Plan," *The New Canadian* 5:24 (A) (February 26, 1942): 1. The article was brief, the topic having been discussed in the previous day's regular issue of the paper: "Ottawa May Announce Total Removal Policy," *The New Canadian* 5:24 (February 25, 1942): 1.

19. Tomoko Makabe has provided an account of intergenerational dynamics. See Makabe, "Canadian Evacuation and Nisei Identity," *Phylon* 41:2 (1980): 116–125; and Makabe, *The Canadian Sansei* (Toronto: University of Toronto Press, 1998). However, cf. a review of the latter written by Michiko Midge Ayukawa in *BC Studies* 121 (Spring 1999): 138–139; and Ayukawa, *Hiroshima Immigrants in Canada*, ch. 7.

20. Salas, interview with Mary Kitagawa, June 17, 2017.

21. Murakami, *Ganbaru*, 16.

22. Salas, interview with Mary Kitagawa, June 17, 2017.

23. Ibid.

24. Decades later, Kimiko recounted how, when she would go to the grocery store, people who had declared themselves her friends a few months earlier could now be heard talking in a theatrical whisper about "those Japs." Murakami, *Ganbaru*, 15–16.

25. Salas, interview with Mary Kitagawa, June 17, 2017.

26. Regarding the Anglican Church's policies, as well as the opinions of some of its members, see Patricia Roy, "An Ambiguous Relationship: Anglicans and the Japanese in British Columbia, 1902–1949," *BC Studies* 192 (Winter 2016–2017): 105–124.

27. "All's Well at Rainbow Says Yosie," *The New Canadian* 5:30 (March 14, 1942): 2.

28. Inouye, interview with Mary Kitagawa, September 2, 2020.

29. Murakami, *Ganbaru*, 17.

30. Salas, interview with Mary Kitagawa, June 17, 2017.
31. Ibid.
32. Inouye, interview with Mary Kitagawa, September 2, 2020.
33. Salas, interview with Mary Kitagawa, June 17, 2017.
34. Inouye, interview with Mary Kitagawa, September 2, 2020.
35. For more on the governmental project of dispossession, see Eric M. Adams, Jordan Stanger-Ross, and the Landscapes of Injustice Research Collective, "Promises of Law: The Unlawful Dispossession of Japanese Canadians," *Osgoode Hall Law Journal* 54:3 (2017): 687–739.
36. Murakami, *Ganbaru*, 26.
37. Salas, interview with Mary Kitagawa, June 17, 2017.
38. Ibid.
39. Ibid.
40. Mary even recalls family heirlooms showing up in a Salt Spring Island antiques shop after the war. Salas, interview with Mary Kitagawa, June 17, 2017.
41. Murakami, *Ganbaru*, 20.
42. Smallshaw, *As If They Were the Enemy*, 57–62. Similar problems arose with respect to Nikkei-owned farms elsewhere in the province (ibid., 67–68).
43. See David Breen and Kenneth Coates, *Vancouver's Fair: An Administrative and Political History of the Pacific National Exhibition* (Vancouver: University of British Columbia Press, 1982).
44. It was renamed the Pacific National Exhibition in 1946.
45. Breen and Coates, *Vancouver's Fair*, 95–96.
46. Frank Moritsugu, ed., *Teaching in Canadian Exile: A History of the Schools for Japanese-Canadian Children in B.C. Detention Camps during the Second World War* (Toronto: The Ghost Town Teachers Historical Society, 2001), 22.
47. Breen and Coates, *Vancouver's Fair*, 94–97. The government initially negotiated for partial use of the site, but once the full extent of its plans became clear, the Vancouver Exhibition Association pushed back. Negotiation came to naught, and eventually the government issued an Order-in-Council (P.C. 1942-2972) on April 14, 1942, that empowered it to expropriate the site. The association managed to secure rental terms the following June (ibid., 98).
48. Muriel Kitagawa, *This Is My Own: Letters to Wes and Other Writings on Japanese Canadians, 1941–1948*, ed. Roy Miki (Vancouver: Talonbooks, 1985), 115.
49. Ibid.
50. Standing between the Women's and Industrial Buildings, one roller coaster fell inside the confinement area. Happyland stood just to the north of it, immediately adjacent to the race track, which abutted both Shoot the Chutes and the Giant Dipper roller coaster. The British Columbia Security Commission was aware of the situation, albeit mainly from the perspective of public relations. See,

for instance, British Columbia Security Commission, *Removal of Japanese from Protected Areas* (Vancouver: BCSC, 1942), 8–9: "The frustrated faces of tiny Japanese children denied association with their erstwhile Canadian companions, who splashed the happy mornings away in the pool, was only one instance which caused Vancouver columnists to decry a system which allowed such paradoxical interpretation of our Laws."

51. See, for instance, British Columbia Security Commission, *Removal of Japanese from Protected Areas*, 7.

52. Lisa Uyeda, interview with Harold Miwa October 6, 2011, as transcribed from the Sedai Project in the Nikkei National Museum's *1942: Japanese Canadian Internment at Hastings Park* commemorative website, http://hastingspark1942.ca/harold-miwa/.

53. Ibid.

54. Moritsugu, ed. *Teaching in Canadian Exile*, 24–25.

55. Ibid., 24.

56. Breen and Coates, *Vancouver's Fair*, 95–96.

57. Salas, interview with Mary Kitagawa, June 17, 2017.

58. Ibid.

59. Ibid.

60. Ibid.

61. Adachi, *The Enemy That Never Was*, 246–249; Sunahara, *The Politics of Racism*, 48–51.

62. Salas, interview with Mary Kitagawa, June 17, 2017.

63. Ibid.

64. Adachi, *The Enemy That Never Was*, 6. Cf. the BCSC's report, which made this boast: "It is interesting to note that, during the operation of Hastings Park as a clearing station, about 8,000 Japanese passed through its portals, and that 1,542,871 meals were served at an average raw food cost of $0.0933 per meal." British Columbia Security Commission, *Removal of Japanese from Protected Areas*, 8.

65. Sunahara, *The Politics of Racism*, 136–138.

66. Salas, interview with Mary Kitagawa, June 17, 2017.

67. Nakagawa, "Reminiscences of My Stay in the Livestock Building," 4.

68. Estimates of the prewar Greenwood population vary considerably. Linda Kawamoto Reid and Beth Carter, *Karizumai: A Guide to Japanese Canadian Internment Sites* (Burnaby, BC: Nikkei National Museum, 2016), 13, estimate there were 200 people in the town prior to the arrival of Nikkei; Oikawa, *Cartographies of Violence*, 132, estimates 150; Tamiko Haraga, "My Experiences during the Second World War," 18, recalls a scant 50.

69. Over 350 came from Steveston, largely because of a concerted effort by residents of the village to cohere even as they were forced from their homes. Kawa-

moto Reid and Carter, *Karizumai*, 13, which also lists 1,177 as the total eventual population.

The welcome was not consistently warm. For instance, Mitsuko Shirley Teramoto remembers being spat on by local children when school began. See Mitsuko Shirley Teramoto, "Memories . . . from the 1930s to the 1950s," *Nikkei Images* 17:3 (2012), 21.

70. Salas, interview with Mary Kitagawa, June 17, 2017.

71. Haraga, "My Experiences during the Second World War," 18.

72. Ibid.

73. Inouye, interview with Mary Kitagawa, June 20, 2022.

74. Ibid.

75. Shimizu, *The Exiles*, 6.

76. Tom I. Tagami, "Still Lingers On: The 60th Anniversary of the Internment, Part 2 'A Ganbare Family,'" *Nikkei Images* 7:3 (2002): 15–16.

77. Timothy M. Nakayama, "Anglican Missions to the Japanese in Canada," rev. ed. (2003), 13, http://anglicanhistory.org/academic/nakayama2003.pdf.

78. Shimizu, *The Exiles*, 19–20 and 110. At least one of Katsuyori's fellow workers at Yellowhead cited the poor treatment of the men as justification for his Japanese nationalist sentiments. In a letter condemned by government censors, he wrote: "Here in this camp every day we pay 75¢ for food that costs 50¢. There is no medical care for us when we need it. The treatment is very cruel, but I think they will have an awakening in a year or so. The news they publish here is only lies. There are no lies in the land of our Emperor, an empire of God and Buddha. Even an old man like myself considers the policy of this country on a level with the mind of a Japanese child" (ibid., 223).

79. David Iwaasa, "Canadian Japanese in Southern Alberta, 1905–1945," in Roger Daniels, ed., *Two Monographs on Japanese Canadians* (New York: Arno Press, 1978), 9.

80. Shimizu, *The Exiles*, 16.

81. See, for instance, Barry Potyondi, *In Palliser's Triangle: Living in the Grasslands, 1850–1930* (Saskatoon, SK: Purich Publishing, 1995).

82. Hugh A. Dempsey, *Treaty Research Report: Treaty Seven* (Ottawa: Department of Indian Affairs and Northern Development, 1987); Alan C. Holman, Daniel J. Bellegarde, and the Canada Indian Claims Commission, *Blood Tribe/Kainaiwa Big Claim Inquiry* (Ottawa: Indian Claims Commission, 2007), esp. 81–159; Blanca Tovías, *Colonialism on the Prairies: Blackfoot Settlement and Cultural Transformation, 1870–1920* (Toronto: Sussex Academic Press, 2011); Treaty 7 Tribal Council with Walter Hildebrandt, Sarah Carter, and Dorothy First Rider, *The True Spirit and Original Intent of Treaty 7* (Montreal–Kingston: McGill-Queen's University Press, 1996). See also David H. Breen, *The Canadian Prairie West and*

the Ranching Frontier, 1874–1924 (Toronto: University of Toronto Press, 1983). On subsequent economic and political developments, see W. Keith Regular, *Neighbors and Networks: The Blood Tribe in the Southern Alberta Economy, 1884–1939* (Calgary: University of Calgary Press, 2009).

83. Salas, interview with Mary Kitagawa, June 17, 2017.

84. Yukinori Peter Takasaki, "Memoirs of Yukinori Peter Takasaki," trans. Mayumi Takasaki, *Nikkei Images* 7:1 (Spring 2002): 6.

85. "Weather Man Feuding Yet As Winter Hits New Low," *The New Canadian* 6:8 (January 23, 1943): 4.

86. Ibid.

87. Karen M. Inouye, interview with Mary and Tosh Kitagawa, September 16, 2022. Takasaki, "Memoirs," 6, described his situation this way: "With no time to rest during summer and winter, I am often amazed at how hard we worked. During my spare time while working in the beet fields, I would do carpentry work for a construction company in town, and after the beet crop was harvested, I would spend the winter working for the construction company."

88. See, for instance, Haraga, "My Experiences during the Second World War," 19.

89. Inouye, interview with Mary Kitagawa, July 12, 2022; Salas, interview with Mary Kitagawa, June 17, 2017. For a brief biography of Jensen, see the finding aid for his papers in the University of Calgary Archives, https://searcharchives.ucalgary.ca/index.php/lalovee-jensen-fonds.

90. *The Cardston News* 37:46 (August 25, 1936): 5: "Lalovee Jensen was a visitor at 'The News' office yesterday. Mr. Jensen is now engaged in the sheep business and has his flock on a Blood Reserve lease. Next spring he will go into farming as well and will have 400 acres of irrigated hay land as well as 1,100 acres under cultivation."

91. Iwaasa, "Canadian Japanese in Southern Alberta," 3.

92. Howard Palmer, "Patterns of Racism: Attitudes toward Chinese and Japanese in Alberta, 1920–1950," *Histoire sociale/Social History* 13:25 (1980): 145, has suggested that the relatively small number of Asian immigrants in the province contributed to the relative lack of activist bigotry.

93. Iwaasa, "Canadian Japanese in Southern Alberta," 1–3.

94. Ibid., 35.

95. Ibid., viii.

96. This analysis builds on Palmer, "Patterns of Racism."

97. Iwaasa, "Canadian Japanese in Southern Alberta," 15–16. See also David Iwaasa, "The Mormons and Their Japanese Neighbors," *Alberta History* 53 (Winter 2005): 7–22.

98. Iwaasa, "The Mormons and Their Japanese Neighbors," 11.

99. Iwaasa, "The Mormons and Their Japanese Neighbors," 12. Raymond Bud-

dhist Church, *A History of Forty Years of the Raymond Buddhist Church* (Raymond, AB: The Raymond Buddhist Church, 1970).

100. Cynthia Carghill, "Japanese in South of Province Making Good," *The Calgary Daily Herald*, December 5, 1931, 22, cols. 7–8. That favorable mention built on the same foundational stereotype as most anti-Japanese sentiment, though. The article was subtitled "Oriental Colony Established Near Raymond Flourishing; Innate Diligence Makes the Jap Excellent Tiller of Soil—Buddhist Temple Is Opened with Picturesque Ceremony—Young Priest Has Large Territory." According to Iwaasa, "Canadian Japanese in Southern Alberta," 42, the article was reprinted from another paper.

101. Iwaasa, "The Mormons and Their Japanese Neighbors," 7.

102. Quoted in Iwaasa, "The Mormons and Their Japanese Neighbors," 15.

103. Palmer, "Patterns of Racism," 145–146.

104. Iwaasa, "Canadian Japanese in Southern Alberta," 70.

105. Ibid., 47ff.

106. Quoted in ibid., 67.

107. Inouye, interview with Mary Kitagawa, June 28, 2022. Cf. Iwaasa, "The Mormons and Their Japanese Neighbors," 19.

108. Inouye, interview with Mary Kitagawa, June 28, 2022; Salas, interview with Mary Kitagawa, June 17, 2017. See also Murakami, *Ganbaru*, 23–24.

109. Salas, interview with Mary Kitagawa, June 17, 2017.

110. Inouye, interview with Mary Kitagawa, June 28, 2022. Mary is not sure, but she thinks Mrs. Jensen may have provided drinking water.

111. Salas, interview with Mary Kitagawa, June 17, 2017.

112. *Catalogue of the Brigham Young College for 1910–1911 with List of Students for 1909–1910* (Logan, UT: The Brigham Young University, 1910), 51.

113. Iwaasa, "The Mormons and Their Japanese Neighbors," 20: "Although a number of Mormons held the same prejudices prevalent among the non-Mormon population, for the majority, it is possible that their own experiences as a displaced people only a generation earlier contributed to their greater willingness to accept the Japanese into their communities."

114. Inouye, interview with Mary Kitagawa, June 28, 2022.

Chapter 3

1. Mary describes the teenaged Alice as having been "mature beyond her years." Inouye, interview with Mary Kitagawa, June 28, 2022.

2. Ibid.

3. Ibid.

4. Inouye, interview with Mary Kitagawa, July 12, 2022.

5. Murakami, *Ganbaru*, 25.

6. Ibid., 25

7. Sunahara, *The Politics of Racism*, 217.

8. "Weather Man Feuding Yet As Winter Hits New Low," *The New Canadian* 6:8 (January 23, 1943): 1. Conditions were even worse in POW camps where many Nikkei expelled from British Columbia found themselves. See, for instance, Carl Yokota, "Angler P.O.W. Camp 101," *Nikkei Images* 7:2 (Summer 2002): 10–12, esp. 11.

9. Sunahara, *The Politics of Racism*, 218.

10. Inouye, interview with Mary Kitagawa, June 28, 2022.

11. Ibid.

12. See William Jantzen, *Limits on Liberty: The Experience of Mennonite, Hutterite and Doukhobor Communities in Canada* (Toronto: University of Toronto Press, 1990); and Julie Rak, *Negotiated Memory: Doukhobor Autobiographical Discourse* (Vancouver: University of British Columbia Press, 2004), both of which provide extensive bibliographies.

13. Rak, *Negotiated Memory*, x.

14. Sunahara, *The Politics of Racism*, 83.

15. Ayukawa, "Lemon Creek Memories," 15.

16. Haraga, "My Experiences during the Second World War," 19.

17. Ayukawa, "Lemon Creek Memories," 15.

18. See, for instance, Office of the Ombudsman for the Province of British Columbia, *Righting the Wrong: The Confinement of the Sons of Freedom Doukhobor Children*, Public Report no. 38, April 1999, to the Legislative Assembly of British Columbia (Victoria, 1999).

19. John Brighton, *Medical Aspects of Evacuation Days, 1942–1946: New Denver–Slocan* (New Denver, BC: self-published, [ca. 1986]), 28–38.

20. Sunahara, *The Politics of Racism*, 84; Moritsugu, ed., *Teaching in Canadian Exile*, 24–25 and 28–38. See also Wakako Ishikawa, "Japanese-Canadian Education during the World War II Internment" (MA thesis, University of Toronto, 2003).

21. Moritsugu, ed. *Teaching in Canadian Exile*, 3.

22. Ibid., 64–67.

23. See, for instance, Gwen Suttie, "With the Nisei in New Denver," ed. Dorothy Blakey Smith, *BC Historical News* 5:2 (1972): 15–25. Regarding Fahrni, see Nancy Knickerbocker, *No Plaster Saint: The Life of Mildred Osterhout Fahrni, 1900–1992* (Vancouver: Talonbooks, 2001).

24. Knickerbocker, *No Plaster Saint*, 150.

25. Ibid., 147

26. Ibid., 148.

27. Ibid.

28. Salas, interview with Mary Kitagawa, June 17, 2017.

29. Ayukawa, "Lemon Creek Memories," 14–15.

30. Ibid., 16.

31. Roy Yasui, "Remembrances of New Denver, 1942–1946," *Nikkei Images* 11:3 (Autumn 2006), 21. Even here, though, the realities of inland exile were inescapable. According to Yasui, the white town handyman had refused to help with cremations for Nikkei, at least until he realized he could profit from the Sanitarium. Camp administrators recruited a cluster of Nisei to cremate the site's first body. The gruesome story of their subsequent misadventure put an end to these evenings for several Nikkei (ibid.). Cf. the account of the crematorium in Brighton, *Medical Aspects of Evacuation Days*, 25.

32. Salas, interview with Mary Kitagawa, June 17, 2017.

33. Inouye, interview with Mary Kitagawa, July 12, 2022; Inouye, interview with Mary Kitagawa, June 28, 2022.

34. Sunahara, *The Politics of Racism*, ch. 5; Smallshaw, *As If They Were the Enemy*, 75. See also Eric M. Adams, Jordan Stanger-Ross, and the Landscapes of Injustice Research Collective, "Promises of Law: The Unlawful Dispossession of Japanese Canadians," *Osgoode Hall Law Journal* 54:3 (2017): 687–739; Jordan Stanger-Ross, Will Archibald, and the Landscapes of Injustice Research Collective, "Unfaithful Custodian: Glenn McPherson and the Dispossession of Japanese Canadians in the 1940s," *Journal of American Ethnic History* 37:4 (2018): 40–72.

35. Jordan Stanger-Ross, "The Economic Impacts of Dispossession," in Stanger-Ross, ed., *Landscapes of Injustice*, 339–365.

36. "Another Blow to Faith," *The New Canadian* 6:10 (April 10, 1942): 2.

37. On those efforts, see Peter Takaji Nunoda, "A Community in Transition and Conflict: 1935–1951" (doctoral thesis, University of Manitoba, 1991), esp. chs. 5 and 6. Regarding interaction among organizations, both within and across national borders, see most recently Bangarth, *Voices Raised in Protest*.

38. Smallshaw, *As If They Were the Enemy*, 80–81.

39. These figures come from Royal Commission to Investigate Claims of Japanese Canadians for Property Losses, Case #625 *In the Matter of the Claim of Katsuyori Murakami: Proceedings at Hearing* (Lethbridge, AB, August 27, 1948), available via the Landscapes of Injustice digital archive, https://landscapesofinjustice.uvic.ca/archive/lac_rg33-69.html. See also Custodian of Enemy Property Case Files 1364 (Katsuyori Murakami) and 6507 (Kimiko Murakami), also available via the Landscapes of Injustice digital archive.

40. Asked why he had not kept an itemized account of his costs at the time, Katsuyori replied through a translator that his labor was an investment in farming, not an exercise in real estate speculation: "I never intended to sell, and I didn't think it would be necessary to keep all that." Royal Commission, *In the Claim of Katsuyori Murakami*, 30.

41. A survey conducted by the Canadian Institute of Public Opinion in De-

cember of 1943—after most properties had been sold—found that "those Canadians who said they favored allowing the Japanese to stay in Canada after the war were almost unanimously in favor of allowing those moved away from their homes to return to them." National Opinion Research Center, *Attitudes toward "The Japanese in Our Midst"* (Denver: University of Denver, 1946), 9.

42. Smallshaw, *As If They Were the Enemy*, 83–86. Regarding the ways Mouat profited from Iwasaki's property over the longer term, see ibid., 100–108.

43. Inouye, interview with Mary Kitagawa, February 10, 2023.

44. Ibid.

45. For more on the Nikkei physicians in and around New Denver, see Brighton, *Medical Aspects of Evacuation Days*, 8, 9, 33, 36, and 40.

46. Ibid. 12.

47. Yasui, "Remembrances of New Denver," 23.

48. Ibid., 24.

49. Ayukawa, "Lemon Creek Memories," 13.

50. On rumor, see Shibutani, *Improvised News: A Sociological Study of Rumor*. Cf. La Violette, *The Canadian Japanese and World War II: A Sociological and Psychological Account*, esp. 154–158, 163–164, and 170–171.

51. Survivor Testimony 3, Healing Fund for Japanese Canadians, recorded in 2018, https://www.anglicanhealingfundforjapanesecanadians.com/testimony-3.

52. Sunahara, *The Politics of Racism*, ch. 6 (esp. 104–106, 109, and 112) and ch. 7.

53. On objections to deportation, see in particular Bangarth, *Voices Raised in Protest*, esp. 60–66.

54. Prime Minister King sold the renewals as a way to ensure order and speed the "dispersal" of Nikkei throughout Canada. By April 1947, Nikkei were free to move anywhere in Canada, so long as their destination was not British Columbia. See Patricia E. Roy, "Lessons in Citizenship, 1945–1949: The Delayed Return of the Japanese to Canada's Pacific Coast," in Fiset and Nomura, eds., *Nikkei in the Pacific Northwest*, 261. The British Columbian racists who backed King pointed to "repatriation" requests as evidence of persistent loyalty to Japanese imperialism. Sunahara, *The Politics of Racism*, 133.

55. The government's actions were based on an electoral miscalculation rather than principle. Prime Minister King figured the renewal would enable his supporters to retain control of the riding where Ian Mackenzie had served. He was wrong; public objections to exclusion, sharpened both by a growing discourse of civil liberties and by lingering disgust at the government's failed deportation plan, eroded public support for the incumbents. The CCF won the riding after the final renewal passed. See Sunahara, *The Politics of Racism*, 134–135. For more on the political debates over Nikkei citizenship and the rights that attend it, see Bangarth, *Voices Raised in Protest*, esp. chs. 2 and 3; Roy, *The Triumph of Citizenship*, esp. chs. 3 and 5.

It should be noted that a handful of white politicians voted against extending the restrictions. These included members of the CCF, Liberal senators Cairine Wilson (1885–1962) and Arthur Roebuck (1878–1971), and, after he left Prime Minister King's cabinet, Thomas Crerar (1876–1975). See Sunahara, *The Politics of Racism*, 94–95.

56. Inouye, interview with Mary Kitagawa, July 12, 2022.

57. Ibid.

58. Sunahara, *The Politics of Racism*, 356–371; and Adachi, *The Enemy That Never Was*, 326–331. Cf. Kaitlin Findlay, "The Bird Commission, Japanese Canadians, and the Challenge of Reparations in the Wake of State Violence" (MA thesis, Uniuversity of Victoria, 2017).

59. Stanger-Ross, ed., *Landscapes of Injustice*, esp. 341–343.

60. Inouye, interview with Mary Kitagawa, September 1, 2022: "My dad couldn't speak English well, so he lived kind of, like, a silent life because he couldn't speak English. But his conversation was always with the family, and he would have Mum translate for him if he wanted to say something to people who came [from outside the family]."

61. Noting that Katsuyori would be unable to reach Lethbridge before 11 a.m., the secretary for the Lethbridge subdivision of the commission directed him to "please come over to the Court House immediately upon the arrival of the bus, as your case will be called shortly after that time." Included in the Murakamis' Bird Commission file (Case #625).

62. Quoted in the transcript of the Murakamis' Bird Commission file (Case #625).

63. Ibid.

64. Inouye, interview with Mary Kitagawa, July 12, 2022.

65. Inouye, interview with Mary Kitagawa, August 13, 2022. For a tentative historical roster of businesses in Cardston, see Pankhurst and Smith, eds., *Chief Mountain Country*, vol. 3, 103–158.

66. "Natural Splendor of Waterton Lakes Is Unsurpassed in Any National Park," *Calgary Daily Herald*, March 14, 1921, 32.

67. Donald G. Wetherell and Irene Kmet, *Useful Pleasures: The Shaping of Leisure in Alberta, 1896–1945* (Regina, SK: Canadian Plains Research Center, 1990), 189–190.

68. Ibid., 191 and 203–204.

69. See, for instance, Graham A. MacDonald, *Where the Mountains Meet the Prairies: A History of Waterton Lakes National Park* (Hull, QC: Canadian Heritage, Parks Canada, 1992).

70. *New Canadian* 11:16 (April 17, 1948): 12.

71. Iwaasa, "Canadian Japanese in Southern Alberta," esp. 10–17 and 45–50.

72. Wetherell and Kmet, *Useful Pleasures*, 197–198.

73. Inouye, interview with Mary Kitagawa, August 13, 2022. Mary remembers one other Nikkei family that lived in Cardston, though only briefly. An unattributed article titled simply "New Business" in the *Lethbridge Herald* (April 23, 1948), 9, describes the Du-Eet café as "the only Japanese [*sic*] business in Cardston at present."

74. Wetherell and Kmet, *Useful Pleasures*, 227–228.

75. Ibid., 229–230.

76. Inouye, interview with Mary Kitagawa, July 12, 2022.

77. Wetherell and Kmet, *Useful Pleasures*, 228.

78. Inouye, interview with Mary Kitagawa, July 12, 2022.

79. Inouye, interview with Mary Kitagawa, August 13, 2022.

80. Brigham Y. Card, "The Canadian Mormon Settlements, 1886–1925: A North-American Perspective," *Canadian Ethnic Studies* 26:1 (1994): 19–39; Neldon Hatch, "A History of the Church of Jesus Christ of Latter-Day Saints in Cardston and Area to 1950," in Keith Shaw, ed., *Chief Mountain Country: A History of Cardston and District*, vol. 1 (Cardston, AB: Cardston and District Historical Society, 1978), 173–182.

81. Wetherell and Kmet, *Useful Pleasures*, 85–91.

82. "Cardston's Present Population 2,486," *Cardston News*, December 8, 1949, 1.

83. Inouye, interview with Mary Kitagawa, August 13, 2022.

84. Inouye, interview with Mary Kitagawa, July 12, 2022; Inouye, interview with Mary Kitagawa, February 10, 2023; "Passes Suddenly," *Cardston News*, November 11, 1949, 1.

85. "Waitress Wanted (Also Extra Help during Stampede Week)—Apply Du-Eet Cafe, Cardston," *Cardston News*, July 13, 1950, 3. This issue of the *News* was virtually a special edition, announcing the Stampede (which started the following week) and running special articles as well as ads keyed to the event.

86. Inouye, interview with Mary Kitagawa, July 12, 2022.

87. Ibid.

88. Ibid.

89. Ibid.

90. Among others, the Cardston Grill and the Rex Cafe were both operational in the early 1950s, to judge by the Christmas greetings each placed in the *Cardston News* in 1951 and 1952. It also appears that the Marquis Cafe was open for business from 1948 onward. Pankhurst and Smith, eds., *Chief Mountain Country*, vol. 3, 148.

91. Inouye, interview with Mary Kitagawa, July 12, 2022.

92. Ibid.

93. Inouye, interview with Mary Kitagawa, August 13, 2022.

94. Ibid. Regarding Atso'toah's efforts as a political leader, see John L. Steckley, *Indian Agents: Rulers of the Reserves* (New York: Peter Lang, 2016), esp. 99–101; and Regular, *Neighbors and Networks*, 54 and 60. Regular casts Atso'toah as a canny mediator, while Steckley sees him as having been more assimilationist.

95. Inouye, interview with Mary Kitagawa, July 12, 2022. Kimiko continued to renew her subscription to the *Cardston News* for several years after the family returned to Salt Spring Island, but most likely for economic reasons. The family continued to own the building that housed the Du-Eet Cafe after they sold the business. Reliant on rent from the property, they needed to keep track of economic and social life in the neighborhood.

96. "Senior Chamber of Commerce Membership," *Cardston News*, December 8, 1949, 1.

97. See, for instance, Michiko Kodama-Nishimoto, interview with Robert Sato, August 25, 1992, https://scholarspace.manoa.hawaii.edu/server/api/core/bitstreams/6b29e879-df8e-478e-854d-4c14db85c52b/content. Although he is talking specifically about the Senior Chamber of Commerce in Hawai'i, Sato's remarks about the perception of belonging track with the political conservativism of the Chamber more generally.

98. "Rod and Gun Club," *Cardston News*, March 31, 1949, 8; Charlie Walker, "Cardston Rod and Gun Club News," *Cardston News*, July 26, 1945, 6.

99. Wetherell and Kmet, *Useful Pleasures*, 249–273. A good example is the Cardston Rotary Club, which in 1936 arranged for a band to perform on Main Street on Saturday evenings. The performances brought people both into contact and into the heart of the commercial zone (ibid., 256).

100. George Colpitts, *Game in the Garden: A Human History of Wildlife in Western Canada to 1940* (Vancouver: University of British Columbia Press, 2003), esp. ch. 3.

101. Wetherell and Kmet, *Useful Pleasures*, 181; J. McIllree and M. H. White-Fraser, "Fishing in Southern Alberta," *Alberta History* 31 (1983): 36–38.

102. "Rod and Gun Club," *Cardston News*, March 25, 1948, 5. The aim of a rearing pond is both to raise fish and to imprint them so that they will reproduce in the area.

103. Quoted in Colpitts, *Game in the Garden*, 90.

104. "Rod and Gun Club," *Cardston News*, March 25, 1948, 5.

105. Alan Artibise, "Boosterism and the Development of Prairie Cities," in R. Douglas Francis and Howard Palmer, eds., *The Prairie West: Historical Readings*, 2nd ed. (Edmonton: University of Alberta Press, 1992), 515–43; Cecily Devereux, "'And Let Them Wash Me from This Clanging World': Hugh and Ion, 'The Last Best West,' and Purity Discourse in 1885," *Journal of Canadian Studies* 32:2 (1997): 100–

115; Gerald Friesen, *The Canadian Prairies: A History* (Toronto: University of Toronto Press, 1984); Doug Owram, *Promise of Eden: The Canadian Expansionist Movement and the Idea of the West, 1856–1900* (Toronto: University of Toronto Press, 1980); and Paul F. Sharp, "The American Farmer and the 'Last Best West,'" *Agricultural History* 21:2 (1947): 65–75.

106. See, for instance, Colpitts, *Game in the Garden*, 87–88.

107. Quoted in Colpitts, *Game in the Garden*, 98.

108. Inouye, interview with Mary Kitagawa, August 13, 2022.

109. According to a 1948 advertisement, "The Central Service Co. is under the very capable management of the proprietors, Messrs. Albert and Fred Widmer, who have had many years' experience in the automobile business. They took over this firm from the previous owner, Mr. K. L. Lee, in February 1946." *Cardston News*, August 5, 1948, 4.

110. Inouye, interview with Mary Kitagawa, August 13, 2022.

111. Ibid.

112. Ibid.

113. The restaurant did occasionally close for brief periods. For instance, in December 1953, Katsuyori, Kimiko, and Bruce spent two weeks in British Columbia visiting Victor Okano, who by then had returned to Salt Spring Island. "Cardston News Items," *Lethbridge Herald*, December 12, 1953, 19.

114. Inouye, interview with Mary Kitagawa, August 13, 2022.

115. Inouye, interview with Mary Kitagawa, July 12, 2022.

116. Ibid.

117. Inouye, interview with Mary Kitagawa, August 13, 2022.

118. Inouye, interview with Mary Kitagawa, July 12, 2022.

119. Ibid.

120. La Violette, *The Canadian Japanese and World War II*, 186, n. 34.

121. Inouye, interview with Mary Kitagawa, July 12, 2022.

122. "Bridal Shower," *Cardston News*, February 15, 1951, 1. Even with the report of this event, it is difficult to gauge how thoroughly Alice was knit into the local community. Several similar showers were mentioned in the *Cardston News* around that time, many of them featuring the same or similar rosters of performers and framed in the same language. This suggests at least some element of ritualized mid-century neighborliness was at work.

123. Inouye, interview with Mary Kitagawa, July 12, 2022.

124. Inouye, interview with Mary Kitagawa, August 13, 2022.

125. Ibid.

126. Ibid.

127. Ibid.

128. Inouye, interview with Mary Kitagawa, July 12, 2022.

129. Ibid.

130. "Education—The Key to Progress," *Cardston News*, December 7, 1950, 1.

131. On this front, at least, Rose and Mary enjoyed an advantage. When the family first moved from the Grey House, their new backyard faced directly onto the high school grounds. Inouye, interview with Mary Kitagawa, August 13, 2022.

132. One critical touchstone for this ethos is the declaration in the Mormon *Doctrine and Covenants* that "the glory of God is intelligence." See *The Doctrine and Covenants of The Church of Jesus Christ of Latter-day Saints* (Salt Lake City: The Church of Jesus Christ of Latter-day Saints, 1981), 93:36. At issue in this declaration is the moral application of an educated mind.

133. Mary has remarked on more than one occasion that these demands were the primary determinant of life in Cardston: "We couldn't take part in too many activities after school because we had to go back home and work in the restaurant. And that took a lot of our time." Inouye, interview with Mary Kitagawa, August 13, 2022.

134. Cardston High School Yearbook Staff, *Milestones, 1951–1952* (Cardston, AB: Cardston High School, 1952), 9. The junior and senior high schools in Cardston shared a building until 1965. See Blaine Bunnage, "Cardston Junior High School," in Bectell, ed., *Chief Mountain Country*, vol. 2, 63. See also Brent Nielsen, "Cardston High School," in Bectell, ed., *Chief Mountain Country*, vol. 2, 64–66.

135. Inouye, interview with Mary Kitagawa, August 13, 2022.

136. Wetherell and Kmet, *Useful Pleasures*, 209.

137. Chuckling at the memory, Mary says, "Rose and I were on the basketball team, so you can tell how small people on the basketball team were." Inouye, interview with Mary Kitagawa, July 12, 2022. Even so, as Mary's yearbook attests, the girls' teammates were noticeably taller: "MARY MURAKAMI: She's a credit to the Cougarette team, though she's tiny, she's got everything." Cardston High School Yearbook Staff, *Milestones, 1951–1952*, 21.

138. Inouye, interview with Mary Kitagawa, August 13, 2022.

139. "Cougarettes Bring Back Trophy," *Cardston News*, April 2, 1953, 1.

140. Inouye, interview with Mary Kitagawa, July 12, 2022.

141. Ibid.

142. While there was an Anglican church in Cardston proper, much of the organization's energy was directed toward the Kainai people. See Rev. Rodney Andrews, "The Reverend Samuel Trivett, First Anglican Missionary with the Blood Indians;" Rev. Rodney Andrews, "A History of St Thomas's Anglican Church, Cardston;" and Rev. Rodney Andrews, "Venerable Archdeacon S.H. Middleton, B.Sc., E.D., C. St.J., F.R.E.S., D.D., 1884–1965," in Shaw, ed., *Chief Mountain Country*, vol. 1, 185–191.

143. Inouye, interview with Mary Kitagawa, August 13, 2022.

144. This is the reason that Seminary buildings in Utah and other predominantly Mormon communities frequently stand directly across the street from school buildings.

145. Inouye, interview with Mary Kitagawa, July 12, 2022.

146. "Passes Suddenly," *Cardston News*, November 10, 1949, 1.

147. Iwaasa, "Canadian Japanese in Southern Alberta."

148. "New Business," *Lethbridge Herald*, April 23, 1948, 5.

149. Cardston High School Yearbook Staff, *Milestones, 1951–1952*, 23, where the editors spelled Mary's family name "Marikami." (Cf. ibid., 9, where the roster of newspaper staff members identifies her as "Mary Murikami.") The category of Hands was not alone in its peculiarity. The "Drool Boy" roster included "Closest Shaven."

150. Inouye, interview with Mary Kitagawa, August 13, 2022.

151. Ibid. A 1962 master's thesis by Cardston High School teacher Lynn M. Beazer heralded plans by the Lethbridge YWCA to establish a dedicated social centre where Kainai could meet and receive "assistance . . . in overcoming the problems of integration." Lynn M. Beazer, "An Historical Study of the Cultural, Social, and Religious Backgrounds of the Education of the Blood Indians, Blood Indian Reservation, Alberta" (MA thesis, Montana State University, 1962), 157. Beazer also notes that white people attended social events at Senator Gladstone Hall, a recreational facility that opened on the reserve in 1959 (ibid., 160).

152. Beazer, "Historical Study," 19, noted that "at present the white population is approximately 2,800 and when the present Blood Indian population of some 3,000 is added thereto, plus shoppers from surrounding communities, Cardston caters to over 6,000 people."

153. Inouye, interview with Mary Kitagawa, August 13, 2022.

154. Inouye, interview with Mary Kitagawa, July 12, 2022.

155. Inouye, interview with Mary Kitagawa, August 13, 2022.

156. Regular, *Neighbors and Networks*.

157. Inouye, interview with Mary Kitagawa, August 13, 2022.

158. See Andrews, "Reverend Samuel Trivett," "History of St Thomas' Anglican Church," and "Venerable Archdeacon;" "History of the Catholic Church in Cardston," in Shaw, ed., *Chief Mountain Country*, vol. 1, 169–173.

"History of the Presbyterian and United Church," *Chief Mountain Country*, vol. 1, 182–185; Beazer, "Historical Study," 142–167. For the larger context of such work, see Kateri Akiwenzie-Damm, "We Belong to This Land: A View of 'Cultural Difference,'" *Journal of Canadian Studies* 31:3 (1996): 24–25; Celia Haig-Brown, *Resistance and Renewal: Surviving the Indian Residential School* (Vancouver: Tillacum, 1989); Katherine Pettipas, *Severing the Ties That Bind: Government Repression of Indigenous Religious Ceremonies on the Prairies* (Winnipeg: University of Manitoba Press, 1994).

159. Eagle Speaker's attendance predated the 1957 agreement that allowed Kainai children to enroll in the Cardston public school system. Jeanne Leishman, "Cardston School Division #2," in Bectell, ed., *Chief Mountain Country*, vol. 2, 59.

160. Inouye, interview with Mary Kitagawa, August 13, 2022.

161. Beazer, "Historical Study," 98–99.

162. Inouye, interview with Mary Kitagawa, August 13, 2022.

163. Inouye, interview with Mary Kitagawa, July 12, 2022.

164. "Calgary's Stampede Queen," *Lethbridge Herald*, July 3, 1954, 4.

165. Ibid.

166. Ibid. See also Susan L. Joudrey, "The Expectations of a Queen: Identity and Race Politics in the Calgary Stampede," in Alvin Finkel, Sarah Carter, and Peter Fortna, eds., *The West and Beyond: New Perspectives on an Imagined Region* (Edmonton: Athabasca University Press, 2010), 133–155.

On the Stampede more generally, see Max Foran, ed., *Icon, Brand, Myth: The Calgary Stampede* (Edmonton: Athabasca University Press, 2008).

167. Inouye, interview with Mary Kitagawa, July 12, 2022.

168. Joudrey, "The Expectations of a Queen," 136.

169. "Blood Indian Girl's Essay on 'Citizenship' Wins Prize," *Lethbridge Herald*, June 30, 1948, 6. The prizes were awarded by the Imperial Order Daughters of the Empire.

Chapter 4

1. Kashima, "Japanese American Internees Return," 108. Writing of Japanese Americans, Kashima rightly argued that "the years between 1945 and 1955, instead of being seen as a transition period, should be viewed as a crisis period" (ibid.).

2. La Violette, *The Canadian Japanese and World War II*, 184, n. 30

3. Harry Burton, "Don Cunningham Talks about the Old Days of Salt Spring Island," part 3, https://vimeo.com/202494241. Cunningham mistakenly dates the Murakami family's return to 1952. Also, it is unclear if he was thinking of Jim and Victor Okano, who also returned to Salt Spring Island from Cardston.

4. Inouye, interview with Mary Kitagawa, February 10, 2023. Patricia Roy, "Lessons in Citizenship, 1945–1949," in Fiset and Nomura, eds., *Nikkei in the Pacific Northwest*, 257, observes that Nikkei Canadians "could only visit the coast for specific purposes, such as specialized medical treatment, and with permission from the Royal Canadian Mounted Police (RCMP)."

5. Inouye, interview with Mary Kitagawa, September 1, 2022.

6. "Du-Eet Cafe Changes Hands," *Cardston News*, September 16, 1954, 1. According to the article, Denver Yip went in with his cousin George to buy the business. It is worth noting, too, that members of their family had been active in the Cardston restaurant trade for some time. George had managed the Rex Cafe since

1936, and he opened the New Rex Cafe with a white business partner in 1948. His mother and two family members also opened the Marquis Cafe in 1948. See Pankhurst and Smith, eds. *Chief Mountain Country*, vol. 3, 148 and 149.

7. Inouye, interview with Mary Kitagawa, July 12, 2022.
8. "Du-Eet Changes Hands," *Cardston News*, September 23, 1954, 3.
9. Smallshaw, *As If They Were the Enemy*, esp. ch. 6.
10. Smallshaw identifies the veterans who bought the Okano and Murakami lands (ibid., 110).
11. Burton, "Don Cunningham Talks about the Old Days."
12. Ibid.
13. Ibid. Although meant to be complimentary, Cunningham's comments echo sentiments that have been widespread for over a century.
14. See Smallshaw, *As If They Were the Enemy*, esp. ch. 5.
15. Inouye, interview with Mary Kitagawa, September 1, 2022.
16. Salas, interview with Mary Kitagawa, June 17, 2017.
17. Inouye, interview with Mary Kitagawa, December 2, 2023.
18. Inouye, interview with Mary Kitagawa, September 1, 2022.
19. Oikawa, *Cartographies of Violence*, 7, observes that white nationalism operated at all levels of British Columbian society.
20. Inouye, interview with Mary Kitagawa, September 12, 2022.
21. Ibid.
22. Inouye, correspondence with Mary Kitagawa, August 13, 2022.
23. Inouye, interview with Mary Kitagawa, July 12, 2022.
24. Mary does not recall exactly when the Murakamis sold the building that housed the Du-Eet Cafe, but late 1957 or early 1958 seems likely. Entries in the *Cardston News* indicate that Kimiko renewed her subscription to the paper through the end of 1957, but not beyond that. See "Subscriptions," *Cardston News*, January 27, 1955, 6; January 3, 1956, 4; and October 10, 1957, 3.
25. Inouye, interview with Mary Kitagawa, September 1, 2022.
26. Ibid.
27. Ibid.
28. Ibid.
29. Ibid.
30. Cf. the observation by Forrest La Violette that "it was generally understood that those [Nikkei] who did go 'east of the Rockies' were symbolizing their intention of remaining in Canada," despite the financial, legal, and logistical obstacles they faced. La Violette, *Canadian Japanese and World War II*, 147–148.
31. Established in 1953, this entity encompassed both the old city of Toronto proper and a number of surrounding towns, villages, and townships.
32. For a brief history of the situation in Toronto, see Roger Obata, "Relocation

to Toronto," in Ad Hoc Committee for *Japanese Canadian Redress: The Toronto Story*, ed., *Japanese Canadian Redress: The Toronto Story* (Toronto: HpF Press, 2000), 63–81. Regarding Montreal, see most recently Christian Roy, "Histoire de la communauté Japonaise du Québec, 1942–1988" (PhD dissertation, Université du Québec à Montréal, 2016), which includes a bibliography.

33. As early as 1951, *The New Canadian* had observed that expense and the limitations of public transportation were only aggravating the situation. See "Toronto JC's Scattered throughout City but Continuing to Disperse," *The New Canadian* 14:45 (June 16, 1951): 1. La Violette, *Canadian Japanese and World War II*, 148, 158, and 185, observed that government policies combined with local racism aggravated the problem for Nikkei.

34. Keibo Oiwa, "The Structure of Dispersal: The Japanese-Canadian Community of Montreal, 1942–1952," *Canadian Ethnic Studies—Études ethniques au Canada* 18:2 (1986), 34. For a measured critique of Oiwa's argument, see Roy, "Histoire de la communauté Japonaise," esp. 168–170.

35. In the case of the *Montreal News Bulletin*, the paper served an explicitly political project, having been founded by a Nikkei organization called the Standing Committee. Nonetheless, it frequently echoed the sentiment that being too visible would work to the detriment of Nikkei in Québec.

36. Inouye, interview with Mary Kitagawa and Tosh Kitagawa, September 29, 2022; Inouye, interview with Mary Kitagawa, February 10, 2023.

37. See Bird Commission (Case #661) and Custodian (Case #1161) files. Murakami owned those two lots, but he could not yet afford to buy his own home. Instead, he leased from one of the canning conglomerates, British Columbia Packers Limited. According to his testimony before the Bird Commission, Murakami bought a five-acre lot for $1,750 in 1927. In 1935, he inherited a 2.5-acre lot from his father; he declined an offer of $1,250 for that property in 1937. In 1942, the Custodian sold Murakami's properties for a total of $1,445, and in 1948 the Bird Commission declared the Canadian government's financial liability to be $658.04. Murakami also had owned a fishing boat, but the Bird Commission refused to take that sale into account because of the technicality that the boat had been seized and forcibly sold by the Japanese Fishing Vessels Disposal Committee, a body formed in January 1942, rather than by the Custodian of Enemy Property.

38. Inouye, interview with Mary Kitagawa, February 10, 2023. Koichi Tsujimura was one of the UBC students for whom Mary secured posthumous recognition in 2012. See Mary Kitagawa, Tosh Kitagawa, et al., eds., *A Degree of Justice: 1942* (Vancouver: n.p., 2017), 162.

39. Inouye, interview with Mary Kitagawa and Tosh Kitagawa, September 29, 2022.

40. Ibid.

41. Inouye, interview with Mary Kitagawa, February 10, 2023.

42. Inouye, interview with Mary Kitagawa and Tosh Kitagawa, September 29, 2022.

43. Ibid.

44. T. A. Reed, *A History of Trinity College, 1852–1952* (Toronto: University of Toronto Press, 1952), 29.

45. The phrase comes from an account of one of the first students to matriculate at Trinity in 1952. Ibid., 50.

46. Ibid., 231–232, makes the organization sound relatively benign. History suggests otherwise, especially from the 1970s onward.

47. Trinity Review Staff, *Trinity, 1852–1952*, a special issue of the *Trinity Review* (1952): 167–168. For the history of women at Trinity College, see Anne Rochon Ford, *A Path Not Strewn with Roses: One Hundred Years of Women at the University of Toronto, 1884–1984* (Toronto: University of Toronto Press, 1984).

48. Inouye, interview with Mary Kitagawa, September 1, 2022.

49. Inouye, interview with Mary Kitagawa and Tosh Kitagawa, September 29, 2022.

50. Inouye, interview with Mary Kitagawa, September 1, 2022.

51. Inouye, interview with Mary Kitagawa and Tosh Kitagawa, September 29, 2022. The invitations did not stick, though the sport did. Mary listed Bowling III as her extracurricular activity in the yearbook commemorating her graduating class. Students' Administrative Council of the University of Toronto, *Torontonensis* (Toronto: University of Toronto, 1958), 410.

Michiko Midge Ayukawa, *Hiroshima Immigrants in Canada*, 111–112, has observed that intraethnic athletic participation was the norm among Nisei. Such participation was at least sometimes more than a mere diversion, since these clubs carried generational, cultural, and religious implications. To judge from the example of Montreal, those implications might go some way toward explaining the unusual durability of that city's bowling club. See Roy, "Histoire de la communauté Japonaise," 172, 301, and esp. 370.

52. Mary has described that period as being "a more or less isolated life" (Inouye, interview with Mary Kitagawa and Tosh Kitagawa, September 29, 2022).

53. Inouye, interview with Mary Kitagawa, September 1, 2022.

54. Inouye, interview with Mary Kitagawa, September 29, 2022.

55. Ibid.

56. Ibid.

57. Ibid.

58. Alice was hardly alone in this respect: "The women in our family were very vocal" (Inouye, interview with Mary Kitagawa, February 10, 2023). The men tended to be more reserved.

59. Inouye, interview with Mary Kitagawa, September 1, 2022.
60. Inouye, interview with Mary Kitagawa, July 12, 2022.
61. Inouye, interview with Mary Kitagawa, September 1, 2022.
62. Inouye, interview with Mary Kitagawa, September 29, 2022.
63. Ibid.
64. A survey of the university's yearbook, *Torontonensis*, gives us a rough idea of the group's public profile. Two of the four graduates who listed that group among their activities were University College students in 1956, with Architecture and St. Michael's providing the other two. In 1957, the college was home to two graduating members; three of its officers that year were University College students, with Trinity providing the fourth. In 1957, the college was home to two graduating members; three of its officers that year were University College students, with Trinity providing the fourth. University College was home to three of its six officers in 1958; the School of General Studies provided another, while Trinity provided two. Of WISA's graduating members, one came from St. Michael's and one from University College. And in 1959, Trinity and University Colleges were home to five graduating seniors each; one officer came from the former, two from the latter, and one University College senior who did not list her affiliation with WISA that year had previously been an officer.
65. *Torontonensis*, 1958, 114.
66. Ibid.
67. *Torontonensis*, 1955, 77. This mission was a central feature of the group's yearbook statements throughout the 1950s.
68. See, for instance, Alan T. Davies, ed. *Antisemitism in Canada: History and Interpretation* (Waterloo, ON: Wilfrid Laurier University Press, 1992).
69. See Ross Lambertson, "'The Dresden Story': Racism, Human Rights, and the Jewish Labour Committee of Canada," *Labour/Le Travail* 47 (Spring 2001): 43–82; Lambertson, *Repression and Resistance*, ch. 7.
70. Josiah Henson, *The Life of Josiah Henson, Formerly a Slave, Now an Inhabitant of Canada, as Narrated by Himself* (Boston: Arthur D. Phelps, 1849).
71. Gordon Burwash, Julian Biggs, and Grant McLean (producers), *Dresden Story* (Montreal: National Film Board of Canada, 1954).
72. According to Stuart McLean, *Welcome Home: Travels in Smalltown Canada* (Toronto: Penguin Books, 1992), provincial racism ran so deep that businesses would take a person's family tree into consideration when deciding whether to deny them service.
73. James W. St. G. Walker, *"Race," Rights, and the Law in the Supreme Court of Canada* (Waterloo, ON: Wilfrid Laurier University Press, 1997), esp. ch. 3.
74. Quoted in Lambertson, "'The Dresden Story,'" 47.
75. On the Committee on Group Relations, which included representation

from, among others, the Japanese Canadian Citizens' Association, see Lambertson, "'The Dresden Story,'" 63.

76. Ibid., 73–79.

77. Ruth Lor, "Report on Dresden," *Varsity* 74 (November 25, 1954): 1.

78. Lambertson, "'The Dresden Story,'" 79, cites a November 16, 1956, visit to Kay's Cafe by representatives of the National Unity Association, when they finally received service, as a symbolic turning point.

79. Quoted in Sunahara, *The Politics of Racism*, 76. Some Nikkei even considered their situation to be better than that of their Jewish and Chinese Canadian neighbors (ibid., 108–109).

80. Obata, "Relocation to Toronto," 65. Cf. Ayukawa, *Hiroshima Immigrants in Canada*, 115–118.

81. Sunahara, *The Politics of Racism*, 76–77. Ernest Trueman, who oversaw the government's relocation efforts in Toronto, suggested in 1943 that almost 90 percent of the Nikkei in the greater Toronto area were Nisei. Some were men who had been forced into the province to work on road gangs; a larger number seem to have been women who performed domestic work or found employment in hospitals. See Nunoda, "A Community in Transition and Conflict," 156.

82. La Violette, *Canadian Japanese and World War II*, 148.

83. Ibid., 148–154.

84. Ibid., 153 n. 14.

85. Elizabeth D. Wangenheim, *The Social Organization of the Japanese Community in Toronto: A Product of Crisis* (MA thesis, University of Toronto, 1956), 6.

86. Ibid., 3 and 5.

87. Far-right parties published ads claiming that support for the CCF would inevitably bring about an extension of the franchise to people of Chinese and Japanese ancestry.

88. Regarding overlap between the two organizations, see Nunoda, "A Community in Transition and Conflict," 166. On the JCCD and its allies, see Nunoda, "A Community in Transition and Conflict"; and Bangarth, *Voices Raised in Protest*; Lambertson, *Repression and Resistance*, ch. 3. Regarding aspects of Nunoda's argument as it pertains to Nisei political efficacy, see Michiko Midge Ayukawa, "Creating and Recreating Community: Hiroshima and Canada, 1891–1941" (PhD dissertation, University of Victoria, 1996), 264–268.

89. Quoted in Carol F. Lee, "The Road to Enfranchisement: Chinese and Japanese in British Columbia," *BC Studies* 30 (Summer 1976), 52.

90. Tomoko Makabe, "Canadian Evacuation and Nisei Identity"; Makabe, *The Canadian Sansei*; Michiko Midge Ayukawa, Review of Tomoko Makabe, *The Canadian Sansei*, BC Studies 121 (Spring 1999): 138–139; Ayukawa, *Hiroshima Immigrants in Canada*, ch. 7.

91. "Montreal Nisei Veto Organizing—Focus Undue Attention on Group," *The New Canadian* 6:13 (March 13, 1943): 1. See also Nunoda, "A Community in Transition and Conflict," esp. chs. 5 and 8; cf. Ayukawa, *Hiroshima Immigrants in Canada*, esp. 116ff.

92. Cf. Ayukawa, *Hiroshima Immigrants in Canada*, 266: "The struggles of the late 1940s emphasize the fact that the Nisei were not all alike, that they varied in their opinions and behaviour—some were strongly outspoken; others wanted to halt the entire appeal process so as not to attract undesireable attention or criticism from white Canadians."

93. Inouye, interview with Mary Kitagawa, September 29, 2022.

94. Ayukawa, *Hiroshima Immigrants in Canada*, 112–113.

95. Inouye, interview with Mary Kitagawa, August 13, 2022; Inouye, interview with Mary Kitagawa, September 1, 2022; Salas, interview with Mary Kitagawa, June 17, 2017.

96. See, for instance, La Violette, *Canadian Japanese and World War II*, 159, on the paradoxically claustrophobic isolation that attended life in places like Slocan and Extension.

97. Inouye, interview with Mary Kitagawa, September 29, 2022.

Chapter 5

1. Inouye, interview with Mary Kitagawa and Tosh Kitagawa, September 16, 2022.

2. Ibid.; Hashizume, *Japanese Community in Mission*, 42–43. Salas, interview with Tosh Kitagawa, June 26, 2017, provides a slightly different sequence of events.

3. Inouye, interview with Mary Kitagawa and Tosh Kitagawa, September 16, 2022; Hashizume, *Japanese Community in Mission*, 6. In Salas, interview with Tosh Kitagawa, June 26, 2017, Tosh mentions one especially lean year when his family had to pick wild blackberries to supplement their income. Hashizume, *Japanese Community in Mission*, 9–10 and 15–17, discusses the primary crops available to the population, as well as the challenges and benefits of growing them.

4. Inouye, interview with Mary Kitagawa and Tosh Kitagawa, September 16, 2022; Hashizume, *Japanese Community in Mission*, 9. The Kitagawas' experience mirrored that of many Mission Nikkei, including the family of William T. Hashizume (Hashizume, *Japanese Community in Mission*, 32–33).

5. The children were, in order of birth, Yoshiko (1926), Hiroshi (1928), Masayoshi (1930), Tosh (1932), Junichi (1934), and Yukio (1936). Inouye, interview with Mary Kitagawa and Tosh Kitagawa, September 16, 2022.

6. While not prominent among the Nikkei leadership, Terajima and Yosokichi Kitagawa were active in the community. Their farm was in a neighborhood that was home to a large number of families that had come from the same prefecture.

Hashizume, *Japanese Community in Mission*, 106. Furthermore, Yosokichi served on a committee that oversaw the construction of a new building to house the Japanese language school (ibid., 18). Hashizume also discusses the economic and administrative structure of the agricultural community in Mission (10–12 and 107), education and religion (18–24), and the relationship with Nikkei communities in nearby towns (13).

7. Inouye, interview with Mary Kitagawa and Tosh Kitagawa, September 16, 2022.

8. Ibid. On the topic of Nikkei moving prior to the restriction expiring in 1949, see Salas, interview with Tosh Kitagawa, June 26, 2017.

9. Lambertson, *Repression and Resistance*, 253.

10. Masumi Izumi, "Reclaiming Powell Street: Reconstruction of the Japanese Canadian Community in Post–World War II Vancouver," in Fiset and M. Nomura, eds., *Nikkei in the Pacific Northwest*, 308–333; Patricia E. Roy, "The Re-creation of Vancouver's Japanese Community, 1945–2008," *Journal of the Canadian Historical Association/Revue de la Société historique du Canada* 19:2 (2008): 127–154.

11. Inouye, interview with Mary Kitagawa and Tosh Kitagawa, October 19, 2022.

12. Ibid.

13. Ibid. During that visit, as during the war, not a word was spoken about expulsion, dispossession, expatriation, or dispersal. Tosh recalls, "I don't know what kind of conversation they had on their own, but the war and the Japanese Canadians working on the farm and that, that was never part of the conversation [he had with them] ever. It was just almost like, 'It's there, and this is how we are coping and dealing with it.' I never heard them ever talk about the process of incarceration or anything like that."

14. Ibid.

15. *Commute* is perhaps too elevated a term: "Basically I used to walk and hitchhike back to Diamond City from Lethbridge every day until I finished my year, my term." As for the riskiness of hitchhiking, in the absence of bus service, "it's either that, or you walk." Inouye, interview with Mary Kitagawa and Tosh Kitagawa, September 16, 2022.

16. Ibid.

17. Ibid.

18. Ibid.

19. Ibid. Cf. the date he provides in Salas, interview with Tosh Kitagawa, June 26, 2017.

20. Inouye, interview with Mary Kitagawa and Tosh Kitagawa, September 16, 2022.

21. Roy, "The Re-creation of Vancouver's Japanese Community," 131.

22. "Return to the Coast," *The New Canadian* 10:2 (January 11, 1947): 2.

23. Regarding economic constraints, see, for instance, "Is Fear Keeping Us Out of the Coast?," *The New Canadian* 12:35 (May 11, 1949): 2, which rebutted claims in the *Pacific Citizen* that demoralization and uncertainty about British Columbian racism were primary motivators.

24. "Disappointed Salesman Finds Only One Couple Returning to Vancouver," *The New Canadian* 12:26 (April 9, 1949): 1.

25. As quoted in Roy, "Lessons in Citizenship," 267. Roy cites the *Vancouver Sun* (September 21, 1945) quoting in turn *The New Canadian*.

26. Inouye, Interview with Mary Kitagawa and Tosh Kitagawa, September 16, 2022.

27. Ibid. The three of them would convince a couple to invite over their friends, would cook dinner for the whole group, and then would pitch their wares. Tellingly, Tosh soon developed his own approach, which involved prioritizing young women engaged to be married. Figuring he could count on a future wedding registry for higher-volume sales, he fared very well.

28. Ibid.

29. Salas, interview with Tosh Kitagawa, June 26, 2017.

30. Ibid.

31. Ibid.

32. I build here on the argument of Oikawa, *Cartographies of Violence*.

33. These assaults continued through the 1980s. Murakami, *Ganbaru*, 33–37.

34. Inouye, interview with Mary Kitagawa, February 10, 2023.

35. Ibid.

36. Ibid.

37. Ibid.

38. Inouye, interview with Mary Kitagawa, October 19, 2022.

39. Inouye, interview with Mary Kitagawa, February 10, 2023.

40. Ibid. Rose eventually secured faculty status in the UBC School of Nursing and served as vice president of nursing at the UBC Health Science Centre Hospital in Vancouver. Murakami, *Ganbaru*, 38.

41. She worked there for a couple of years before earning graduate degrees at McGill and, after that, Boston University. Inouye, interview with Mary Kitagawa, February 10, 2023; Murakami, *Ganbaru*, 38.

42. Inouye, interview with Mary Kitagawa and Tosh Kitagawa, September 16, 2022.

43. Ibid.

44. Inouye, interview with Mary Kitagawa and Tosh Kitagawa, October 19, 2022.

45. Inouye, interview with Mary Kitagawa and Tosh Kitagawa, September 16, 2022. Cf. Salas, interview with Tosh Kitagawa, June 26, 2017.

46. Inouye, interview with Mary Kitagawa and Tosh Kitagawa October 19, 2022.

47. Inouye, interview with Mary Kitagawa and Tosh Kitagawa September 16, 2022.

48. Ibid.

49. Ibid.

50. Ibid.

51. This chronology builds on Inouye, interview with Mary Kitagawa and Tosh Kitagawa September 16, 2022.

52. Ibid.

53. Salas, interview with Mary Kitagawa, September 17, 2017.

54. Inouye, interview with Mary Kitagawa and Tosh Kitagawa September 16, 2022; Inouye, interview with Mary Kitagawa and Tosh Kitagawa October 19, 2022.

55. Izumi, "Reclaiming Powell Street," in Fiset and Nomura, eds., *Nikkei in the Pacific Northwest*, 58.

56. Rick Shiomi, "Community Organizing: The Problems of Innovating and Sustaining Interest," in K. Victor Ujimoto and Gordon Hirabayashi, eds., *Asian Canadians Regional Perspectives: Selections from the Proceedings, Asian Canadian Symposium V, Mount Saint Vincent University, Halifax, Nova Scotia, May 23 to 26, 1981* (Guelph, ON: University of Guelph, 1982), 339–354, especially 342–344 (regarding the Wakayama group) and 348–352 (regarding the slide show).

57. Michiko Sakata, "Tonari Gumi," *Rikka* 4:2 (Summer 1977): 4–11; Takeo Yamashiro, "Tonari Gumi: Powell Street Positively Revisited," in Cassandra Kobayashi and Roy Miki, eds. *Spirit of Redress: Japanese Canadians in Conference* (Vancouver: JC Publications, 1989), 55–58.

58. Japanese Canadian Centennial Project Committee, *A Dream of Riches: The Japanese Canadians, 1877–1977* (Vancouver: Japanese Canadian Centennial Project, 1978).

59. Inouye, interview with Mary Kitagawa and Tosh Kitagawa, September 29, 2022.

60. See, among others, Maryka Omatsu, *Bittersweet Passage: Redress and the Japanese Canadian Experience* (Toronto: Between the Lines, 1992); Roy Miki, *Redress: Inside the Japanese Canadian Call for Justice* (Vancouver: Raincoast Books, 2004); Daniel Tsuruo Tokawa, *Vancouver Rashomon: Redress Stories* (Altona, MB: Friesen Press, 2022).

61. See Miki, *Redress*, esp. 230–235 and 306–307.

62. Inouye, interview with Mary Kitagawa and Tosh Kitagawa, September 29, 2022.

63. Inouye, interview with Mary Kitagawa and Tosh Kitagawa, September 16, 2022.

64. Inouye, interview with Mary Kitagawa and Tosh Kitagawa, September 29, 2022.

65. See Omatsu, *Bittersweet Passage*; Miki, *Redress*; Tokawa, *Vancouver Rashomon*.

66. Salas, interview with Mary Kitagawa, June 17, 2017.

67. Inouye, interview with Mary Kitagawa and Tosh Kitagawa, September 29, 2022.

68. Ibid.

69. One First Nations speaker made a strong impression on Tosh, who particularly liked the man's definition of "white justice" as "just us." Inouye, interview with Mary Kitagawa and Tosh Kitagawa, September 29, 2022.

70. Norm Masaji Ibuki, "Art Miki: Canadian Redress Leader and Human Rights Champion—Part 2," *Discover Nikkei* 13 (January 2016), https://discovernikkei.org/en/journal/2016/1/13/art-miki-2/.

71. National Association of Japanese Canadians, "Presentation to the Special Joint Committee on a Renewed Canada," *Minutes of Proceedings and Evidence*, no. 16 (*Winnipeg, November 4, 1991*) (Ottawa: Government of Canada Publications, 1992).

72. Inouye, interview with Mary Kitagawa and Tosh Kitagawa, September 29, 2022.

73. Inouye, interview with Mary Kitagawa, February 10, 2023.

74. Inouye, interview with Mary Kitagawa, December 2, 2023.

75. René Goldman, *A Childhood Adrift* (Toronto: Azrieli Foundation, 2017).

76. Inouye, interview with Mary Kitagawa, February 10, 2023.

77. Goldman has remarked that his time in China was a relief, since being Jewish was of no consequence to the people around him. He felt that the people there simply did not possess the anti-Semitic framework that so many Europeans, Americans, and Canadians continue to nurture. See Goldberg, "Turning to China," video, Re:collection, https://memoirs.azrielifoundation.org/recollection/#display-asset|29658.

78. Inouye, interview with Mary Kitagawa, February 10, 2023.

79. Ibid.

80. Murakami, *Ganbaru*, 33–36.

81. The JCCA is a member of the National Association of Japanese Canadians. Founded in 1952, the JCCA changed its name to the Greater Vancouver Japanese Canadian Citizens' Association in 2015.

82. Inouye, interview with Mary Kitagawa, February 10, 2023.

83. Murakami, *Ganbaru*, 36.

84. Inouye, interview with Mary Kitagawa and Tosh Kitagawa, September 29, 2022.

85. Ibid.; Salas, interview with Tosh Kitagawa, June 26, 2017.

86. Inouye, interview with Mary Kitagawa and Tosh Kitagawa, September 29, 2022.

87. The Powell Street Festival Society Board, "The Powell Street Festival: Into the New Millennium?," *The JCCA Bulletin* 41:10 (1999): 11.

88. The range of issues raised in this article was much broader. See ibid., 7–11, 14.

89. Inouye, interview with Mary Kitagawa and Tosh Kitagawa, September 29, 2022.

90. Ibid.

91. Tosh's father, for instance, was a devout Buddhist who played a key role in the wartime establishment of a temple in Picture Butte. Inouye, interview with Mary Kitagawa and Tosh Kitagawa, September 16, 2022.

92. Tosh recalls relatively little racism in Diamond City "because Diamond City used to be a coal-mining town, and so a lot of Europeans worked in the mines. And when the mines closed, many of them stayed because there was nowhere else to go. So, it was very cosmopolitan [in the sense of being culturally diverse]. Like, we had just about everyone from every European country, and we were *all* minorities, you know. Basically, I don't think, I don't recall very many people from Great Britain being in our community; it was mostly eastern—not eastern, *yeah*, eastern—Europeans." He adds, "There weren't that many, sort of, real white supremacists or real hard-core whites. They were [immigrant] Europeans, and they weren't in much better shape than we were financially. And I think if there was a class distinction in those days, it was an economic distinction. I don't think there was that much racism, as we know it today." Inouye, interview with Mary Kitagawa and Tosh Kitagawa, September 16, 2022.

93. Inouye, interview with Mary Kitagawa and Tosh Kitagawa, October 19, 2022.

94. This section builds on Inouye, *The Long Afterlife of Nikkei Wartime Incarceration*, ch. 5; and Mary Kitagawa, Tosh Kitagawa, et al., eds., *A Degree of Justice: 1942*.

95. Quoted in Knickerbocker, *No Plaster Saint*, 152.

96. Salas, interview with Mary Kitagawa, June 17, 2017; Salas, interview with Tosh Kitagawa, June 26, 2017.

97. Inouye, interview with Mary Kitagawa, August 13, 2022.

Afterword

1. On the politics of such recognizability, see Oikawa, *Cartographies of Violence*, esp. 57–66.

2. Cf., for instance, Saidiya Hartman, "Venus in Two Acts," *Small Axe* 12:2

(2008): 1–14; Hartman, *Wayward Lives, Beautiful Experiments: Intimate Histories, Riotous Black Girls, Troublesome Women, and Queer Radicals* (New York: W. W. Norton, 2019).

3. Inouye, interview with Mary Kitagawa, July 12, 2022.

4. See, first and foremost, https://www.anglicanhealingfundforjapanesecanadians.com, which provides additional resources, including an important archive of survivors' stories. See also "Anglican Church Apology," *The Bulletin*, July 23, 2015; Mary Kitagawa, "Speaking to the Apology by the Anglican Clergy, June 15, 2015," *The Bulletin*, July 23, 2015; "Reverend Nakayama Disclosure Project Working Group," *The Bulletin*, May 29, 2014; Joy Kogawa, *The Rain Ascends* (Toronto: Penguin, 2003); Dana Swift, "Bishops Apologize for Priest's History of Abuse," *Anglican Journal* 141:7 (2015): 1 and 12.

5. I borrow this formulation from Oikawa, "'Driven to Scatter Far and Wide," which documents the Canadian government's program in painstaking detail.

6. It is unclear how or whether Bruce recalled the incident. Although he died in 2008, after Richard's revelation, Mary has no recollection of him speaking about Nakayama. Inouye, interview with Mary Kitagawa, August 13, 2022.

7. See the transcript of remarks Mary offered at the ceremony marking the official apology by Anglican leaders: https://www.anglicanhealingfundforjapanesecanadians.com/testimony-8.

8. Kashima, "Japanese American Internees Return," 108–109.

9. Think of Powell Street, which went from being a lively Nikkei cultural hub to a disused industrial zone as a direct consequence of wartime injustice. Even now, that history is knit into the fabric of the neighborhood, from the re-established Vancouver Buddhist Temple to the boarded-up storefronts of businesses that tried and failed to gain a foothold. See Izumi, "Reclaiming Powell Street," in Fiset and Nomura, eds., *Nikkei in the Pacific Northwest*, 308–333.

10. Inouye, interview with Mary Kitagawa and Tosh Kitagawa, September 29, 2022.

11. See, for instance, Bill Hosokawa, *Nisei: The Quiet Americans* (New York: William Morrow, 1969). It must be noted, however, that Hosokawa changed considerably as a political thinker in subsequent years.

12. Oikawa, *Cartographies of Violence*, 51, observes that silence often serves as a complex form of political and cultural negotiation.

Bibliography

Newspapers
The Bulletin (Greater Vancouver Japanese Canadian Citizens Association)
The Calgary Daily Herald
The Cardston News
The Lethbridge Herald
Maclean's
Montreal News Bulletin
The New Canadian
Varsity (University of Toronto)

Interviews and Correspondence
Norm Masaji Ibuki, "Art Miki: Canadian Redress Leader and Human Rights Champion—Part 2," *Discover Nikkei* 13 (January 2016) https://discovernikkei.org/en/journal/2016/1/13/art-miki-2/
Inouye, Karen M. Correspondence with Mary Kitagawa, May 5, 2022.
———. Correspondence with Mary Kitagawa, January 26–27, 2024.
———. Interview with Mary Kitagawa, June 28, 2022.
———. Interview with Mary Kitagawa, July 12, 2022.
———. Interview with Mary Kitagawa, August 13, 2022.
———. Interview with Mary Kitagawa, September 1, 2022.
———. Interview with Mary Kitagawa, February 10, 2023.
———. Interview with Mary Kitagawa, December 2, 2023.
———. Interview with Mary Kitagawa and Tosh Kitagawa, September 16, 2022.
———. Interview with Mary Kitagawa and Tosh Kitagawa, September 29, 2022.

———. Interview with Mary Kitagawa and Tosh Kitagawa, October 19, 2022.
Kodama-Nishimoto, Michiko. Interview with Robert Sato, August 25, 1992. https://scholarspace.manoa.hawaii.edu/server/api/core/bitstreams/6b29e879-df8e-478e-854d-4c14db85c52b/content.
Salas, Rebecca. Interview with Mary Kitagawa, June 17, 2017.
———. Interview with Tosh Kitagawa, June 26, 2017.

Published Sources

Ad Hoc Committee for *Japanese Canadian Redress: The Toronto Story*, ed. *Japanese Canadian Redress: The Toronto Story* (Toronto: HpF Press, 2000).
Adachi, Ken. *The Enemy That Never Was: A History of the Japanese Canadians* (Toronto: McClelland and Stewart, 1976).
Adams, Eric M., Jordan Stanger-Ross, and the Landscapes of Injustice Research Collective. "Promises of Law: The Unlawful Dispossession of Japanese Canadians," *Osgoode Hall Law Journal* 54:3 (2017): 687–739.
Akiwenzie-Damm, Kateri. "We Belong to This Land: A View of 'Cultural Difference,'" *Journal of Canadian Studies* 31:3 (1996): 24–25.
Artibise, Alan. "Boosterism and the Development of Prairie Cities." In R. Douglas Francis and Howard Palmer, eds., *The Prairie West: Historical Readings*, 2nd ed. (Edmonton: University of Alberta Press, 1992), 515–543.
Ayukawa, Michiko Midge. "Creating and Recreating Community: Hiroshima and Canada, 1891–1941" (PhD dissertation, University of Victoria, 1996).
———. *Hiroshima Immigrants in Canada, 1891–1941* (Vancouver: University of British Columbia Press, 2008).
———. "Lemon Creek Memories," *Nikkei Images* 17:1 (2012): 11–16.
———. Review of Tomoko Makabe, *The Canadian Sansei*, *BC Studies* 121 (Spring 1999): 138–139.
———. "Yasutaro Yamaga: Fraser Valley Berry Farmer, Community Leader, and Strategist." In Fiset and Nomura, eds., *Nikkei in the Pacific Northwest*, 71–94.
Bangarth, Stephanie. *Voices Raised in Protest: Defending North American Citizens of Japanese Ancestry, 1942–1949* (Vancouver: University of British Columbia Press, 2008).
Beazer, Lynn M. "An Historical Study of the Cultural, Social, and Religious Backgrounds of the Education of the Blood Indians, Blood Indian Reservation, Alberta" (MA thesis, Montana State University, 1962).
Bectell, Beryl, ed. *Chief Mountain Country: A History of Cardston and District*, vol. 2 (Cardston, AB: Cardston and District Historical Society, 1987).
Breen, David H. *The Canadian Prairie West and the Ranching Frontier, 1874–1924* (Toronto: University of Toronto Press, 1983).
Breen, David, and Kenneth Coates. *Vancouver's Fair: An Administrative and Polit-*

ical History of the Pacific National Exhibition (Vancouver: University of British Columbia Press, 1982).
Brighton, John. *Medical Aspects of Evacuation Days, 1942–1946: New Denver–Slocan* (New Denver, BC: self-published, ca. 1986).
British Columbia Security Commission, *Removal of Japanese from Protected Areas* (Vancouver: British Columbia Security Commission, 1942).
Bunnage, Blaine. "Cardston Junior High School." In Bectell, ed., *Chief Mountain Country*, vol. 2, 63–64.
Burton, Harry. "Don Cunningham Talks about the Old Days of Salt Spring Island," Part 3, video, https://vimeo.com/202494241.
Burwash, Gordon, Julian Biggs, and Grant McLean (producers), *Dresden Story* (Montreal: National Film Board of Canada, 1954).
Cail, Robert E. *Land, Man, and the Law: The Disposal of Crown Lands in British Columbia, 1871–1913* (Vancouver: University of British Columbia Press, 1974).
Card, Brigham Y. "The Canadian Mormon Settlements, 1886–1925: A North-American Perspective." *Canadian Ethnic Studies* 26:1 (1994): 19–39.
Cardston High School Yearbook Staff. *Milestones, 1951–1952* (Cardston, AB: Cardston High School, 1952).
Catalogue of the Brigham Young College for 1910–1911 with List of Students for 1909–1910 (Logan, UT: The Brigham Young University, 1910).
Champagne, Anne. *Kyowakai: Memory and Healing in New Denver* (New Denver, BC: Nikkei Internment Memorial Center, 2020).
Chang, Kornel. *Pacific Connections: The Making of the U.S.-Canadian Borderlands* (Berkeley: University of California Press, 2012).
Colpitts, George. *Game in the Garden: A Human History of Wildlife in Western Canada to 1940* (Vancouver: University of British Columbia Press, 2003).
Daniels, Roger. "Words Do Matter: A Note on Inappropriate Terminology and the Incarceration of Japanese Americans" In Fiset and Nomura, eds., *Nikkei in the Pacific Northwest*, 190–214.
Davies, Alan T., ed. *Antisemitism in Canada: History and Interpretation* (Waterloo, ON: Wilfrid Laurier University Press, 1992).
Dempsey, Hugh A. *Treaty Research Report: Treaty Seven* (Ottawa: Department of Indian Affairs and Northern Development, 1987).
Devereux, Cecily. "'And Let Them Wash Me from This Clanging World': Hugh and Ion, 'The Last Best West,' and Purity Discourse in 1885," *Journal of Canadian Studies* 32:2 (1997): 100–115.
The Doctrine and Covenants of The Church of Jesus Christ of Latter-day Saints (Salt Lake City: The Church of Jesus Christ of Latter-day Saints, 1981).
Elliott, Marie. *Mayne Island and the Outer Gulf Islands: A History* (Mayne Island, BC: Gulf Islands Press, 1984).

Findlay, Kaitlin. "The Bird Commission, Japanese Canadians, and the Challenge of Reparations in the Wake of State Violence" (MA thesis, University of Victoria, 2017).

Fiset, Louis, and Gail M. Nomura, eds. *Nikkei in the Pacific Northwest: Japanese Americans and Japanese Canadians in the Twentieth Century* (Seattle: University of Washington Press, 2005).

Foran, Max, ed. *Icon, Brand, Myth: The Calgary Stampede* (Edmonton: Athabasca University Press, 2008).

Ford, Anne Rochon. *A Path Not Strewn with Roses: One Hundred Years of Women at the University of Toronto, 1884–1984* (Toronto: University of Toronto Press, 1984).

Friday, Chris. *Organizing Asian American Labor: The Pacific Coast Canned-Salmon Industry, 1870–1942* (Philadelphia: Temple University Press, 1994).

Friesen, Gerald. *The Canadian Prairies: A History* (Toronto: University of Toronto Press, 1984).

Fukawa, Masako. "Lifting the Veil on Nanaimo's Nikkei Community: From Settlement to Return," *BC Studies* 204 (Winter 2019–2020): 151–170.

Fukawa, Masako, with Stan Fukawa and the Nikkei Fishermen's History Book Committee. *Spirit of the Nikkei Fleet: British Columbia's Japanese Canadian Fishermen* (Madeira Park, BC: Harbour Publishing, 2009).

Fukawa, Stan. "Rescuing Wayward Men and Raising the Status of the Japanese in Canada: Early Goals for a Chapel/Hospital," *Nikkei Images* 17:2 (2012): 14–16.

Geiger, Andrea. *Converging Empires: Citizens and Subjects in the North Pacific Borderlands, 1867–1945* (Chapel Hill: University of North Carolina Press, 2022).

———. "Disentangling Law and History: Nikkei Challenges to Race-Based Exclusion from British Columbia's Coastal Fisheries, 1920–2007," *Southern California Quarterly* 100:3 (2018): 263–296.

———. "Reframing *Nikkei* Histories: Complicating Existing Narratives," *BC Studies* 192 (Winter 2016–2017): 13–18.

———. *Subverting Exclusion: Transpacific Encounters with Race, Caste, and Borders, 1885–1928* (New Haven, CT: Yale University Press, 2011).

Geiger-Adams, Andrea. "Reframing Race and Place: Locating Japanese Immigrants in Relation to Indigenous Peoples in the North American West, 1880–1940," *Southern California Quarterly* 96:3 (2014): 253–270.

———. "Writing Racial Barriers into Law: Upholding B.C.'s Denial of the Vote to Its Japanese Canadian Citizens, Homma v. Cunningham, 1902." In Fiset and Nomura, eds., *Nikkei in the Pacific Northwest*, 20–43.

Goldman, René. *A Childhood Adrift* (Toronto: Azrieli Foundation, 2017).

Greenaway, John Endo. "Kimiko Murakami: A Portrait of Strength," *The Bulletin* (December 2005): 3–5.

Haig-Brown, Celia. *Resistance and Renewal: Surviving the Indian Residential School* (Vancouver: Tillacum, 1989).
Haraga, Tamiko. "My Experiences during the Second World War," *Nikkei Images* 7:3 (2002): 18–19.
Hartman, Saidiya. "Venus in Two Acts," *Small Axe* 12:2 (2008): 1–14.
———. *Wayward Lives, Beautiful Experiments: Intimate Histories, Riotous Black Girls, Troublesome Women, and Queer Radicals* (New York: W.W. Norton, 2019).
Hashizume, William T. *Japanese Community in Mission: A Brief History, 1904–1942* (Scarborough, ON: self-published, 2002).
Hatch, Neldon. "A History of the Church of Jesus Christ of Latter-Day Saints in Cardston and Area to 1950." In Shaw, ed., *Chief Mountain Country*, vol. 1, 173–182.
Healing Fund for Japanese Canadians. https://www.anglicanhealingfundforjapan esecanadians.com.
Henson, Josiah. *The Life of Josiah Henson, Formerly a Slave, Now an Inhabitant of Canada, as Narrated by Himself* (Boston: Arthur D. Phelps, 1849).
"History of the Catholic Church in Cardston." In Shaw, ed., *Chief Mountain Country*, vol. 1, 169–173.
Holman, Alan C., Daniel J. Bellegarde, and the Canada Indian Claims Commission. *Blood Tribe/Kainaiwa Big Claim Inquiry* (Ottawa: Indian Claims Commission, 2007).
HoSang, Daniel Martinez, and Natalia Molina, "Introduction: Toward a Relational Consciousness of Race." In Molina, HoSang, and Gutiérrez, eds., *Relational Formations of Race*, 1–18.
Hosokawa, Bill. *Nisei: The Quiet Americans* (New York: William Morrow, 1969).
Inouye, Karen M. *The Long Afterlife of Nikkei Wartime Incarceration* (Stanford, CA: Stanford University Press, 2016).
Irby, Charles B. "The Black Settlers on Salt Spring Island in the Nineteenth Century," *Phylon* 35:4 (1974): 368–374.
Ishikawa, Wakako. "Japanese-Canadian Education during the World War II Internment" (MA thesis, University of Toronto, 2003).
Iwaasa, David. "Canadian Japanese in Southern Alberta, 1905–1945." In Roger Daniels, ed., *Two Monographs on Japanese Canadians* (New York: Arno Press, 1978).
———. "The Mormons and Their Japanese Neighbors," *Alberta History* 53 (Winter 2005): 7–22.
Izumi, Masumi. "The Japanese Canadian Movement: Migration and Activism before and after World War II," *Amerasia Journal* 33:2 (2007): 49–66
———. "Reclaiming Powell Street: Reconstruction of the Japanese Canadian Community in Post–World War II Vancouver." In Fiset and Nomura, eds., *Nikkei in the Pacific Northwest*, 308–333.

Jantzen, William. *Limits on Liberty: The Experience of Mennonite, Hutterite and Doukhobor Communities in Canada* (Toronto: University of Toronto Press, 1990).

Japanese Canadian Centennial Project Committee. *A Dream of Riches: The Japanese Canadians, 1877–1977* (Vancouver: Japanese Canadian Centennial Project, 1978).

Joudrey, Susan L. "The Expectations of a Queen: Identity and Race Politics in the Calgary Stampede." In Alvin Finkel, Sarah Carter, and Peter Fortna, eds., *The West and Beyond: New Perspectives on an Imagined Region* (Edmonton: Athabasca University Press, 2010), 133–155.

Kahn, Charles. *Saltspring: The Story of an Island* (Vancouver: Harbour Publishing, 1998).

Kanesaka, Rumiko, and Brian Smallshaw, eds. *Island Forest Embers: The Japanese Canadian Charcoal Kilns of the Southern Gulf Islands* (Ganges, BC: Japanese Garden Society of Salt Spring Island, 2018).

Kashima, Tetsuden. "Japanese American Internees Return, 1945 to 1955: Readjustment and Social Amnesia," *Phylon* 41:2 (1980): 107–115.

Kawamoto Reid, Linda, and Beth Carter. *Karizumai: A Guide to Japanese Canadian Internment Sites* (Burnaby, BC: Nikkei National Museum, 2016).

Kilian, Crawford. *Go Do Some Great Thing: The Black Pioneers of British Columbia*, 3rd ed. (Madeira Park, BC: Harbour Publishing, 2020).

Kitagawa, Mary, Tosh Kitagawa, et al., eds. *A Degree of Justice: 1942* (Vancouver: n.p., 2017).

Kitagawa, Muriel. *This Is My Own: Letters to Wes and Other Writings on Japanese Canadians, 1941–1948*. Edited by Roy Miki. (Vancouver: Talonbooks, 1985).

Knickerbocker, Nancy. *No Plaster Saint: The Life of Mildred Osterhout Fahrni, 1900–1992* (Vancouver: Talonbooks, 2001).

Kobayashi, Audrey L. "Camp Road." In Daniel J. Keyes and Luis L.M. Aguiar, eds., *White Space: Race, Privilege, and Cultural Economies of the Okanagan Valley* (Vancouver: University of British Columbia Press, 2021), 117–126.

———. "Emigration from Kaideima, Japan, 1885–1950: An Analysis of Community and Landscape Change" (PhD dissertation, University of California, Los Angeles, 1983).

Kogawa, Joy. *The Rain Ascends* (Toronto: Penguin, 2003).

La Violette, Forrest. *The Canadian Japanese and World War II: A Sociological and Psychological Account* (Toronto: University of Toronto Press, 1948).

Lambertson, Ross. "'The Dresden Story': Racism, Human Rights, and the Jewish Labour Committee of Canada," *Labour/Le Travail* 47 (Spring 2001): 43–82.

———. *Repression and Resistance: Canadian Human Rights Activists, 1930–1960* (Toronto: University of Toronto Press, 2005).

Lee, Carol F. "The Road to Enfranchisement: Chinese and Japanese in British Columbia," *BC Studies* 30 (Summer 1976): 44–76.
Lee, Erika. *At America's Gates: Chinese Immigration during the Exclusion Era, 1882–1943* (Chapel Hill: University of North Carolina Press, 2003).
Leishman, Jeanne. "Cardston School Division #2." In Bectell, ed., *Chief Mountain Country*, vol. 2, 58–61.
Lipsitz, George, George J. Sánchez, and Kelly Lytle Hernández, with Daniel Martinez HoSang and Natalia Molina, "Race as a Relational Theory: A Roundtable Discussion." In Molina, HoSang, and Gutiérrez, eds., *Relational Formations of Race*, 22–42.
MacDonald, Graham A. *Where the Mountains Meet the Prairies: A History of Waterton Lakes National Park* (Hull, QC: Canadian Heritage, Parks Canada, 1992).
Makabe, Tomoko. "Canadian Evacuation and Nisei Identity," *Phylon* 41:2 (1980): 116–125.
———. *The Canadian Sansei* (Toronto: University of Toronto Press, 1998).
———. *Picture Brides: Japanese Women in Canada* (North York: Multicultural History Society of Ontario, 1995).
Marlatt, Daphne, ed. *Steveston Recollected: A Japanese-Canadian History* (Vancouver: Provincial Archives of British Columbia, 1975).
Matsumura, Janice. "More or Less Intelligent: Nikkei IQ and Racial/Ethnic Hierarchies in British Columbia and Imperial Japan," *BC Studies* 192 (Winter 2016–17): 51–69.
Mawani, Renisa. *Colonial Proximities: Crossracial Encounters and Juridical Truths in British Columbia, 1871–1921* (Vancouver: University of British Columbia Press, 2009).
McAllister, Kirsten Emiko. *Terrain of Memory: A Japanese Canadian Memorial Project* (Vancouver: University of British Columbia Press, 2010).
McLean, Stuart. *Welcome Home: Travels in Smalltown Canada* (Toronto: Penguin Books, 1992).
McIllree, J., and M. H. White Fraser. "Fishing in Southern Alberta," *Alberta History* 31 (1983): 36–38.
Miki, Roy. *Redress: Inside the Japanese Canadian Call for Justice* (Vancouver: Raincoast Books, 2004).
Molina, Natalia, Daniel Martinez HoSang, and Ramón Gutiérrez, eds. *Relational Formations of Race: Theory, Method, and Practice* (Berkeley: University of California Press, 2019).
Moritsugu, Frank, ed. *Teaching in Canadian Exile: A History of the Schools for Japanese-Canadian Children in B.C. Detention Camps during the Second World War* (Toronto: The Ghost Town Teachers Historical Society, 2001).

Murakami, Rose. *Ganbaru: The Murakami Family of Salt Spring Island* (Ganges, BC: Japanese Garden Society of Salt Spring Island, 2005).
Nakagawa, Frances Kuniko. "Reminiscences of My Stay in the Livestock Building," *Nikkei Images* 18:2 (2013): 4–5.
Nakayama, Goichi Gordon. *Issei: Stories of Japanese Canadian Pioneers* (Toronto: NC Press, 1984).
Nakayama, Timothy M. "Anglican Missions to the Japanese in Canada," rev. ed. (2003): 1–17. http://anglicanhistory.org/academic/nakayama2003.pdf. Originally published in the *Journal of the Canadian Church Historical Society* 8:2 (1966): 26–48.
National Association of Japanese Canadians, "Presentation to the Special Joint Committee on a Renewed Canada," *Minutes of Proceedings and Evidence*, no. 16, Winnipeg, November 4, 1991 (Ottawa: Government of Canada Publications, 1992).
National Opinion Research Center, *Attitudes toward "The Japanese In Our Midst"* (Denver: University of Denver, 1946).
Nielsen, Brent. "Cardston High School," in Bectell, ed. *Chief Mountain Country*, vol. 2, 64–66.
Nikkei National Museum. "Harold Miwa," interview by Sendai Project (n.d.). 1942: Japanese Canadian Internment at Hastings Park. http://hastingspark1942.ca/harold-miwa/.
Nunoda, Peter Takaji. "A Community in Transition and Conflict: 1935–1951" (Doctoral thesis, University of Manitoba, 1991).
Obata, Roger. "Relocation to Toronto." In Ad Hoc Committee for *Japanese Canadian Redress: The Toronto Story*, ed., *Japanese Canadian Redress: The Toronto Story* (Toronto: HpF Press, 2000, 63–81.
Ohashi, Ted, and Yvonne Wakabayashi. *Tasaka* (North Vancouver: self-published, 2005).
Oikawa, Mona. *Cartographies of Violence: Japanese Canadian Women, Memory, and the Subjects of the Internment* (Toronto: University of Toronto Press, 2012).
———. "'Driven to Scatter Far and Wide:' The Forced Resettlement of Japanese Canadians to Southern Ontario, 1944–1949" (MA thesis, University of Toronto, 1986).
Oiwa, Keibo. "The Structure of Dispersal: The Japanese-Canadian Community of Montreal, 1942–1952," *Canadian Ethnic Studies/Études ethniques au Canada* 18:2 (1986): 20–37.
Omatsu, Maryka. *Bittersweet Passage: Redress and the Japanese Canadian Experience* (Toronto: Between the Lines, 1992).
Omi, Michael, and Howard Winant. *Racial Formation in the United States: the 1960s to the 1980s*, 3rd ed. (New York: Routledge, 2015).

Owram, Doug. *Promise of Eden: The Canadian Expansionist Movement and the Idea of the West, 1856–1900* (Toronto: University of Toronto Press, 1980).

Palmer, Howard. "Patterns of Racism: Attitudes toward Chinese and Japanese in Alberta, 1920–1950," *Histoire sociale/Social History* 13:25 (1980): 137–160.

Pankhurst, Robert, and Susan Smith, eds. *Chief Mountain Country: A History of Cardston and District*, vol. 3 (Cardston, AB: Cardston and District Historical Society, 2005).

Pettipas, Katherine. *Severing the Ties That Bind: Government Repression of Religious Ceremonies on the Prairies* (Winnipeg: University of Manitoba Press, 1994).

Potyondi, Barry. *In Palliser's Triangle: Living in the Grasslands, 1850–1930* (Saskatoon, SK: Purich Publishing, 1995).

Powell Street Festival Society Board, "The Powell Street Festival: Into the New Millennium?," *The JCCA Bulletin* 41:10 (1999): 7–11, 14.

Rak, Julie. *Negotiated Memory: Doukhobor Autobiographical Discourse* (Vancouver: University of British Columbia Press, 2004).

Raymond Buddhist Church. *A History of Forty Years of the Raymond Buddhist Church* (Raymond, AB: The Raymond Buddhist Church, 1970).

Reed, Thomas Arthur. *A History of Trinity College, 1852–1952* (Toronto: University of Toronto Press, 1952).

Regular, W. Keith. *Neighbors and Networks: The Blood Tribe in the Southern Alberta Economy, 1884–1939* (Calgary: University of Calgary Press, 2009).

Robinson, Greg. "Quebec Newspaper Reactions to the 1907 Vancouver Riots: Humanitarianism, Nationalism, and Internationalism," *BC Studies* 192 (Winter 2016–2017): 25–49.

———. *A Tragedy of Democracy: Japanese Confinement in North America* (New York: Columbia University Press, 2009).

Roy, Christian. "Histoire de la communauté Japonaise du Québec, 1942–1988" (PhD dissertation, Université du Québec à Montréal, 2016).

Roy, Patricia E. "An Ambiguous Relationship: Anglicans and the Japanese in British Columbia, 1902–1949," *BC Studies* 192 (Winter 2016–2017): 105–124.

———. "Lessons in Citizenship, 1945–1949: The Delayed Return of the Japanese to Canada's Pacific Coast." In Fiset and Nomura, eds., *Nikkei in the Pacific Northwest*, 254–277.

———. "The Re-creation of Vancouver's Japanese Community, 1945–2008," *Journal of the Canadian Historical Association/Revue de la Société historique du Canada* 19:2 (2008): 127–154.

———. *The Triumph of Citizenship: The Japanese and Chinese in Canada, 1941–1967* (Vancouver: University of British Columbia Press, 2007).

———. *A White Man's Province: White Politicians and Chinese and Japanese Immigrants, 1858–1914* (Vancouver: University of British Columbia Press, 1989).

Sakata, Michiko. "Tonari Gumi," *Rikka* 4:2 (1977): 4–11.
Sandwell, Ruth W. *Contesting Rural Space: Land Policy and Practices of Resettlement on Saltspring Island, 1859–1891* (Montréal–Kingston: McGill University Press, 2005).
Sharp, Paul F. "The American Farmer and the 'Last Best West,'" *Agricultural History* 21:2 (1947): 65–75.
Shaw, Keith, ed. *Chief Mountain Country: A History of Cardston and District*, vol. 1 (Cardston, AB: Cardston and District Historical Society, 1978).
Shibutani, Tamotsu. *Improvised News: A Sociological Study of Rumor* (Indianapolis: Bobbs-Merrill, 1966).
Shimizu, Yon. *The Exiles: An Archival History of the World War II Japanese Road Camps in British Columbia and Ontario* (Wallaceburg, ON: self-published, 1993).
Shiomi, Rick. "Community Organizing: The Problems of Innovating and Sustaining Interest." In K. Victor Ujimoto and Gordon Hirabayashi, eds., *Asian Canadians Regional Perspectives: Selections from the Proceedings, Asian Canadian Symposium V, Mount Saint Vincent University, Halifax, Nova Scotia, May 23 to 26, 1981* (Guelph, ON: University of Guelph, 1982), 339–354.
Smallshaw, Brian. *As If They Were the Enemy: The Dispossession of Japanese Canadians on Saltspring Island* (Victoria: University of Victoria Press, 2020).
———. "The Murakami Women of Saltspring Island," *BC Studies* 204 (Winter 2019–2020): 183–204.
Stanger-Ross, Jordan, "The Economic Impacts of Dispossession," In Jordan Stanger-Ross, ed. *Landscapes of Injustice: A New Perspective on the Internment and Dispossession of Japanese Canadians* (Montréal–Kingston: McGill–Queen's University Press, 2020), 339-365.
Stanger-Ross, Jordan, Will Archibald, and the Landscapes of Injustice Research Collective. "Unfaithful Custodian: Glenn McPherson and the Dispossession of Japanese Canadians in the 1940s," *Journal of American Ethnic History* 37:4 (2018): 40–72.
Stanger-Ross, Jordan, and Pamela Sugiman, eds. *Witness to Loss: Race, Culpability, and Memory in the Dispossession of Japanese Canadians* (Montréal–Kingston: McGill-Queen's University Press, 2017).
Steckley, John L. *Indian Agents: Rulers of the Reserves* (New York: Peter Lang, 2016).
Stewart, Todd, and Karen J. Leong, with John Tateishi and Natasha Egan. *Placing Memory: A Photographic Exploration of Japanese American Internment* (Norman: University of Oklahoma Press, 2008).
Stielow, Timothy Mark. "No Quarter Required: Japanese Experiences and Media Distortions in the Steveston Fishers' Strike of 1900" (MA thesis, Simon Fraser University, 2012).

Students' Administrative Council of the University of Toronto. *Torontonensis* (Toronto: University of Toronto, 1954–1963).

Sugiman, Pamela. "Memories of Internment: Narrating Japanese Canadian Women's Life Stories," *The Canadian Journal of Sociology/Cahiers canadiens de sociologie* 29:3 (2004): 359–388.

Sugimoto, Howard Hiroshi. *Japanese Immigration, the Vancouver Riots, and Canadian Diplomacy* (New York: Arno Press, 1978).

Sunahara, Ann Gomer. *The Politics of Racism: The Uprooting of Japanese Canadians during the Second World War*, rev. ed. (Burnaby, BC: Nikkei National Museum, 2020).

Suttie, Gwen (Dorothy Blakey Smith, ed.). "With the Nisei in New Denver," *British Columbia Historical News* 5:2 (1972): 15–25.

Swift, Dana. "Bishops Apologize for Priest's History of Abuse," *Anglican Journal* 141:7 (2015): 1, 12.

Tagami, Tom I. "Still Lingers On: The 60th Anniversary of the Internment, Part 2, 'A Ganbare Family,'" *Nikkei Images* 7:3 (2002): 12–17.

Takasaki, Yukinori Peter. "Memoirs of Yukinori Peter Takasaki." Trans. Mayumi Takasaki. *Nikkei Images* 7:1 (Spring 2002): 6–7.

Teramoto, Mitsuko Shirley. "Memories . . . from the 1930s to the 1950s," *Nikkei Images* 17:3 (2012): 18–23.

Thompson, E. P. *Witness against the Beast: William Blake and the Moral Law* (New York: New Press, 1993).

Thompson, Grace Eiko. "National Association of Japanese Canadians President's Report: JC Community Loses a Good Friend," *Nikkei Voice* 22:2 (2008): 10.

Tokawa, Daniel Tsuruo. *Vancouver Rashomon: Redress Stories* (Altona, MB: Friesen Press, 2022).

Tovías, Blanca. *Colonialism on the Prairies: Blackfoot Settlement and Cultural Transformation, 1870–1920* (Toronto: Sussex Academic Press, 2011).

Treaty 7 Tribal Council, with Walter Hildebrandt, Sarah Carter, and Dorothy First Rider. *The True Spirit and Original Intent of Treaty 7* (Montreal–Kingston: McGill-Queen's University Press, 1996).

Trinity Review Staff. *Trinity, 1852–1952*, a special issue of the *Trinity Review* (1952).

Van Vliet, L. J. P., A. J. Green, and E. A. Kenney. *Soils of the Gulf Islands of British Columbia*. Vol. 1, *Soils of Saltspring Island* (Victoria: Ministry of the Environment, 1987).

Vandenberg, Helen Elizabeth Ruth. "Race, Hospital Development, and the Power of Community: Chinese and Japanese Hospitals in British Columbia, 1880–1920" (PhD dissertation, University of British Columbia, 2015).

Walker, James W. St. G. *"Race," Rights, and the Law in the Supreme Court of Canada* (Waterloo, ON: Wilfrid Laurier University Press, 1997).

Wangenheim, Elizabeth D. *The Social Organization of the Japanese Community in Toronto: A Product of Crisis* (MA thesis, University of Toronto, 1956).

Ward, Peter. *White Canada Forever: Popular Attitudes and Public Policy toward Orientals in British Columbia*, 3rd ed. (Montréal–Kingston: McGill University Press, 2014).

Wetherell, Donald G., and Irene Kmet, *Town Life: Main Street and the Evolution of Small Town Alberta, 1880–1947* (Edmonton: University of Alberta Press, 1995).

———. *Useful Pleasures: The Shaping of Leisure in Alberta, 1896–1945* (Regina, SK: Canadian Plains Research Center, 1990).

Yang Murray, Alice. *Historical Memories of the Japanese American Internment and the Struggle for Redress* (Stanford, CA: Stanford University Press, 2007).

Yamashiro, Takeo. "Tonari Gumi: Powell Street Positively Revisited." In Cassandra Kobayashi and Roy Miki, eds., *Spirit of Redress: Japanese Canadians in Conference* (Vancouver: JC Publications, 1989), 55–58.

Yasui, Roy. "Remembrances of New Denver, 1942–1946," *Nikkei Images* 11:3 (Autumn 2006): 20–25.

Yesaki, Mitsuo. *Sutebusuton: A Japanese Village on the British Columbia Coast* (Vancouver: Peninsula Publishing, 2003).

Yesaki, Mitsuo, Harold Steves, and Kathy Steves. *Steveston Cannery Row: An Illustrated History*, rev. ed. (Vancouver: Peninsula Publishing, 2005).

Yokota, Carl. "Angler P.O.W. Camp 101," *Nikkei Images* 7:2 (Summer 2002): 10–12.

Index

Page numbers in italics refer to figures.

A Dream of Riches. See Japanese Canadian Centennial Project
A.P. Slades, 38
Adachi, Ken, 13
Alberta, 5, 9, 11, 12, 13–15, 53, 54, 62, 64–72, 84, 85–111, 114, 115, 116, 133–136, 137, 138, 141, 158, 164, 165, 166, 168
Alberta Farmer, 67
Alberta Sugar Beet Growers Association, 66, 68–69. *See also* beet farming
alliances, inter-group, 6, 8, 49, 81, 123–126, 155, 162, 170
Anglican church, 6, 8, 101, 102, 103, 106, 197 n. 42; attitudes toward Nikkei, 184 n. 26; exclusion of the Murakami family from, 49, 113, 120. *See also* Nakayama, Goichi Gordon; University of Toronto
anti-Semitism, 123–126, 209 n. 77
arson, 32

Asian Canadian and Asian Migration Studies Program. *See* University of British Columbia
assimilation, 94, 127, 128, 183 n. 10, 195 n. 94
Atso'toah, 94, 195 n. 94
Ayukawa, Michiko Midge, 23, 76, 78, 84, 129

B'nai B'rith Hillel Foundation. *See* University of Toronto
Baptism, 113
Barnet, I.T., 82
basketball, 101, 105, 197 n. 137
Bay Farm. *See* Slocan and Extension
beet farming, 5, 12, 14, 53, 54, 62, 65–66, 68, 70, 81, 84, 86–87, 89, 98, 116, 133, 134–135, 138, 142, 162, 168, 188 n. 87. *See also* Alberta Sugar Beet Growers Association
Bennett, Karen (Kitagawa), 145–146, 151, *163*

225

berry farming, 19, 80, 133, 136
Bird, Henry, 86
Bird Commission. *See* Royal Commission to Investigate Claims of Japanese Canadians for Property Losses
birds of passage. *See* watari-dori
Black migrants. *See* Salt Spring Island: Stark family; Whims family; Wood family
Blood Indians. *See* Kainai
Blum, Sid, 124, 125
Bondaruk farm (Magrath), 85
Booth Canal Road. *See* Salt Spring Island
Bowling, 92, 107, 121, 129, 202 n. 51
Brigham Young University, 66, 70
British Columbia: as destination for Nikkei migrants, 19–23; expulsion of Nikkei from, 43–54; *See also*, Hastings Park; Vancouver
British Columbia Electric Company, 58
British Columbia Security Commission, 54, 59, 61, 68–69, 71–72, 75, 77, 80, 102, 186 n. 50, 186 n. 64
Bulletin, 156. *See also* Japanese Canadian Citizens Association
Burnett, Hugh, 124–125

Calgary Daily Herald, 89, 189 n. 100
Calgary Elks Club, 108
Calgary Stampede, 107–108, 168
Canadian Girls in Training, 101
Canadian Jewish Labour Committee, 124–125
Canadian Race Relations Foundation, 147
Card, Charles Ora, 91
Cardston, 9, 12, 13, 54, 65, 67, 88–91, 94, 97–99, 100, 102–107, 108; Cardston Junior-Senior High School, 99–101, 104, 106–107; Rod and Gun Club, 94–95, 103; Senior Chamber of Commerce, 94; Social Centre, 105, 107; "Grey House" in, 88, 91, 96, 97, 197 n. 131; Du-Eet Cafe, 88–94, 96–97, 101, 103, 104, 105, 106, 110, 111, 112, 114, 117, 195 n. 95, 199 n. 6, 200 n. 24; *Cardston News*, 99, 100, 104, 195 n. 95, 196 n. 122, 200 n. 24. *See also* basketball; Kainai; Locker, Evelyn; wildlife policy in southern Alberta
Carpenter Creek. *See* Slocan and Extension
Catholicism, 106, 124
Chang, Kornel, 17
Chief Shot Both Sides. *See* Atso'toah
childhood: experience of, 9, 12, 26–27, 30–31, 39–41, 43, 49, 57–60, 65, 72, 76–80, 102, 105, 142; as racialized construct, 4–5, 48, 55–56; *See also* Hastings Park
Chinese: immigrants, 10, 15, 18, 20, 21, 27, 34, 67; communities descended from, 67, 90. *See also* Yip family (Cardston)
Chinese Student Christian Association. *See* University of Toronto
Church of Jesus Christ of Latter-day Saints, 6, 67, 88, 91, 94, 99, 101, 103, 104, 105, 168, 197 n. 132, 198 n. 144
Coaldale: town, 89; Anglican Church of the Ascension in, 164
Committee on Group Relations, 125
Cooperative Committee for Japanese Canadians, 81, 127, 128
Co-operative Commonwealth Federation, 78, 127, 192 n. 55, 204 n. 87

Crerar, Thomas, 193 n. 55
Custodian of Enemy Property, 46, 47, 50, 52, 80, 110, 111, 118, 201 n. 37. *See also* Mouat, Gavin; Royal Commission to Investigate Claims of Japanese Canadians for Property Losses
Cunningham, Don, 112

dancing, 78, 105, 107, 123
Daniels, Roger, 14, 162
dekasegi, 20–21, 22, 23, 24
Department of Fisheries, 35
deportation. *See* expatriation
Diamond City, 133, 135, 158, 169, 210 n. 92
dispossession, 1, 9, 11, 15, 53, 86, 89, 90, 98, 100, 108, 109, 121, 128, 129, 130, 133, 138, 141, 142, 143, 148, 162, 163, 165, 168, 170, 175, 206 n. 13. *See also* Custodian of Enemy Property; Royal Commission to Investigate Claims of Japanese Canadians for Property Losses
Doukhobors, 15, 66, 75–77, 168
Dresden, 124–125
Dresden Story, 124
Du-Eet Cafe. *See* Cardston
Duck Bay. *See* Salt Spring Island
Ducks Unlimited. *See* wildlife policy in southern Alberta

Eagle Speaker, Evelyn. *See* Locker, Evelyn (Eagle Speaker)
Edmunds Act, 91
Elizabeth, Queen Mother and Consort of George VI, 38
Elizabeth II, Queen of the United Kingdom, 115
Episkopon. *See* University of Toronto

expatriation, 7, 9, 14, 54, 85, 127, 128, 147, 192 n. 55, 206 n. 13
"evacuation:" as euphemism, 13. *See also* forced dispersal, dispossession, inland exile, expatriation
ethnic cleansing, 7, 9, 15, 85, 117, 128, 143, 147, 163, 165, 168, 169, 183 n. 10, 192 n. 54, 201 n. 35. *See also* intermarriage

Fahrni, Mildred, 78, 158, 162,
Finlay, Reverend James, 126, 129
forced dispersal, 2, 9, 14, 15, 51, 53, 54, 74, 78, 82, 84, 85, 87, 88, 89, 100, 116, 121, 130, 136, 142, 147, 159, 165
franchise: exclusion of immigrants and First Nations peoples from, 18, 204 n. 87; pursuit of by Nikkei, 18–19, 127
Fraser River, 27

Galbus, Gus, 112
Gentlemen's Agreement, 25, 37. *See also* immigration, restrictions on
George VI, King of England, 38
"ghost towns," 14, 53, 130, 162. *See also* forced dispersal
Gibb, Shirley, 101
Goldman, René, 151–153, 154, 161, 171, 209 n. 77
Green, Howard Charles, 2, 159
Greenwood, 53, 61–62, 64, 74, 75, 76, 102, 186 n. 68
"Grey House." *See* Cardston
Gulf Islands, 6, 15, 26, 27, 28–29, 85, 102, 154; Islands Trust, 154–155. *See also* Salt Spring Island; preemption

hanafuda, 86
Haraga, Tamiko, 62, 76

Hastings Park: Automotive and Ice Rink Building, 54, 55; Exhibition Park Race Track, 55, 185 n. 50; facility, 14, 53, 54–60, 185 n. 47; Garden Auditorium, 55, 57; Happyland, 54, 55, 185 n. 50; Horseshow Building, 54; Livestock Building, 55, 56, 58–59, 60; Manufacturers' Building (Machinery Hall), 55, 56, 57, *58*; Shoot the Chutes, 55, 185 n. 50
Hirano, Ruth. *See* Tsujimura, Ruth (Hirano)
Hiroshima, 16, 22, 23, 117
Holocaust. *See* Shoah
Homma, Tomekichi, 19, 24, 176 n. 11
Hong Kong, Japanese invasion of, 44
Hutterites, 94

immigration: restrictions on in British Columbia, 17–18, 20, 25, 34–35, 37; patterns of among Issei, 19, 20–21, 23. *See also* Qualification and Registration of Voters Act; franchise
Imperial Order Daughters of the Empire, 199 n. 169
incarceration as term for forced dispersal, 14
Indian Affairs Department, 106
inland exile, 5, 9, 10, 14, 60, 75, 84, 87, 105, 116, 129, 133, 138, 142, 162, 163, 165, 171, 191 n. 31
Innoshima, 16, 32, 33, 37
Inouye, Ron, *63*
intermarriage, 143, 152
internment: as provisional term for forced dispersal, 13–15
Inuit peoples, 120
Islands Trust. *See* Gulf Islands

Issei, 19, 44, 46–47, 55, 67, 84, 136, 146, 147
Iwasaki, Torazo, 52–53, 82, 112–113, 168, 169–170

Japanese Canadian Centennial Project, 147
Japanese Canadian Citizens Association, 2, 132, 155, 156, 203 n. 75, 209 n. 81. *See also* National Association of Japanese Canadians
Japanese Canadian Citizens' League, 19, 127
Japanese Canadian Committee for Democracy, 81, 123, 127, 128
Japanese Community Volunteers Association, 147
Japanese Fishing Vessel Disposition Committee, 44, 46
Jensen, Lalovee, 66, 71–72
Jung, Douglas, 2, 159

Kainai: Nation, 64–65, 94, 106, 108; relations with surrounding communities, 103–105, 198 n. 151; Reserve, 90, 103; restrictions on movement of, 106–107; schooling of, 106; treaty enforcement, 95. *See also* Atso'toah; Evelyn Locker; Treaty Day; wildlife policy in southern Alberta
Kashima, Tetsuden, 109, 167
Kaslo, 74, 77
Kay's Cafe. *See* Dresden
Kearl, Arminto, 100, 101
Keeler family (Magrath), 53, 65, 85
King, William Lyon Mackenzie, 44, 85, 192 n. 54, 192 n. 55, 193 n. 55
Kitagawa, Landon, 135, 145, 146, 151, *163*

Kitagawa, Muriel, 55, 126
Kitagawa, Nobuko (Yamaura), 133, 134
Kitagawa, Takejiro, 133
Kitagawa, Tosh, 2, 13, 132, 133–138, 140–146, *145*, 147, 148, 149, 152, 155–158, 159–161, *160*, 162, *163*, 169, 171
Kitagawa, Yosokichi, 133, 135, 143, 144, 205 n. 6
Knight Sugar Company, 67
Kobayashi, Audrey L., 19, 21
Kootenays, 5, 7, 13, 39, 53, 64, 69, 71, 72–77, 78, 82, 101, 102. *See also* Greenwood; New Denver; Slocan and Extension

L.D.S. Church. *See* Church of Jesus Christ of Latter-day Saints
La Violette, Forrest, 98, 110, 126, 130, 200 n. 30
labor unions, 124–125, 171. *See also* salmon: fishers' unions
Landscapes of Injustice Project, 2
Last Best West mythos, 95
Lee Creek, 91, 95
Lemon Creek. *See* Slocan and Extension
Lethbridge, 64, 67, 68, 71, 87, 91, 104, 108, 113, 133, 134, 135, 136, 137, 141, 142, 157, 193 n. 61, 198 n. 151, 206 n. 15
Lethbridge Herald, 68, 104, 108, 194 n. 73,
Locker, Evelyn (Eagle Speaker), 106–108, 166, 168, 199 n. 159
Lor, Ruth. *See* Malloy, Ruth (Lor)
loyalty survey. *See* expatriation

Mackenzie, Ian, 85, 192 n. 55
MacLean's, 125

Magrath, 53, 54, 62, 64–70, 71–72, 77, 82, 85, 87, 88, 89, 90, 91, 98, 102, 161
Magrath, Charles A., 68
Magrath Trading Company, 70
Malloy, Ruth (Lor), 125
Manitoba, 14, 138, 165
Mayne Island, 29, 53. *See also* Gulf Islands
McAllister, Kirsten Emiko, 43
McArthur, W.T., 61
Meiji Emperor, 22
Methodism, 24
Mission City, 133, 142, 157, 206 n. 6
Miwa, Harold, 56, 60
Miwa, Katherine. *See* Suzuki, Katherine (Miwa)
mochi, 30, 41
model minority myth, 109
Montreal, 14, 117, 121, 128, 202 n. 51
Montreal News Bulletin, 117, 201 n. 35
Mormonism. *See* Church of Jesus Christ of Latter-day Saints
Mouat, Gavin, 47, 50, 51, 53, 82, 113, 170, 192 n. 42
Mouat family (Salt Spring Island), 38
Mounties. *See* Royal Canadian Mounted Police
Murakami, Alice, 12, 39, *40*, 42, 48–49, 51, 52, 62, 70, 71, *73*, 78, 92, 96, 98–99, 100, 102, 106, 116, 122, 158, 169, 196 n. 22, 202 n. 58
Murakami, Asamatsu, 24
Murakami, Katsuyori, 37–39, *40*, 41, 42, 47, 49, 50, 54, 62, *63*, 64, 66, 69–70, 71, *73*, 74, 80–82, 86–88, 90, 92, *93*, 94, 96–97, 98, 103, 110–114, 115, 116, 139, 154, 170, 172, 182 n. 102, 182 n. 1, 187 n. 78, 191 n. 40, 193 n. 61, 196 n. 113

230 Index

Murakami, Kimiko (Okano), 9, 24, 26, 29, 30, 32–33, *35*, *36*, 37, 38–39, *40*, 41, 49, 50–52, 53, 58, 59, 60, 62, 64, 66, 70, 73, 80, 82, 85, 86–88, 90, 92, *93*, 94, 96, 97, 98, 110, 112–114, 115, 116, 139, 154, 165, 170, 172, 178 n. 32, 182 n. 99, 184 n. 24, 195 n. 95, 196 n. 113, 200 n. 24

Murakami, Luke, *63*

Murakami, Philip, *63*

Murakami, Richard, 39, 59, *73*, 92, 96, 97, 111, 113, 116, 122, 139, 143, 154–155, 158, 164–166, 211 n. 6

Murakami, Rose, 12, 16, 25, 29, 30, 32, 38, 39, *40*, 49, 50, 54, 72, *73*, 92, 95, 97, 99–101, 105, 111, 113, 116, 139–140, 143, 154, 158, 164, 197 n. 131 and n. 137, 207 n. 40

Murakami, Ryoichi, 39, 113

Murakami, Sukini, 38, 63

Murakami, Violet, 39, *40*, *73*, 82–83, 92, 97, 111, 116

Nagano, Manzo, 20, 21

Naganobu, Harry, 127

Nakayama, Goichi Gordon, 62, 64, 84, 103, 164–165, 166; protection of by Anglican authorities, 165

National Association of Japanese Canadians, 2, 147, 151, 209 n. 81

National Unity Association, 124, 204 n. 78

naturalization, 19, 45, 46, 184 n. 17

New Canadian, 45, 47–48, 50, 62, 65, 74, 81, 89, 117, 128, 136–137, 139, 143, 201 n. 33

New Denver, 54, 69, 74, 77, 80, 83, 191 n. 31

Nikkei labor camps, 14, 45, 46, 49–50, 62, *63*, 64, 71, 138. *See also* Yellowhead Pass

Nisei, 19, 44, 55, 65, 77, 85, 121, 123, 125, 126–130, 134, 136, 150, 154, 169, 191 n. 31, 202 n. 51, 204 n. 81, 204 n. 88, 205 n. 92

Nisei Students' Club. *See* University of Toronto

Nuremberg Race Laws, 152

Oikawa, Mona, 138

Okada, Henry, *160*

Okano Creek. *See* Salt Spring Island

Okano, Ayanosuke and Tsuruka, 25

Okano, James, 33, 85, 88, 90–92, 94–96, 97, 103, 111, 116

Okano, Kazue, 27, 31, 32, 33

Okano, Kimiko. *See* Murakami, Kimiko (Okano)

Okano, Kumanosuke, 9, 10, 16, *17*, 20, 21, 22, 24, 25, 26, 29, 30–31, 32–34, *35*, 39, 51, 65, 85, 90, 91, 92, 104, 118, 172

Okano, Miyoko, 32

Okano, Riyo (Kimura), 9, 10, 16, *17*, 21, 22, 24, 25–26, 29, 30, 32, 33, 38, 39, 51, 65, 85, 91, 92, 97, 104, 111, 116, 118, 172, 177 n. 21

Okano, Sayoko, 27, 32, 33, *35*, *36*, 179 n. 48

Okano, Victor, 33, 85, 94–96, 110–111, 116, 196 n. 113, 199 n. 3

Ontario, 62, 117, 118, 125, 126, 127, 165

Order-in-Council P.C. 1486, 158

Order-in-Council P.C. 1665, 50, 80

Order-in-Council P.C. 469, 80–81

Oshiro, Roy, *160*

Pacific Citizen, 143, 207 n. 23

Palliser Triangle, 64

Pearl Harbor, 2, 5, 9, 10, 12, 13, 42, 43, 44, 55, 78, 81, 84, 102, 138, 140, 158, 165, 183 n. 10

Philip, Duke of Edinburgh and Consort to Queen Elizabeth II, 115
picture brides, 16, 21, 25, 27
polygamy. *See* Edmunds Act
Popoff. *See* Slocan and Extension
Powell Street, 2, 60, 80, 134, 146–147, 155, 157, 211 n. 9
Powell Street Festival, 2, 132, 147, 156–157
Powell Street Review, 147
preemption, 28–29, 168
Price, John, 2, 160
Prince of Wales Hotel. *See* Waterton Lakes National Park
Princess Mary, 52–53

Qualification and Registration of Voters Act, 18. *See also* franchise
Quebec, 14, 165

Rainbow Road. *See* Salt Spring Island
Raymond, 65, 67–68, 89
redress, 2, 8, 9, 132, 147–151, 154, 159, 161, 169, 171
Regular, Keith, 105
relationality, 3–10, 11, 12, 13, 14, 15, 21, 70, 72, 105–106, 123, 132–161, 166, 167–170, 171, 172
repatriation. *See* expatriation
Richmond, 145, 146
Ririe, James Alfred, 70, 71
road camps. *See* Nikkei labor camps
Roebuck, Arthur, 193 n. 55
Rosebery, 54, 72, *73*, 74, *79*, 80, 82, 102
Royal Canadian Mounted Police, 5, 14, 42–43, 44, 47, 49, 50, 59, 60, 72, 84, 155, 165, 199 n. 4
Royal Commission to Investigate Claims of Japanese Canadians for Property Losses, 86–87, 111, 113, 127, 193 n. 61, 201 n. 37
Russell family (Diamond City), 134–135, 141, 169

salmon: canneries, 20, 26–27, 31, 34; fishers' unions, 14, 171, 181 n. 86; housing for fishers and cannery workers, 24, 26–27; licensing, 31–35. *See also* labor unions; Steveston; Sutebusuton Gyosha Jizen Dantai
Salt Spring Island: Anglican church, 49, 113; Booth Canal Road, 35–36; charcoal production on, 20, 29–30; Consolidated School, 30; Duck Bay, 27, 29, 30, 31, 32, 33; Ganges, 30, 36, 38, 52, 154; Islands Trust, 154; location of, 4; Murakami family return to, 111–116; Nikkei cemetery, 11, 39, 113–114; Okano Creek, 36; Rainbow Road, 35, 112, *115*; Sharp Road, 35, 37, *40*, 110, 112. *See also* Gulf Islands; Stark family; Tasaka family; Whims family; Wood family
San, the. *See* Slocan and Extension: Sanitarium
Sandwell, Ruth, 30, 39
Sansei, 146–147, 171
Saskatchewan, 14, 75, 95
sexual predation, 84. *See also* Nakayama, Goichi Gordon
Sharp Road. *See* Salt Spring Island
Shoah, 152
Shimizu, Hide (Hyodo), 77
Shin-Issei, 146–147, 171
Shogunate, Tokugawa, 21, 22
Shoot the Chutes. *See* Hastings Park
Slocan and Extension: Bay Farm, 54, 72; Carpenter Creek, 23–24; Lemon

Slocan and Extension (*cont.*)
Creek, 54, 76, 77, 78, 79; Popoff, 54, 72; Sanitarium, the, 77, 83, 191 n. 31; Slocan City, 54, 72; Slocan Lake, 54, 74, 77, 83; Slocan River, 54, 72, 79
Smallshaw, Brian, 111
Spam, 156–157
Special Committee on Orientals in British Columbia, 43–44
Speed, T. Frank, 82
Standing Committee (Montreal), 128, 201 n. 35
Stark family (Salt Spring Island), 28, 41
Steveston, 19, 21, 24–27, 29, 34, 60, 76, 118, 128, 147, 178 n. 37, 179 n. 48, 186 n. 69. *See also* salmon
Steveston Fishermen's Benevolent Society. *See* Sutebusuton Gyosha Jizen Dantai
Stoney Point Band (First Nation), 151
Streng Verboten Day, 47–48
Stringham, Briant W., 114
Sumiya, Mits, 159
Sunahara, Ann Gomer, 13
surveillance, 56
Sutebusuton Gyosha Jizen Dantai, 19, 24, 34
Suzuki, Katherine (Miwa), 122, 129, 130, 142–143, 144, 152, 153, 154, 161
Suzuki, Umanosuke and Moto, 25

Tagami, Tom, 62
Takasaki, Yukinori Peter, 65, 188 n. 87
Tanaka, Ted, 99, 106
Tasaka family (Salt Spring Island), 29. *See also* Salt Spring Island: charcoal production
Thompson, E.P., 8

Thompson family (Toronto), 118–119, 121, 122
Tonari Gumi, 147
Toronto: as destination for Nikkei, 6, 14, 117, 126–127; infrastructure, 117–118, 119, 122; Nikkei awareness of anti-Semitism in, 125–126; Nikkei sense of community in, 129–130, 170–71; as "New Niseiville," 126, 128; resistance to Nikkei arrivals in, 117, 126. *See also* Finlay, Reverend James; United Church
Toronto Association of Civil Liberties, 125
Toronto Star, 125
Toronto Telegram, 125
Treaty Day, 105
Trinity College. *See* University of Toronto
Tsujimura, Koichi, 118, 201 n. 38
Tsujimura, Ruth (Hirano), 54, 118

Uchida, Matasaburo, 83
United Church, 77, 126. *See also* Finlay, Reverend James
University College. *See* University of Toronto
University of British Columbia: Asian Canadian and Asian Migration Studies Program, 2, 132, 159, 160; diploma ceremony, 2, 12, *160*; expulsion of Nikkei students from, 2, 12, 118, 132; Mary Kitagawa's studies at, 140, 151–152; Richard Murakami's enrollment in, 139; Senate Tributes Committee, 158, 159
University of Toronto: B'nai B'rith Hillel Foundation, 123; Chinese Student Christian Association, 123;

Episkopon, 119–120, 202 n.46; Nisei Students' Club, 121, 123, 129; Trinity College, 100, 116, 119–122, 203 n. 64; *Torontonensis*, 203 n. 64; University College, 123, 203 n. 64; West Indian Students' Association, 123, 203 n. 64

Vancouver Asiatic Exclusion League, 27
Vancouver: city of, 4, 16, 21, 26, 27, 29, 31, 32, 33, 53, 60, 83, 116, 122, 133, 140, 145, 154, 156, 159, 211 n. 9; General Hospital, 140; Japanese Language School, 150; Junior Board of Trade, 47; Nikkei awareness of anti-Asian sentiment in, 126, 136, 139; Nikkei postwar return to, 109, 111, 133, 136–137, 139–140, 147–148; race riots, 27, 29, 179 n. 48. *See also* British Columbia; Hastings Park; Powell Street
Vancouver Island, 19, 29, 32, 38, 48
Vancouver News-Herald, 47
Vancouver Sun, 151
Veterans Land Act, 86

violence, state-sponsored, 43, 49, 50, 60, 109, 144, 147, 150–151, 167, 168

watari-dori, 22, 23
Waterton Lakes National Park, 88–89, 101
West Indian Students' Association. *See* University of Toronto
Whims family (Salt Spring Island), 41
Widmer, Sylvia, 96, 104
wildlife policy in southern Alberta, 94–95
Wilson, Cairine, 193 n. 55
Wood family (Salt Spring Island), 41
work camps. *See* Nikkei labor camps

Yasui, Roy, 57, 79, 83, 191 n. 31
Yasui, Yosie, 50
Yellowhead Pass, 62, 63, 69–70, 71, 92, 187 n. 78. *See also* Nikkei labor camps
Yip family (Cardston), 111
Yobiyose, 37, 39, 182 n. 102
Young Women's Christian Association, 101

The authorized representative in the EU for product safety and compliance is:
Mare Nostrum Group
B.V Doelen 72
4831 GR Breda
The Netherlands

www.ingramcontent.com/pod-product-compliance
Lightning Source LLC
Chambersburg PA
CBHW030106170426
43198CB00009B/509